Private Government

Private Government

INTRODUCTORY READINGS

Edited by
Sanford A. Lakoff
University of Toronto

with the assistance of
Daniel Rich
University of Delaware

Scott, Foresman and Company
Glenview, Illinois *London*

From the collection of C. V. S. Roosevelt, Washington, D. C., *Cube with Magic Ribbons* by M. C. Escher.

Library of Congress Catalog Card Number: 70-171856
ISBN: 0-673-07612-1

Printed in the United States of America.

Regional offices of Scott, Foresman and Company are located in Dallas, Oakland, N.J., Palo Alto, and Tucker, Ga.

Preface

Although the concept of private government is still something less than a household word, the issues that fall within its purview—such as the responsibilities of corporate management, the rights of rank-and-file trade unionists, and the structure of government in universities—have become subjects of keen interest. This book brings together for the first time readings on the theory and practice of a range of "private governments" including business corporations, trade unions, professional associations, and universities. The basic question posed by such a collection of readings about private government is whether the supposedly voluntary associations, which in our highly organized society exert so much power over members and nonmembers, are or can be democratic.

Private Government: Introductory Readings is designed to serve as an introduction to the topic as a whole and to several of the leading subcategories. The book is appropriate for undergraduate and graduate courses in political science, sociology, public administration, higher education, and business administration. In addition, it has particular relevance to courses in labor relations and to courses involving the study of formal organizations. We hope that the availability of these materials will not only encourage teachers to include the subject in course work but also will stimulate further research.

In a number of instances, we have been compelled by space limitations to shorten the original text and to delete footnote references. We have tried to be as judicious as possible in making the alterations; they are noted before the selections and by ellipses within them.

Daniel Rich and I met in the spring term of 1970, when he was completing his graduate studies at Massachusetts Institute of Technology and I was there as a visiting professor. A word of thanks is therefore due to the Department of Political Science at M.I.T. My friend Martin Shapiro also deserves thanks for insisting that I put this volume together. A special word of appreciation should go to the publisher for making it possible for venturesome political scientists to probe the uncertain frontiers of their discipline. The editor first in charge of the project was George Vlach, who, unfortunately, did not live to see it come to fruition. His untimely death was a misfortune for his profession and for all who were privileged to work with him.

S. A. L.

Contents

Introduction: Private Government and the New Pluralism

In ordinary usage, the term *private government* is still rare. Increasingly, however, political scientists are recognizing that it is both necessary and useful to distinguish between two types of government—public versus private. Public governments, on the one hand, are those general as well as special-purpose associations and agencies either to which all inhabitants of a given locality are subject or of which all citizens are members. Private governments, on the other hand, are those limited-purpose associations or organizations, usually voluntary in membership, which exist both alongside and subordinate to public governments. Private associations are considered governments when they exhibit, to a significant extent, certain fundamental political characteristics. In varying degrees and in ways circumscribed by the ultimate coercive sanctions of public governments, private governments exercise power over both members and nonmembers, often in vital areas of individual and social concern. They make and apply rules affecting and limiting the behavior of members. Often they have well-developed systems of legislation, adjudication, and execution, and at least rudimentary electoral and federal systems. In organizational form, they run the gamut from authoritarian to populist.

Private governments are, along with local public governments, the key organizational entities of the democratic social structure often designated by the term *pluralism*. As a pure ideal, pluralism envisions a society which is "an assembly of autonomous groups, living in harmony with each other, but offering individuals a wide variety of alternative opportunities for self-expression and self-fulfillment."[1] Although the study of private government is interesting and important in itself (and is therefore in no need of ulterior justification), the very discovery of the concept and the empirical research inspired by this discovery point to a theoretical issue of broader significance. That issue is the reexamination and the renewal—a need of all fundamental political ideas from time to time—of pluralism.

[1] Maurice Cranston and Sanford A. Lakoff, eds., *A Glossary of Political Ideas* (New York: Basic Books, Inc., Publishers, 1969).

When pluralism made its appearance in Europe during the early decades of this century, it was put forward both as a normative and as an analytic theory of politics. Those who advanced it were eager to refute a more conventional theory derived from earlier notions grounded in the idea of the social contract. According to that conventional view, society was composed of discrete individuals who had joined together to form the state. The state, in turn, was endowed with authority to grant or withhold charters for less inclusive associations. The state's decision in each case would presumably follow from a judgment as to whether or not any particular association might be expected to contribute to the general welfare.

The pluralists contended that the theory upon which those conclusions rested was riddled with invalid and unhistorical assumptions about the ways in which political life had actually developed. Worse still, they claimed, the abstract idea of the contract could be used to justify the most arbitrary and irresponsible practices. This contention had an understandable appeal for religious dissenters who suffered from discrimination in states where one faith had been recognized as the established church.[2] A similar indignation was felt by supporters of the labor movement, who could point to a no less discriminatory policy in the economic sphere: The same states that were freely granting charters to companies of merchants, sometimes with rights to monopolize whole areas of trade, adamantly denied the employees of those companies any right to organize and bargain collectively. Such unfairness, the pluralists maintained, could only be eradicated by a wholesale revision of the underlying theory of political association upon which the state relied for its justification.

The new view which they proposed began from the premise that groups, rather than discrete individuals, are the basic units of the social system. Individuals, they pointed out, cannot fulfill themselves in isolation; for reasons rooted in human nature and social interdependence, they can only define their purposes and protect their interests in association with others who share similar concerns. According to this view, the state is only one association among many entitled to compete for the loyalty of the individual. Its aims cannot exhaust the range of individual concerns; nor can its protection suit the special needs of all the groups bound to arise in a flourishing state of civilization.

Some pluralists went so far as to deny that there was any need for a state at all. If the state were eliminated, so they believed, the various groups would soon realize the need to come to terms with each other through a series of mutual accommodations. Others conceded the need for a modified state—perhaps reconstituted as a parliament of associations—that would serve only as an umpire in cases of conflict between those associations. All warned that unless the autonomy of voluntary associations were guaranteed, constitutionally and politically, the liberty of the individual would suffer a continual erosion as state control was expanded over every facet of social life.

Some of the theorists who posted this warning lived to see their worst forebodings realized in the rise of authoritarian and totalitarian regimes. Their critics have pointed out, however, that pluralist arguments—especially the more radical ones—played into the hands of the enemies of liberty by weakening support for

[2] One of the best statements of the pluralist case is presented by J. N. Figgis in *Churches in the Modern State* (New York: Longmans, Green and Company, 1913).

the constitutional state. In theory, at least, the pluralist attack upon the "omnicompetent state" left society vulnerable to takeover attempts by aggressive minorities. And, in practice, groups have often been a good deal less tolerant of rivals than some of the more optimistic pluralists imagined they would be, particularly in the absence of a watchdog state.

Wherever the truth may lie in this controversy, the fact remains that the appeal of normative pluralism was seriously undermined by actual events. Two world wars and the chaotic results of the violent swings of the business cycle persuaded many that the hand of the state needed to be made stronger rather than weaker. In this politically charged atmosphere, the pluralist argument seemed out-of-date and romantic.

As an analytic theory, however, pluralism became extremely popular, especially in the United States. American political scientists convinced themselves—sometimes with the fanatic zeal of the newly converted—that they had committed a gross error in taking the legal and constitutional apparatus of government as the real stuff of politics. Behind the textbook facade, they then realized, lay the hard reality of interest groups—economic, regional, ethnic, and (to a lesser extent in the U.S. than elsewhere) ideological. The political system was renamed the political process; public policy was defined as the resultant of group interaction.

Even apart from sins of exaggeration, American-style pluralism is by no means as "value-free" as its advocates sometimes claim. It is easy to see that it reflects the liberal ideology which has been so powerful a factor in American political thinking. Adam Smith's free, competitive individuals have been replaced by autonomous groups; the invisible hand of the market that was supposed to transform private greed into public welfare has become the seamless web of government. In this view, the best policy is once again "laissez faire, laissez passer": Let the groups alone so they can bargain and trade with each other; so long as there is a "polyarchic" distribution of power, then checks and balances (or "countervailing power") will arise from within the social system. According to this theory, there is no need for a powerful state; the state's only function, as in the ideal universe of Adam Smith, is to assure that all the competitors have an equal chance and that none is able to gain a monopoly.

Not surprisingly, the weaknesses of American pluralism are reminiscent of the weaknesses of earlier laissez faire theory. Once again, it is too easily assumed that any competitor can find free entry into the market. The coercive possibilities that are open to combinations and to oligopolies go largely unrecognized. And the capacity of narrow but well-organized private interests as, for instance, manufacturers to disarm and subordinate broader but unorganized groups such as consumers can be conveniently neglected.

Notwithstanding those serious weaknesses, it remains true that analytical pluralism has greatly improved the understanding of American political experience. By examining group interaction, political scientists are able to explain much that happens and much that does not happen in political life. Whether a bill is passed in a legislature or prevented from passing, the chances are excellent that the attitudes and behavior of pressure groups concerned with the bill will play a decisive role in the outcome. The character of American political parties and the distribution of community power would be unintelligible without the help of analytical pluralism. Nor is the theory useful only to apologists for the status quo. Originally, it was a potent weapon in the hands of muckrakers eager to expose the vested interests who corrupted the political process. Even now, those who are quickest to condemn pluralism as an American liberal myth are just as quick to resort to it when they explain American foreign policy as the work of a nefarious "military-industrial complex" or when they criticize regulatory agencies for subservience to interests they are supposed to control.

This is not to say that analytical pluralism is a flawless key to the mysteries of the political universe. It is not well designed, for example, for the analysis of institutions and policies in which the role of domestic interest groups is minimal. At a time when international crises are a major preoccupation, this is no small failing. Nor has pluralism shed much light on the internal operation of private associations. The normative pluralists ignored the subject because they had defined those associations as voluntary and had assumed away any possibility of coercion that such associations might direct toward their members. The analytical pluralists, having defined the role of the associations exclusively in terms of their impact upon public policy, have treated those associations as "pressure groups" rather than as political entities or governments in their own right.

The examination of private government opens the way toward the development of a fuller and more realistic pluralism. It is often stated that the annual budget of General Motors Corporation is larger than that of many public governments. Its decisions have a profound impact upon its own corporate citizens —including its employees, shareholders, and distributors—and upon the environment and the social system generally. Earl Latham and Anthony Jay show that GM and many other corporations have all the earmarks of political systems, including legislatures, executives, judiciaries, electoral processes, and internal factions. Much the same is true for other types of private association. How can the study of government possibly be comprehensive if it takes no account of such obviously political subsystems?

It was precisely because he recognized this gap in political science that Charles Merriam called for an examination of private government. As the selections brought together in this book indicate, Merriam's call has begun to be answered, though it must be admitted that thinking and research in this area of study are still at a relatively early stage. Grant McConnell's essay on the special characteristics of private government is one of a small body of reflective efforts devoted to the topic as a whole. The literature is extensive in some areas —notably the government of trade unions, which has for some time been of keen interest to sociologists and students of labor relations—and almost nonexistent in others. Very little of an analytical nature has been written about the government of churches, intriguing as that subject might seem. The study of the governments of professional associations has likewise been limited; Corinne Gilb's examination of the governmental functions exercised by professional organizations, the Hyde and Wolff and Hapgood studies of the American Medical Association, the examination of the Roman Catholic priesthood by Ference et al., and Daniel Rich's research on scientific societies are among the very few that have been produced.

It is no exaggeration to say that recent events have made further study of private government of more than academic interest. Since the New Deal period the problem of assuring democratic procedures in trade unions has evoked wide concern, as Seymour Lipset's comprehensive account indicates. Paul Sultan shows that the problem has been especially acute for union dissenters. Efforts such as Ralph Nader's "Campaign GM" to ensure that the management of large corporations will make socially responsible decisions provide vivid evidence of the "constitutional crisis of the corporation" described by Richard Eells and discussed by Eugene Rostow and by Barnekov and Rich. The recent turmoil over the government of the university points to a similar "crisis of legitimacy" which Clark Kerr, Charles Frankel, and Daniel Bell have examined.

One conclusion that runs through virtually all of these studies is that private governments should not be regarded as havens for democracy in this age of big and bureaucratic government: The fact is that the private sector reflects many of the same pathologies that beset public government. Because the supporting instruments of democracy—such as competitive parties and communications media, an independent judiciary, and other facets of public government—are often weak or absent in the case of private governments, the environment for individual freedom in relatively small associations is not necessarily better. Indeed, there is reason to believe that the tendency toward managerial elitism on the one hand and mass alienation on the other is even more pronounced in the private sector than it is in the public. This issue is examined in the context of a fuller discussion of the study of private government in the essay which concludes this volume.

But it would be premature and unduly pessimistic to decide on the basis of what we now know that there is no prospect of improving the climate for democracy in private governments. We do not yet have a reliable indication of the variations that are possible; movements of reform and renovation now underway may change the picture considerably. One of the virtues of examining what we do know is that we will not be tempted to embark on programs of change that ignore the special characteristics of private governments. It may be more defensible, for example, to delineate classes of citizenship in a corporation or in a university than it would be in a public democracy. And insisting upon total "participatory democracy" in private associations could well be a self-defeating tactic, if only because the fragile unity of the private polity could disintegrate under the strain.

From the point of view of political theory and political science, the further study of private government could contribute to a much needed revision of traditional pluralism, both as a normative and as an analytical doctrine. A New Pluralism can emerge from the recognition that in nontotalitarian social systems political power is shared by a continuum of associations, including some that are public and others that are private. It must be understood that these distinctions are not absolute, especially when public authority is formally and informally devolved upon private associations. The political character of a society depends upon the various ways in which power is exercised by all of those associations—how power-holders are kept accountable to their constituents in private as well as public associations and how the rights of the individual to free expression and to influence over decisions that affect his life are protected in all types of political association, both private as well as public. International private governments—in particular the multinational corporations—must be examined alongside public federations and alliances if we are to attain a better understanding of the global political system. These considerations, at any rate, must be part of any thoroughgoing theoretical and empirical study. If this volume indicates how the examination of private government can contribute to a creative renewal of pluralist thinking, it will have served its underlying purpose.

1

Private Government and the Science of Politics

Charles E. Merriam

THE STUDY OF PRIVATE GOVERNMENT

Since the "thread of governance" runs through all the institutions of society, including churches, universities, and business corporations, why not recognize that private governments of all sorts exist within the larger framework of public government? So argues one of the most distinguished political scientists of his generation, Charles E. Merriam, who also contends that the healthy existence of "sound private government" is essential in a free society.

When I was much younger and much more innocent than I now am, I supposed in this innocence that politics was always political. My father was a postmaster, with all that postmastership involved in the early days of "offensive partisanship." But he was also an elder in the Presbyterian church. One day following a church meeting I noticed he looked somewhat depressed. I asked him what had happened at the meeting. He said, "Nothing," except that he was not reelected as an elder. "I thought," said I, "there was no politics in the church." "So did I," he said. "But just wait till the next election." But if he had been widely read in church history, he might have anticipated occasional turns of politics, even in the house of God.[1]

I need not remind you that there is not only common law but canon law; and now and then we observe some scholar who has the J.U.D., doctor of either law. There are business law and patent law and labor law and a thousand laws of all the various groups that make up our social network. These laws may, of course, be called rules or regulations, or go unnamed. The thread of governance runs through all the web of social life in varying forms, in varying units. The problem of systems of rules, the problem of consent, and the problem of leadership are common to all units of association, whether labeled public or private . . . .

An anthropologist surveying the social behavior of Indiana University might think he had found a private government, but on reflection he would discover that he was dealing with a public government, a branch of the state of Indiana. If, however, he were to observe the behavior of the University of Chicago, he would find himself dealing with a private government. But when the Illinois Senate investigates the University, the academic institution becomes public. Yet if the observer looked for essential and characteristic differences between this public government in Indiana and this private government in Illinois, he would have difficulty in identifying and classifying them. He would find wide

[1] When I was a student in the University of Berlin many years ago they showed me the university jail which was separate from the town jail. In this academic hoosegow distinguished men such as Bismarck had been confined when students. This was a revelation to me, for in my day the school authorities could throw a man out but they could not throw him in.

Reprinted with permission from Charles E. Merriam, *Public and Private Government* (New Haven, Conn.: Yale University Press, 1944), pp. 2-19.

differences, to be sure, but would they be differences related primarily to the government of these respective institutions? In any modern university, you know, you can find traces of monarchy, aristocracy, along with dictatorship, oligarchy, and mob rule. Dare I say that even universities may have their bureaucracies, their leaders, their bosses, their budgets, their common law, their manifestations of mass psychology bursting out from time to time and difficult to control? The "community of scholars" does not like the role of sheep or of goats either, though both are found there. And what a treatise might be written on university presidents as a House of Lords!

You may recall that, when Woodrow Wilson was asked whether he had much difficulty in accustoming himself to practical politics, he said that after his experience with the campus politics of Princeton University everything else seemed simple. I have sometimes made the same observation myself after contacts with some of my colleagues who were wiser than serpents but not essentially dovelike . . . .

If we compare the operation of the Commonwealth Edison Company in Chicago with the T.V.A. down in Knoxville, each engaged in the primary task of generating electric power with a huge staff of men, we would find many similarities and, of course, some dissimilarities. The problems of ownership would vary, but the complexities of management and labor would present many of the same questions. Dr. Floyd Reeves, who organized the T.V.A. personnel system so admirably, might with little change in form have been asked to organize the personnel system of the Southern Electric or the Commonwealth Edison.

In some of these organizations the plus or minus of profit may mark a differential, some would say. But in great organizations like universities, churches, and other large-scale cultural-social groups the main concern is not with profit but with results measured by something else than the cash register or the accounting system of the pecuniary order. But we might also find salaried managers of great industrial establishments who are not primarily interested in personal profits but in low-cost service to large markets of consumers. Rewards in these cases may be accumulated by managers whose income is derived from salaries and not from dividends. At the same time we might also find thrifty university presidents who are shrewdly interested in profits as was President Butler when Columbia leased the site of Rockefeller Center. You might readily find men of God interested in canny and profitable investment of their trust funds, as keenly concerned as if the funds were their own private enterprise—more so, indeed.

These varying social groups are of many types and colors. Some are territorial, some are ethnic, some are religious, some are professional, some are economic, some are cultural in the broadest sense of the term. Their advantages and limitations have constituted a major object of theoretical and practical interest in recent times. My old professor in the University of Berlin, Otto Gierke, patiently evolved through three fat volumes the history of the theory of the untranslatable *Genossenschaft*—a cross between the community and a corporation. Proudhon built a theory of anarchism on the foundations of what was called economic federalism, a federalism so complete in its functioning as to make the political state superfluous. Duguit, brilliant professor of jurisprudence in France, developed elaborate legal and political theories about the meaning of associations. Guild socialists in recent times have developed and revived somewhat the medieval doctrine with variations of their own. Various forms of guilds may be held together in the system of G. D. H. Cole, merely by "a democratic supreme court of functional equity." He has since forgotten this phrase or must have wished to forget it. Advocates of industrial self-government have favored various forms of cooperative organization ranging from highly developed industrial autonomy to types of corporatives which become units in the corporative state, as in the recent unhappy experiment with Fascism in Italy. Somewhat similar forms are found in the Austrian-German development of the "estate-state" (the German word is *Ständestaat*) in which elements of feudalism are intermingled with totalitarianism in strange blends with curious colors and effects.

The huge structural and functional developments of our day have given rise to much analysis and speculation. I need only refer to treatises such as Burnham's *Managerial Revolution*, Brady's *Business as a System of Power*, Zweig's *The Planning of Free Societies*, along with many other discussions of the emergence of organizations within the state or across the lines of states. The modern organization of labor, the modern organization of agriculture, the modern organization of industry, the modern organization of education, law, medicine, engineering, and other professions, monopolies, trusts, trade associations are by now as impressive structurally as the organization of the church or of military force.

Many of these associations are of course not restricted to national boundaries but reach into wider political domains, in the form of international cartels, associations, and agreements of varying types and behavior. Sometimes their bonds of cohesion are as strong as those of rival political aggregations. The budget of a powerful international association and administration may be more impressive than the budget of a small state—even though a sovereign nation. The reconciliation of the powers and purposes of these struggling organizations is one of the major problems of political association and administration in our day. Is the effective government under all these circumstances properly characterized as public or as private?

It is not my purpose on this occasion to deal with the theory and practice of groupism but only to direct attention to the vast proliferation of what might be called private government within the general framework of the political state.[2]

All of these organizations have their own rules and regulations. All have their own personnel. All have their own plans and programs, formal and informal. All have their own codes, common understandings, and expectancies as to courses of action. Many of them have their own bureaucracies, their own factions or parties, their own leaders and demagogues, their own politics—petty or noble. There have been "parties" of a sort in the College of Cardinals.

I have frequently remarked to those who wondered at what they termed the mysteries and complications of politics that public government is much like private government. If you wish to understand the political, do not try too hard. Look around you at the associations of which you are a member—how many,

[2] See Helen Hill, "The Group and the State," University of Chicago. Unpublished doctoral dissertation.

you know better than I. Is there no nonvoting in your association? Are there no leaders whose vaulting ambition impedes the purpose of the group? Are there no inflexible interpretations of outworn rules? Is there no petty bureaucracy? Are there no efforts to seize power in what we call a dictatorial manner? Are there those seeking or holding power without responsibility? An accurate behavioristic study of your own organizations might reveal many of the same traits which seem to puzzle you so when thrown on the larger screen of the nation. The "mystery in the soul of state" is an old phrase. But there is much the same mystery, if so it may be called, in the soul of any organization you please to consider—the Chamber of Commerce, the Masonic Order, the Knights of Columbus, the Y.M.C.A., the labor union, the farm associations. The organization of direction and consent runs through them all.

Sometimes, in fact, these organizations become the directors of the political state or political unit, but without assuming political responsibility. The business organization may give orders to the rulers, and so may the labor union or a farm bloc. Commonly the directions given by special groups to the political organization are limited to special problems in which these social organizations are especially interested. But at times the control of public government by private organizations is comprehensive and complete.

All of these groups have their own sanctions or penalties. The state can throw a man into prison. But an employer can take away his job. As the state can deprive a man of his life, the church can threaten his happiness for the future and make him extremely uneasy and unhappy while he lives. The state may tax, but the monopoly may raise prices and lower standards.

Areas of Conflict

But what happens when the commands and sanctions of the political state conflict with those of the so-called private organizations? What if the state says "Yes" and the other group says "No"? What if the other group says "Must not" and the political group says "Must"? In certain classes of cases the issue may be resolved by adjudication or by violence, but this is not the whole story. In many cases the outcome is determined by an appeal to values and interests other than the political. The church, or the industry, or the labor union may protest effectively without the sword or even in extreme cases against the sword. What I have elsewhere called "the Poverty of Power"[3] may in certain cases reveal in a lightning flash the weakness of those who seem to be invincible.

"It may even happen that authority is like the hard-boiled, hard-faced person who is in point of fact compensating for an inner shyness and timidity. One with insight realizes that some faces are harder than humanity can possibly be." The same may be said of governments with the same rigidity. What seems to be granite is sometimes found to be putty. Naked hands and empty pockets may obstruct and antagonize the action of authority by means which authority cannot successfully oppose without destroying the basis of human association itself. The state cannot break up all christenings and weddings and funerals even

[3]Charles E. Merriam, *Political Power* (1934), chap. 6.

though they may be occasions of antistate demonstrations. Even if all games are prohibited, certainly all gossip cannot be suppressed.

One of the sharpest conflicts between rival authorities was that of the medieval Church and the Empire. Here were two associations competing in a sense for priorities in allegiance and obedience. The mixed feudal and imperial system in which these rivalries were set made the antagonism more marked. Such rivalry reaches its highest point when there is a combination of religion, region, and race together with a mixture of unreconciled economic interests.

In our day the sharpest conflict has been that between industry and government. Within industry itself there has been of course the rivalry of ownership and labor—to say nothing of management. Many industries have developed governments of their own with personnel, budgetary, and planning agencies; with widely ramifying hierarchies and bureaucracies; with laws and regulations enforcible by severe penalties. In some instances, in addition, they have taken over in effect the government of political units as in some mining and manufacturing towns where the company is practically the government, and the personnel of the industry and that of the political authority are almost interchangeable. Were the policies then company policies or public policies? Were the company police public or private in their activities? In Zion City under Dowie they could not tell me whether oysters and cigarettes were forbidden by the City Council or the Church Council—being the same persons. In some cases there has been reached what amounts to private socialism as distinguished from public socialism since property and political power were alike in the hands of the same persons. Grover Cleveland once referred to "the communism of pelf."[4] I do not say private feudalism, since the essence of feudalism was the private-public identity. Inside the state there has been conflict traditionally between the military and civil types of governmental hierarchy and order.

The Meaning and Interdependence of Public and Private

But perhaps we should have inquired earlier, what is public and what is private? And how do we draw the line between them? At first blush this seems very clear, but on closer examination it is not so evident. On further analysis, lines of demarcation emerge again but of a different type from those often traced.

Public and private systems of law and government, as far as modern civilization is concerned, emerged three or four hundred years ago at the time of the transition from the feudal system to the national state. Under the feudal system private law and public law were much the same. The ruler ruled the land and the people on the land because he owned the land; and he owned the land because the law gave him the land! And he gave the law. Obedience was personal; and law was private law, although also in a sense public law. That great monument of erudition, *The Restoration of Political Science* (6 vols.), by Ludwig von Haller (1816-34), was dedicated to the thesis that there is and can be no genuine distinction between public law and private law, or between private rights and public rights, or between personal leadership and public authority. The state, he held,

[4] Allan Nevins, *Grover Cleveland: A Study in Courage* (New York: Dodd, Mead and Company, 1966), p. 586.

does not differ in kind from the family or the church or the school, since the real integrating principle is leadership supplemented by force. This was earlier known as the patrimonial theory. When once the nation-state appeared, however, this doctrine was blended into the doctrine of sovereignty and the power of the sovereign.

I looked in my book of synonyms and found that "'private' literally denotes the abstract quality of private." Not very illuminating. Further that "privacy is most suitable for such as are in circumstances of humiliation, whether from their misfortune or their fault." The *Oxford Dictionary* defines "private" as "individual, personal, not affecting the community."[5] The *College Dictionary* says "not common or general, special."[6]

"Public" on the other hand signifies "pertaining to or affecting the people at large," relating to, etc., a nation, state, or community at large. The conclusion might be drawn that private is not public and that public is not private. But how does it happen, one may ask, that a private soldier is not public? Obviously this refers to the order of rank rather than to the distinction between public and private. But again a "privateer" was really almost as private as piracy.

The question whether work performed for a public authority is public or private has given rise to much business for lawyers. It becomes a delicate question whether the government is acting in the capacity of the political or the commercial. This led to the long-famous controversy over the liability of the state for its own torts. This may seem a matter of dry legality to you, unless you happen to be hit by a brick falling from a building in construction, public or private, and begin an effort to collect damages therefor. When we come to deal with mixed agencies, authorities, and corporations, the issue between public and private becomes all the more confusing.[7]

Is a public utility public or private, or is it both? Public and private are not words with which all problems can be solved; nor do the phrases "public utility" and "private enterprise" settle everything.[8] The struggle between absolute individualism and absolute collectivism is intellectually a sham battle. There are no such complete alternatives. The individual is born into and works within a social system without which he cannot even begin to operate. On the other hand, the collective is inevitably rooted in the personality of man and presumably serves his purposes. The end goal—even of collectivist systems, however violent their methods—is alleged to be the release of the personality. In the Marxian theory, anarchy is the goal. The purpose of individualism—whatever its methods—includes the promotion of common good. Private enterprise is not unmindful of the common good, from the days of the English Common Law until now.

What religion or philosophy ventures to make the ego the supreme end of life? Is it Christianity? Is it Mohammedanism? Or some other member of the group of comparative religions? No. Along with self goes sacrifice, without which

[5] Grimm's *Deutsches Woerterbuch,* Vol. 7, traces the development of definitions of "privat" through the 16th, 17th, 18th, and 19th centuries.

[6] See Webster's *Dictionary of Synonyms* (1942).

[7] McDougal and Miller, "Public Purpose in Public Housing," *Yale Law Journal,* 52, 1 (1942).

[8] See Merriam, *The Role of Politics in Social Change,* chap. 2.

the personality cannot be explained. Soldiers who volunteer for services that almost certainly mean death, missionaries who devote themselves to colonies of lepers, mothers who go down into the valley of the shadow of death to bring children into the world—all these are inspired by other than purely selfish motives. Of course you may call sacrifice a form of selfishness; and if this dry husk is soothing to you, take it along and gnaw it as you go. What we are really saying is that public and private interests are often so inseparably intertwined that it is impossible to tear one strand away from the others and leave anything living.

The formalized philosophies of anarchism and totalitarianism are alike in their failure to effect a sound reconciliation between the state and the personality, between public government and private government. The anarchistic solution, namely, the abolition of the state, was a violent and futile reaction against juristic theories and economic and social practices building up the power of arbitrary rulers, not only in the field of public government, it may be noted, but also in the field of private economic government. This particular doctrine no longer moves men as it did a generation ago, but it is a recurrent philosophy from the days of Chinese theorists on down through the course of philosophy.

The totalitarian doctrine stresses shrilly the complete priority of the state and the subordination of the individual. But Hitler and Mussolini did not discover patriotism or the common good. They borrowed an idea and pulled it out of shape. The supremacy of the state from the point of view of juristic hierarchy is not new or at any rate not newer than three hundred years. It was stated by Bodin in 1576; and the nature of juristic sovereignty one hundred years ago by the English jurist Austin. To this the totalitarian has added only the sadism of frustration, the razzle-dazzle of the demagogues, and the drunken attempt to put in universal practice what had hitherto been a convenient legal tool rather than a god to worship. I shall discuss the doctrine of sovereignty more fully in paragraphs that are to follow.

The individual interests that profess to serve the common good at the sacrifice of the common good are not the interests around which we build our value systems. The man who consistently places his private good above the common good is characterized as a parasite and never as a great creator. Private enterprise conflicting with the common good is not the creative enterprise we cherish. Public enterprise which treats the human personality only as a pawn is not the common good we hope for.[9]

All this does not prove, and is not intended to prove, that there is no substantial and important difference between public and private interest in all groupings, between what is the common good and personal good. These comments are designed to demonstrate that lines between "public" and "private" are not absolutes, but that there are zones of cooperation and cohesion in the common cause and on a common basis in many fields of human action. As Aristotle said centuries ago, the isolated individual could not exist except as a stone hand. The lone individual does not figure either in family relations, in neighborhood relations, in state relations, in social relations, or in the higher values of religion. Nowhere is he left without guiding social groups, personalities, and principles.

[9] See Beardsley Ruml, "Looking Ahead," *Survey Graphic* (May 1943), p. 224.

Nor does the state exist for itself alone. Whatever the legal possibilities of eminent domain and the juristic jargon of omnipotence and irresistibility, the wise state does not wish to dominate everything or to master everything. Government is the tool of the common good, a symbol of common interests. The state is not a god. The ruler is not a mortal god as Bishop Bossuet maintained in the days of Louis XIV. The state is us. We are the state. Its functions and powers are ours.

Many of the common distinctions between states and other societies distinguish little on close analysis. That the state has a universal jurisdiction over its territories and a monopoly of violence is usually declared, and at times this conclusion may serve a useful purpose, with value as a broad historical observation. But if traditional forms of violence are superseded by milder forms of aggression not definable as violence, such as economic or psychological intimidation or pressure? What if the state should be a world state?

In times of crisis, such as pestilence, flood, fire, famine, war, the state is driven to undertake nearly all activities in the category of human behavior and may be applauded for the activity. Commonly, the functions of the state are listed as external defense, internal order; and alongside these are justice, common welfare, the development of the human personality through liberty and happiness. But private governments may also promote the general welfare, may aid in the maintenance of internal order, help in national defense, and promote both personal liberty and the common good. In a free society a state promotes the common welfare. In a free society a state promotes and encourages freedom of enterprise, private or public, fitting in with free society.

The state from time to time undertakes functions in behalf of the group deemed to be common and wise. These actions may not be in accord with an enlightened view of the end of the state. This may not satisfy the demands of the precisionists for rigid demarcation, but it goes as far as the order of precision in which the political society is set. This leaves always a zone of uncertainty, but this zone of uncertainty is the life of the pluralism of societies which make up the free society. This zone is indeed a margin of safety which prevents too great precision in an area where it is not indicated, and where too precise decision for that very reason becomes arbitrary and absolutistic. But just government, public or private, is an end, whatever the forms of regulation or direction or cooperation. Behind political power are value, purpose, end—justice, liberty, order, security, welfare. Government itself may be a value, but a value leading to other values.[10]

Finally, in a democratic system, the rivalry sometimes arising between public and private organizations may most readily be reconciled. In a democracy all agencies and authorities are, or profess to be, servants of the common good. They are linked together theoretically in cooperative enterprise. They are aids in obtaining the genuine consent of the governed effectively, with a maximum of reason and persuasion and a minimum of violence and brutality, with an end result of justice. There are parties and pressure groups and ambitious aspirants for more and more power in these various groups. But they must all pledge allegiance to the common good, in theory if not in practice, and the

[10] See Merriam, *Political Power,* chap. 5, "The Shame of Power," and chap. 7, "The Morbidity and Mortality of Power."

superior claims of the community they profess to serve. The democratic forms of free association respect most fully the dignity of man, his possibilities for growth, the unfolding of the human personality in its widest forms. Under these conditions private enterprise and public enterprise, private rights and public rights are not in opposition but in apposition—free industrial and free political society—in the course of becoming the realization of the common good. We would not destroy all private governments if we could, but on the contrary encourage and foster them. Sound private governments of private groups will not destroy public government. They are themselves a part of the system of order and justice, of which the state is a symbol and an instrument for the realization of human values. The first step of despots is the disintegration of legal bodies, of parties, of churches and schools, of unions, of industrial and agricultural associations.

In a government of one or of a few, all associations may be suspect except those of a small ruling clique. They are all possible centers of resistance and hence dangerous. In a government of the many, on the contrary, these associations are the bases of liberty, order, justice, democratic habit and practice, bulwarks of the republic. Out of the energies, the enterprise, the rivalries, the adjustments of these associations arises what we call public opinion, the final stabilizer and judge of liberty, justice, order.

In any political society, if private governments or associations disclaim or disregard community responsibilities, either ignorantly or intelligently, then confusion and dangers arise. But in a free society the general recognition of the significance of the common good makes these dangers and tensions less likely to arise than in an absolute state. The democratic process may be slower when we employ patience, good will, adjustment as instruments rather than the tools of command and violence; but the end result is a higher level of morale and a closer cooperation of vital elements in the community, a higher standard of human achievement and happiness.

Grant McConnell

PUBLIC AND PRIVATE GOVERNMENT

Grant McConnell agrees with Merriam that private government is an unstated assumption of American political thinking, but he doubts that individual liberty is likely to be protected or enhanced by most private governments. More often than not, he points out, they are prime examples of Michels' "iron law of oligarchy," for reasons that relate to the structure and composition of limited-purpose associations.

I

Massive endorsement of the private association as an essential of democracy is one of the most striking features of American political thought. Freedom of association has virtually become a fundamental guarantee of the Constitution.[1] The ideas of self-government and self-regulation have entered deeply into the doctrines of the political order, and they have been institutionalized to an unheralded degree. The private association, moreover, has been linked with the values of decentralization and federalism. It has also been pictured as the source of stability in politics and held up as the medium of the public interest. Most frequently, however, it has been seen as the guarantor of liberty. This is the most essential part of the general argument, and any examination of the doctrine must deal with this claim.

There is no doubt that pluralism belongs in the liberal tradition. The pluralist attack upon the state's assertion of unlimited power was one of the most incisive ever made. The defense of the private association against attempts to suppress it or to subordinate it to the state has almost always been a defense of liberty itself; the elaboration of this defense by pluralist writers has provided some of the noblest statements on constitutionalism and the limits of state action. Pluralist discussions of law carried important insights on the roots of law in sources other than compulsion. Moreover, the pluralists for the most part spoke out of a genuine dedication to individual liberty. Perhaps the most important aspect of pluralist doctrine in the present context is its adherence to the distinction between the state and society, a distinction closely related to that between the public and the private spheres of life.[2]

There can be equally little doubt that the preference of those American

[1] Cf. Robert A. Horn, *Groups and the Constitution* (Stanford, Calif.: Stanford University Press, 1956).

[2] On the distinction between state and society as a liberal principle see Guido de Ruggiero, *The History of European Liberalism* (London and New York: Oxford University Press; 1927), pp. 383-86. See also Lord Acton, *Essays on Freedom and Power* (Glencoe, Ill.: The Free Press, 1949), pp. 247-48.

writers who are sometimes classed as pluralists is for liberty.[3] More conspicuously, however, the private associations of the United States have fought with great vigor to protect themselves from government encroachments. The organizations of business and labor have been the most vociferous in this regard, but perhaps the churches have made greater contributions; certainly separation of church and state is a more firmly established principle in America than in most countries.

When all this has been recognized, however, some very important questions remain. Since the private association has made its claim against the state in the name of liberty, how has the liberty of the individual fared vis-à-vis the private association? If the private association is to maintain the right of self-government and self-regulation, how is it governed itself? What is its conception of government within its own boundaries? These questions were not asked by the pluralists, and only comparatively recently have they been asked by more than a few others. Nevertheless, they are not easily avoidable today.

Since early in the present century enthusiasts for the private association have been confronted with Robert Michels' very troubling analysis of the sociology of membership organizations.[4] Ostensibly, his work dealt with political parties, and his concrete information related almost wholly to the social democratic parties of central Europe. The sweep of his work, however, was much broader, extending by implication to all organizations in which membership could be said to exist. Michels' thesis was one of the boldest and most provocative in all of social science: the "iron law of oligarchy"—who says organization says oligarchy. Nevertheless, for long periods of time, it has been ignored. Not that Michels was an obscure figure,[5] nor that his argument, despite its somewhat disorderly presentation, was easily disposed of. From time to time Michels' work has been rediscovered and the controversy begun anew.[6] Refutations have been offered, but the need for further refutation seems consistently to remain.

Michels' argument was phrased in perhaps too sensational terms. A generalization framed as an "iron law" invites the discovery of exceptions, particularly when it runs contrary to popular and cherished beliefs. Nevertheless, this "law" was supported with the citation of many factors of which increasing numbers of people have had personal experience. The argument rested, first, upon the characteristics of organization, and organization in the twentieth century was increasingly becoming the setting for the myriad activities in which Americans engaged. The situation was not new. Indeed, Alexis de Tocqueville, with his extraordinary prescience, had remarked during the previous century on the American propensity for forming associations. Where in Europe some large undertaking appeared, a prominent nobleman stood at its head; in America a

[3] Classification of American writers as pluralists or nonpluralists is somewhat risky. However, to take one writer who is quite clearly in the pluralist tradition, Mary Parker Follett, it is evident that (whatever the confusions that may seem to exist in her writings) her purpose was liberal. Cf. *The New State* (New York: Longmans, Green, 1918).

[4] Robert Michels, *Political Parties,* reprinted (Glencoe, Ill.: The Free Press, 1949). The first English edition was printed in 1915, but the original German appeared in 1913.

[5] For example, he is one of the real-life figures who appear in the early volumes of Jules Romains' *Men of Good Will.*

[6] This is most particularly true in the English-speaking world. For example, see Sylvia Kopald, *Rebellion in Labor Unions* (New York: Boni and Liveright, 1924).

similar undertaking would have an association of equals established for its furtherance.[7] This trait was incalculably more intensified in the twentieth century, when national associations were formed for everything from abrasives and absorbent paper to Zionism and zirconium; a thousand-page volume could do little more than list them and the addresses of their headquarters,[8] and it took no account of the multitude of local groups organized for seemingly every purpose the human mind could conceive. Thus many people had direct experience of the behavior of organizations, although few were willing to question the official doctrine about it. But such of those few who encountered Michels' argument found disturbing corroboration from their personal experience with many modern American associations.

Michels deliberately limited the scope of his work on private associations to the social democratic parties—those presumed to be most wholeheartedly devoted to a democratic ideal. If democracy existed in organizations, where more logical to look for it than among these parties? Or if it were not to be found there, what hope was there of finding it elsewhere?

Michels' entire work rested on a distinction between leaders and led that to a certain extent recalled the Marxist distinction between classes and was akin to ideas about the elite. The particular dimension he traced was formal organization. Organization requires leadership, since as a matter of technical necessity direct government by the membership is "mechanically" impossible. Moreover, because of their sheer incompetence without leaders, the masses or membership need, approve, and even crave leadership. The leaders control not merely by virtue of their superior abilities and the submissive tendencies of the masses, but also by an array of simple but crucial devices. The list of members, the files, the organization press—the apparatus of organization—all are in the leaders' hands.

To the extent that the "iron law of oligarchy" means that leadership is inevitable in organization, it is a truism; but there is a much more disturbing implication in the argument. Leaders develop within a different milieu from members. They engage in different activities and come to enjoy a different status. Most important, they acquire different interests. Organization becomes conservative; leaders tend to identify their own interests with those of the organization and seek to preserve the foundations of their own position, thus laying the foundation for conflict of interests between leaders and led. The identity that is commonly assumed to exist among the interests of all within the organization is therefore false. And in contests between leaders and led, the former have virtually all the advantages.

Plainly, this argument is very sweeping. It is also very disturbing, particularly for those drawn to the pluralist belief that the freedom and self-determination of private associations are close to the essence of democracy. If private associations themselves should be undemocratic, as the Michelian thesis would seem to assert, how can they be essential to democracy?

Perhaps the simplest answer offered to this question is that the internal arrangements of the private associations are irrelevant to the question. In the

[7] Alexis de Tocqueville, *Democracy in America* (New York: Alfred A. Knopf, 1945), Vol. 2, p. 106.

[8] Cf. *National Organizations of the U.S.* (Detroit: Gale Research Co., 1961).

first place, so the argument goes, the private associations as centers of power stand in opposition to the assumption of total power by any all-encompassing tyranny. With such associations in vigorous and separate existence, a sudden *Putsch* or mob action is insufficient to assume complete domination over the nation. Totalitarianism is defeated unless it can either absorb or destroy the private associations; hence, it is argued, private associations preserve democracy against the totalitarian threat.

The contention has much merit if the threat of totalitarianism is considered imminent. Certainly, twentieth-century experience indicates that totalitarianism is an evil greater than almost any other. By comparison with what went on in Hitler's Germany and Stalin's Russia occasional breaches of the democratic ideal inside private associations in America are insignificant. The force of this argument diminishes, however, if the threats of totalitarianism in America appear remote. On a lesser score, this ground for indifference to the internal arrangements of the private associations stands against the pluralist argument that the private associations are schools in democracy for the larger community. If such they are to be, they can hardly be other than models for behavior in the larger arena of national politics.

Another reason sometimes offered for dismissing Michels' charge is that the private associations are mutually countervailing—a modern gloss on the argument of Madison and his colleagues in the Federalist Papers. It tends to merge with the preceding contention that private associations are barriers to totalitarianism, but it goes somewhat further: by opposing each other, private associations supposedly check any overly greedy attempts by particular associations to extend their power. One association protects against another to the extent that in the large community democracy is insured.

This argument is relevant to the fear that one or more associations may exploit the general public. Except under special and unusual circumstances, however, it does not bear on the problem Michels posed. A trade union and a corporation may check each other in the making of decisions affecting the scale of wages and production costs; a high-tariff interest group may find itself confronted by a low-tariff interest group. Yet although each of these contests and the many others commonplace in modern political life may protect the economy and the polity from the extremist policies that might be followed if opposing or countervailing private groups were not active, they do not protect the members of any of these groups when they are threatened by their own organizations. To provide such protection, countervailing organizations would have to exist *inside* the associations, or, alternatively, there would have to be very nearly parallel or rival associations between which members might move without being deprived of the benefits that go with association membership.

In practice, however, private associations tend to be jealous of rivals. They seek to prevent the rise of competitors in the fields they have marked as their own. Often, when such rivals do exist, there is bitter conflict between them, conflict that has as its object the destruction of one or the other. Sometimes, when the conflict cannot be brought to this point, an accommodation takes place and jurisdictional boundaries are agreed upon, so that as a result the condition of monopoly is restored. An entire ethos within the American labor movement holds "dual unionism" to be the worst of sins, but this ethos is not unique to labor; it is found to some degree among farm organizations, veterans' organizations, and others. The appeal made to support this ethos is for unity. The fear is that with two or more organizations in a particular field, competition among them may lead one to appeal to a common foe, with consequent losses to the interests the organizations and their members share. In one degree or another many, if not most, private associations see themselves arrayed against some external enemy and are warring organizations.

If it is unrealistic to look for an escape from the problem through parallel or rival associations, there remains the first alternative: to look inside the associations. This, however, poses the question of how the associations govern themselves. Although the question is plainly relevant in view of the emphasis placed upon the private association as an essential of democracy, it is sometimes suggested that examination of the private association as a form of government is improper, probably because of the fear that such inquiry is a preliminary to suggestions for state regulation. But it can also be objected that the private association is not the same as the state and that the tests applied to public government are not applicable to the government of the private association.

Certainly state and private association are different, but the differences are hard to define. Both are to some extent based on territorial lines. The state, if it is a constitutional state, has, like the private association, limited ends. Both state and association exercise some form of authority. Each makes rules or laws (not infrequently the term "laws" is used by private associations for their own rules). These rules are enforced with penalties of varying degrees of severity, but some organizations' penalties are more severe than many punishments of the states. Fines, suspension, and expulsion, all exacted by private associations, are serious matters where the associations involved control the right to practice a particular trade or profession. This is especially true where, as with medicine, a large investment of money and years in education, training, and experience are also involved. Perhaps (at least for devout communicants) the most awesome penalty of all, excommunication, is enforced by the church, a private association. Of course not all private associations exist in spheres of interest with such degrees of importance. Yet some do, and where they do the problem of authority is substantially the same as it is in the state.

This problem is considerably more far-reaching than conflict between leaders and led, or the prospect of tyrannical leaders, for it is also a problem of conflict among members. Such conflict is very conspicuous in the state and constitutes a major part of the substance of politics. But it is far less apparent in the private association. Much of the ethos of these associations revolves about the belief that there are no differences among members, or at least no important differences. This is the tradition of the *Gemeinschaft,* expressed in the very language with which many associations cloak their proceedings: brotherhood, solidarity, fellowship, and so on. The members are likened to the members of a family, in which the ties of blood relationship reduce all transitory causes of dispute to insignificance. The roots of this tradition are ancient, and it is not to be despised. But not all associations have this communal quality. The distinction between the community and the more mundane society with narrow ends is familiar. In the latter, presumably, cohesion is markedly less than in the former, but since it exists for ends on which all members are agreed, there is no problem of government as found in the state. Different arguments thus apply to different kinds of association, but they arrive at the same conclusion: that the private association does not have the problem of government which the state exhibits.

Unfortunately for this conclusion, there are very genuine differences among the members of most associations, differences, for example, of age, opinion, taste, sex, religion. Some of these differences are trivial and do not represent conflicts, but others are important, some of them involving direct conflicts of both interest and belief. They occur even in the associations that lay claim to the quality of community, in some of which it would be difficult to claim that the tradition of community actually overrides the differences and the conflicts. In associations with narrow ends the absence of differences is also an illusion. In both types the problem of government does exist, and unless (as with hierarchical churches) there is a superior source of authority, there is also a problem of legitimacy.

Beyond all these factors, two considerations are stressed by the pluralists themselves. First, according to their argument, the state is but one of many forms of association. Accordingly, if it stands on the same ground as the other associations, and if its exercise of authority is open to question, so too is the exercise of authority in the other associations. Second, the pluralists correctly insist that the activities and ends of private associations are profoundly important. Some of them have moral purposes higher than the state's; the activities of some are in practice intrinsically more important than many state activities. Thus, while many associations have trivial aims, engage in activities of little general concern, and may be safely ignored, other associations are genuinely important to the large community. It is therefore unreasonable to assert that private associations are both important to the general polity and yet so unimportant that their political life may be ignored. Unless it can be established that problems of authority and government within private associations stand on different grounds from those of the state, examination of such problems in the private association is not only proper but necessary.

II

The initial difficulty confronting any attempt to examine the government of private associations is their great number. In the United States, as we have seen, they exist by the thousands. Many are national, but regional, state, and local associations are beyond counting, not merely because of their multiplicity but because they appear and disappear with the luxuriance of tropical vegetation. Indeed, even those that have attained national scope have different degrees of vitality, some being exceedingly vigorous while others are clearly moribund. Moreover, many organizations are associations in name only. Some bear titles which suggest large memberships, but in any realistic sense they have no members at all. This is particularly true of numerous "associations" and "institutes" with Washington offices which not infrequently consist of small rooms occupied by one or two individuals who may represent six or more organizations; the organizations may be little more than fictions used by individual lobbyist entrepreneurs. This is not to say that professional lobbyists do not necessarily represent genuine groups; some of the groups so represented are very real.

Still other organizations which maintain substantial office establishments and which claim many members are not membership organizations at all. In these, the so-called members are no more than subscribers to a cause or to a service carried on wholly by the office professionals. The "members" have no voice whatever in the determination of organizational policy or choice of officers, and there is no pretense that they do. The supporter (a better term here than "member") may receive reports and information, and sometimes even a membership card. Nevertheless, he is quite outside the organizational reality, and his only recourse if he disagrees with policy is to end his support—a condition that is often quite openly stated. However, the distinction between this and the situation in which safeguards are deliberately established to prevent a genuine membership from exercising influence on policy is in practice sometimes difficult to perceive. The motive for such safeguards is usually to prevent enemies of the association from joining and disrupting it or diverting it from its avowed objectives—as, in somewhat analogous fashion, constitutional barriers are erected against the subversion of a state. But there is a very great difference of degree in that the purposes and policies that the private association seeks to defend are usually much more narrow and concrete.

The governments of still other associations present problems that fall outside the democratic tradition and can only be noted here. The outstanding example is the organization of the Catholic Church. Although this is an organization of extraordinary complexity with an involved political life of its own, it has no presumption of democracy within itself. The principle of authority in the Church is, accordingly, much clearer than in many other organizations: Authority derives from God and extends downward on a hierarchical pattern. There is no problem of deriving authority from the will of the members and, so long as the faith of the communicants is maintained, the major problem of government is efficient administration. The same situation prevails in other hierarchical churches. The problem of government is, of course, more prominent in sects which emphasize the role of individual conscience in the interpretation of divine authority.

Perhaps the most difficult problem is presented by the corporation, probably the most important form of private government in America today. The evidence of its role in modern life is pervasive and inescapable. In a formal sense, however, the corporation is a creation of the state, and presumably what the state may create it may destroy—or regulate. Nevertheless, many have claimed in recent years that here is in fact a genuine private government. The corporation makes rules, it is argued, and is thus within the category.[9] Moreover, in a realistic view, the part played by the state in the creation of corporations is minimal and unimportant. And, to understand the actual behavior of corporations, a political analysis must be added to the more traditional economic analysis.

These considerations have been very persuasively argued and they carry much force. Some of the major corporate units of American business exercise

[9]Thus "A business is a *government* because within the law it is authorized and organized to make rules for the conduct of its affairs. It is a *private* government because the rules it makes within the law are final and not reviewable by any public body." Beardsley Ruml, quoted in Richard Eells, *The Government of Corporations* (New York: The Free Press of Glencoe, 1962), p. vi.

great power, and it is significant that business economists have been urging extended consideration of the corporation in explicitly political terms.[10] Concepts such as legitimacy, authority, power, and constitutionalism have now entered deeply into the discussion of the modern business corporation. Nevertheless, this approach exposes a serious dilemma. On the one hand, the corporation is today an intrinsic part of the economy and society. It is the dominant way of doing business and of producing and distributing most of the goods by which men live and earn their living. Its organizations reach deep into the patterns of daily life for millions. At different points it stands in opposition to the spirit of the nation's historic antitrust policy, but that policy has, to a significant extent, begun to give way. The brute fact that the corporation exists cannot be wished away. On the other hand, the existence of the modern corporation does not accord with long-standing conceptions of political organization, and no theory exists by which it can be reconciled with such conceptions.

The difficulty is apparent as soon as the corporation is regarded as a political body, that is, as having power. So long as one can maintain a fiction that the corporation is solely an economic unit exercising no power within the market, the problem is to some degree disguised. Even so, the fiction does not touch the difficulty of assessing political life inside the corporation, and it is this internal aspect that discussions of the corporation increasingly emphasize. Both critics and defenders of the corporation make the point that it is an association of people.[11] Whether it is a fellowship or a form of tyranny, however, it poses a problem of authority within itself. It possesses no claims, like the church's, to superior heavenly sanction. It can rely upon a theory of concession or delegation from the state, but to do so exposes it to the claims of external political control.

The traditional theory of corporate government—and it is of some interest that there is such a theory—is that stock ownership confers votes, which in turn control the choice of directors. In this sense, the government of the corporation has been derived from democratic theory. There was always a difficulty in that votes are attached to shares of stock rather than to individual human beings. This may have some precedent in the long-standing property-holding qualifications for the vote in the state, but the comparison is not really valid, since wealth is much more explicitly represented in the corporation than people. However, the theory at least was clear on one point: the constituency of the corporation's government consisted of the stockholders.

For some time (at least three decades) this theory has been untenable in the light of common knowledge about the realities of corporate life. The now-classic work of Berle and Means exploded the idea that ownership meant control in the large corporations of America.[12] Their demonstration of the actual separation of these factors created a sensation, but the demonstration withstood attack and in any event only confirmed what many observers had long sensed. The sheer size of the significant American corporations and the minute fractions of total

[10] Especially Robert Aaron Gordon, *Business Leadership in the Large Corporation* (Washington: The Brookings Institution, 1945). Most recently, Richard Eells, op. cit., has become the most articulate advocate.

[11] For example, Roger Blough, *Free Man and the Corporation* (New York: McGraw-Hill, 1959); also, "General Motors is People" (national advertising of General Motors).

[12] Adolph A. Berle and Gardiner C. Means, *The Modern Corporation and Private Property* (New York: Macmillan, 1932).

stockholdings that any one owner might possess made obsolete the idea of simple control by ownership (except in a very few corporations, notably the Ford Motor Company). The development of numerous legal devices and the control of the proxy machinery by management made a mockery of any belief that management could be readily challenged by any faction of the corporate citizenry. Proxy fights occurred during the period following World War II in somewhat greater numbers than Berle and Means expected, but they remained exceptional.[13]

The question of control, once raised, proved a Pandora's box. As questioners sought to discover the reality of control, it became apparent that to a very large degree management was in control. By virtue of its possession of the proxy machinery, it was more likely to select the directors than the directors the management.[14] Uneasily, many observers felt that they had passed through the looking glass. In one sense they found themselves in a Michelian world: organization was indeed conservative in that the leaders of the corporation carefully and effectively preserved their positions, and were, in fact, virtually self-perpetuating. The files, the membership list, the control of meetings—most of the devices Michels noted as accruing to the advantage of leadership in a membership organization—were in management's hands. Moreover, the presumed "members" were either apathetic about the exercise of their rights of self-governance or quite frankly determined not to exercise them. Indeed, at this point the reality of stockholder "membership" was so blatantly contrary to the formal theory of corporation government that the Michelian analysis collapsed by virtue of its success as explanation: the question arose whether the stockholders were indeed entitled to the control the formal theory gave them. In the eyes of some critics, the stockholder was not only incompetent and helpless in his role of "member"; he was also irresponsible and deserved the powerless state to which corporate reality had consigned him.[15] In short, the stockholder could not be considered a member of the corporation at all.

This, however, was not the last of the questions unleashed by the initial query. Just who could be considered a "member"? What was the corporation's constituency? For a long time leaders of major corporations have toyed with these questions and have been tempted to proclaim that their responsibilities extend far beyond the welfare of mere stockholders. But then how far do they reach? To the customer? Certainly no corporate executive could be expected to exclude this group. To the employees? This is less simple, since the conflict of interest between stockholders and employees is rather obvious; moreover, too bold or aggressive an assertion of this responsibility might even arouse charges of unfair labor practices under the National Labor Relations Act, since it could be taken as an attack on unions. To the general public? But what is the general public? The trend of business thought has sometimes been to deny that this concept is meaningful when it is invoked by government.

[13] See David Karr, *Fight for Control* (New York: Ballantine Books, 1956).

[14] Cf. R. A. Gordon, op. cit., p. 121.

[15] Abram Chayes, "The Modern Corporation and the Rule of Law," in Edward S. Mason, *The Corporation in Modern Society* (Cambridge, Mass.: Harvard University Press, 1959). See also the article by Eugene V. Rostow, "To Whom and for What Ends Is Corporate Management Responsible?" in the same volume.

A variety of motives were at work to release these questions. The muckrakers' attacks upon "the soulless corporation" invited the response that corporations had souls and were not merely machines for the enrichment of their owners. This was an especially tempting trap, and for a long time its dangers were not apparent; thus Judge Elbert Gary, first Chairman of United States Steel, insisted that his giant firm had not abused its power and had behaved responsibly, and the corporation's official historian even went so far as to assert that U.S. Steel *had* a soul.[16] With Gary's passing, however, whether because the danger in the position had become apparent or for other reasons, the firm's defense reverted to the blander assertion that it had no power. Perhaps there was also a motivation arising from a realistic sense of the behavior of corporations. Certainly it cannot have been very satisfactory to believe that the good that corporate leaders were convinced they were doing in the world was sheer inadvertence. At any rate, it is now almost fashionable for industrial chieftains to consider themselves statesmen and to enlarge in public upon the responsibilities they feel toward stockholders, consumers, employees, and the public. A few crusaders continue to struggle for "shareholder democracy," but their efforts are futile, and they are generally regarded with indulgent amusement.[17]

Although opinion may now be tending toward acceptance of the view that corporation leaders have just such a broad constituency, the questions still do not end. The really difficult ones remain: if, for example, there is a responsibility to a constituency that includes consumers, employees, and the public, how is it enforced? What are the means of accountability? These are very unpleasant questions indeed, and although the reply is seldom made loudly, it seems to be that corporation leaders are good men and make good decisions.

Obviously, this is a dangerous assertion. By what standards are they good? By what criteria can it be said that they do good? By what right do they claim to rule? What is this but an arrogation of power? Here are all the questions that must converge on power, and the questions have no answers. Richard Eells, a former corporate executive, has stated very justly that there is a constitutional crisis in the corporation.[18] The problem, in fact, is so acute that some sympathy may be given to the critics who would rather turn their backs upon it and take refuge in an extreme positivism which rejects the baleful notion of power entirely.[19] Unfortunately, however, the problem of legitimacy is not so easily induced to go away.

A number of points regarding the corporation are, then, quite clear. Power is one of its principal characteristics, exercised not merely over significant sectors of the economy, but over members of its own "family" as well. As might be expected, criticisms are not lacking that such power amounts to a form of

[16] Arundel Cotter, *United States Steel: A Corporation with a Soul* (Garden City, N.Y.: Doubleday Page & Co., 1921).

[17] Mr. Lewis D. Gilbert reportedly attended 150 annual meetings of different corporations during the annual meeting "season" of 1963. See his book, *Dividends and Democracy* (Larchmont, N.Y.: American Research Council, 1956).

[18] Eells, op. cit., chap. 2.

[19] Bayless Manning, "Corporate Power and Individual Freedom: Some General Analysis and Particular Reservations," *Northwestern University Law Review*, Vol. 55, no. 1 (March-April 1960), pp. 38-53.

tyranny.[20] The Michelian theory of oligarchy in organization seems all too well substantiated by the corporation, however numerous the various pressure-group influences on it may be; in fact, the reality is so plain that to dispute the thesis of oligarchy is scarcely worth undertaking. Second, there is no available theory by which this power can be regarded as legitimate, and without some such conception there are no guidelines for rendering it legitimate. Probably the only available ground for exonerating the corporation's present form of rule is the fact that stockholders generally find a ready market for their shares when they are sufficiently dissatisfied to resign their membership. This view, however, rests upon the theory that shareholders are the only true constituency of the corporation, a theory that is today acceptable to few people. Until its constitutional crisis has been solved, then, the corporation cannot be used as a model of private government for analytical or any other purposes.

In many ways the corporation presents a peculiar problem, and is untypical of the many associations with which the United States is endowed. If corporations, churches, and the various organizations lacking membership in any realistic sense are excepted, the overwhelming number of the remainder are founded on a conception of authority which derives from the democratic ethos of the surrounding culture. In most, membership has a defined meaning, and the will of the membership provides the basis of authority.

Although genuine membership organizations of this sort are exceedingly numerous, they have similar characteristics and share the same problems, much of the similarity being the result of their mutual imitation of organizational form. Constitutions for new organizations are quite frequently simple copies of those of existing organizations, with only trivial changes of names and detail. This borrowing takes place even where the substantive interests of the organizations involved are very different; thus, for example, the constitution of the International Typographical Union was apparently based upon that of the Order of Odd Fellows.[21] Beyond this, it is to be expected that experience gained with organization in one sphere should be applied in others. The general conception of government in membership organizations, for whatever reasons, appears to be much the same. To understand the character of this conception, then, it is useful to follow the example of Michels and examine its operation in the practice of the organizations most devoted to the ideal of democratic association.

III

In the United States, as in a number of other countries, the associations which have most vociferously dedicated themselves to an ideal of democratic organization are the trade unions. Although their claim to superiority in this regard may be contested by various other groups, the unions are on the whole the most

[20] See the general indictment in William H. Whyte, Jr., *The Organization Man* (New York: Simon & Schuster, 1956).

[21] See George E. Barnett, "The Government of the Typographical Union," in Jacob H. Hollander and George E. Barnett, eds., *Studies in American Trade Unions* (New York: H. Holt & Co., 1912), p. 19.

conspicuous claimants, and it would be mistaken to doubt their fundamental sincerity. They were born of a profound desire to establish democracy in the daily working conditions of industrial life. Whatever the American labor movement's aberrations in predatory unionism, the institution of industrial democracy has undeniably been one of its fundamental objectives. Here, if anywhere in the nation, the democratic vision should be clear and practice enlightened. What, then, are the conceptions at work, and how have they evolved?[22]

The source of authority in a trade union is the same as in a democratic state: the membership or the whole of the citizen body. In a small organization, such as a local, the membership (or a given portion of it defined as a quorum) meets and makes its own governing decisions. Ideally the presiding officer is no more than a moderator acting to preserve the conditions of orderly discussion and decision; the meeting itself is the sovereign body. Here is the ideal of the town meeting, of direct democracy. In a large organization, however, the meeting of the whole citizenry or membership cannot be approximated by these devices. The effective substitute is the convention, which has some similarities to a legislature, but also important differences. The delegates are not representatives in the same sense as are, say, members of Congress who meet continuously for extended periods. They are a much closer approximation to the town meeting of the citizenry.[23]

Accordingly, the convention frequently passes not only resolutions stating policies and "laws" or "statutes," but also constitutional amendments. This latter practice is not universal among trade unions, but it is nonetheless widespread. It underlies the fact that the convention in session is generally regarded as the embodiment of the sovereign power of the general membership and not merely as an ordinary legislature. An incident in the 1944 convention of the United Mine Workers will illustrate. At this convention the union's president, John L. Lewis, received a personal telegram from the Secretary of the Interior. Lewis referred the telegram to the convention, and a reply was sent to the Secretary in the convention's name. A second telegram addressed personally to Lewis arrived, and he then proposed the following reply before the assembled delegates:

You do not seem to understand that our telegram to you was adopted by the unanimous vote of 2700 delegates elected by the mine workers of the nation in their home communities. This convention is the supreme authority of the Union. We are the employers of John Lewis and he is responsible to our orders. While this convention is in session we will answer his telegrams if we elect to

[22] Much of what follows in the remainder of this chapter previously appeared in Grant McConnell: "The Spirit of Private Government," *The American Political Science Review,* Vol. 52, no. 3 (September 1958), pp. 754-70.

[23] The convention's similarities to the British Parliament are superficially greater. To press this analogy, however, is to ignore the strong constitutional restraints that have developed to circumscribe the actions of Parliament, a development that has not occurred in American trade union conventions. For a vivid descriptio . of the convention in the Teamsters Union see Sam Romer, *The International Brotherhood of Teamsters, Its Government and Structure* (New York: John Wiley & Sons, 1962), chap. 2. There is an extended account of the American Federation of State, County and Municipal Employees in Leo Kramer, *Labor's Paradox* (New York: John Wiley & Sons, 1962), chap. 3.

do so. When we go home you can move in on him if you desire but watch your guard and protect your wind. We think he will go around you like a cooper around a barrel.[24]

With but one dissenting vote the telegram was adopted by the convention as its own.

The fiction that union leadership is no more than the servant of the assembled membership was perhaps transparent in this instance. Nevertheless, the underlying theory was consistent with the temper of the reply. Moreover, the existence of the theory sometimes has important consequences. Thus during the steel crisis of 1952, which resulted in President Truman's seizure of the steel mills, Philip Murray, president of the Steelworkers, persuaded the union to pass a measure forbidding the union leadership to accept a truce plan without approval of a special convention. As a tactical measure it almost precipitated extreme action by the federal government and Murray and the union leadership had to repudiate it hastily.[25]

While the convention is in session, then, the leadership in theory serves only as moderator. The leadership has no authority for independent action, and can only carry out the mandate of the collective decisions. To fulfill the many tasks facing it in a short span of time, the convention is compelled to rely on the work of temporary committees, but these too are merely the agents and servants of the larger body. This rationale also applies to the periods between convention sessions. In a great variety of provisions, from arrangements for election at conventions to requirements of ratification of officers' actions by the next convention, the pattern is made clear. From time to time, as in the examples given above, the fictional character of the pattern becomes apparent, but generally these instances are regarded as exceptional.

In theory, then, the union's executive body is a committee or group of officers of the whole membership as embodied in the convention. Although it may make a very real practical difference whether the officers are elected in convention or by referendum vote, the theoretical conception is not greatly different here. The officers are in theory definitely subordinate to the convention, a term which implies a body with constituent powers. The convention will usually dissolve at the end of its meeting. The president will often have power to summon a new convention, but its members then will be newly elected and possessed of a completely fresh mandate. Its authority, whatever the variations of practice, will be virtually unlimited, far greater than that of any legislature. And this authority in turn will serve to justify the leadership's exercise of power after the convention has been dissolved.

The officers, in fact, have very great power when the convention is not in session—real and authorized power, not normally considered as usurped. In some organizations the president's actions are specifically made subject to the approval of the executive board—of which he is, of course, the chairman. Some students have regarded this as a check on his power, but it is important to see that such a provision is intended less as a check on power than as a form of insurance that

24 Quoted in J. Kovner, *Report on Conventions,* typescript, p. 337.

25 The incident is told in Grant McConnell, *The Steel Seizure of 1952* (Published by the University of Alabama Press, University, Alabama, 1960, for Inter-University Case Program), p. 17.

the will of the membership is carried out. Actually, however, such a provision is a very slight check in any sense upon presidential power.[26] Whatever the facts, it is quite clear that the purpose is not the division of power.

In a larger sense, the evaluation of private government in terms of its checks and balances is beside the point. For, as with the checks on executive power, there is little conception of checks and balances as a system. The convention is not a legislature, and the executive is only an instrument of the general membership as represented in convention; the executive board is only an agent and the president is its continuing chairman. These bodies do not check each other, nor are they intended to. It is true that measures are taken in some unions for auditing funds (in which experience has been most disillusioning) and for the unseating of officers. But these devices are frequently weak and have appeared as grafts on a scheme of government to which they are intrinsically foreign. There is no *system* of checks and balances here.

If we look within the government of unions—and most other associations—for other important features of public government in the United States, we find additional important differences. The most striking is the absence of a bill of rights. In almost any union constitution it is possible to cull a list of membership duties which could stand as a "bill of obligations," but almost never a list of members' rights comparable in importance to those in the first amendments to the federal Constitution. Such enumerations of rights as are found are apt to be those not accorded to nonmembers; they are not the rights of members against the association or its government. On the other hand, the items of the "bill of obligations" are both numerous and inclusive. Thus, "conduct unbecoming a union man," "creating dissension," "slandering an officer," and "undermining the union" are frequently named as punishable offenses.[27]

There are rudimentary guarantees for trials and appeals. They need to be viewed, however, against the common provision of penalties for members who seek redress of grievances against the associations in public courts of law. The public courts are generally unwilling to take jurisdiction over such issues where there is a system of internal appeals and the entire system has not yet run its course. Typically, the system calls for an original trial by a trial committee of the local organization; decision by the local; appeal to the president or executive council of the national organization; appeal to the convention, with action by a trial committee; and final decision rendered by majority vote of the convention. This system may in some stable situations permit the development of a body of case law and a rule of stare decisis, but it is hardly conducive to either.

A discussion of United States government, or that of any Western democracy, would be very unrealistic if it did not treat the party system. In union government, however, parties have almost no place; the practice of most unions is, indeed, antagonistic to parties. In some organizations, parties are in effect forbidden by constitutional rules against circulating partisan electioneering

[26] See Philip Taft, "Constitutional Power of the Chief Officer in American Labor Unions,' *Quarterly Journal of Economics,* Vol. 62 (May 1948), pp. 459-71. However, compare the tenor of that discussion with Taft's *The Structure and Government of Labor Unions* (Cambridge, Mass.: Harvard Univ. Press, 1954), chap. 8.

[27] See the tabulation and discussion in Philip Taft, "Judicial Procedure in Labor Unions," *Quarterly Journal of Economics,* Vol. 59 (May 1945), pp. 370-85; however, see also his *The Structure and Government of Labor Unions,* pp. 123-25, for an apologia.

materials or participating in "outside" meetings relating to union affairs. Thus, the Constitution of the International Brotherhood of Electrical Workers makes the following offenses punishable by fine, suspension, or expulsion:

Attending or participating in any gathering or meeting whatsoever, held outside meetings of a L.U. [local union], at which the affairs of the L.U. are discussed, or at which conclusions are arrived at regarding the business and the affairs of a L.U. or regarding L.U. officers or a candidate or candidates for L.U. office.

Mailing, handing out, or posting cards, handbills, letters, marked ballots or political literature of any kind, or displaying streamers, banners, signs or anything else of a political nature, or being a party in any way to such being done in an effort to induce members to vote for or against any candidate or candidates for L.U. office, or candidates to conventions.[28]

These provisions are somewhat more stringent than those in some other union constitutions, but the point of view is widely shared. Thus Philip Murray, one of the most justly revered of American labor leaders, warned the 1942 convention of the Steelworkers at its first meeting:

I do not want—as a matter of fact, I shall fight any attempt that is made to have little back room caucuses while this convention is going on. There is going to be one convention in the city of Cleveland and it is going to be held in this hall. We are not going to permit sharp practices and petty politics to be played in the Steelworkers. So if any of the boys are thinking right now of midnight sessions in strange places in the city of Cleveland, just begin to forget about it right now. There is only going to be one convention . . . . That is the democratic way to do business . . . .[29]

Statements in a similar spirit have been made by numerous other prominent labor leaders and convey the orthodox doctrine. Some factionalism does occur in many unions, but it is generally deplored within them and tends to die out with the complete victory of some of the contenders. Only one private association of importance, the International Typographical Union, has an *institutionalized* system of parties. This organization, the subject of an intensive study,[30] is so atypical that it only sharpens the impression of an almost universal distaste for disunity and division within other unions.

The amendment process of many unions is also quite different from that provided in the United States Constitution, and ordinarily much easier to operate. Practice is somewhat varied. Although some union constitutions may be amended only by a two-thirds vote, sometimes in convention and sometimes by general referendum, it is not at all uncommon for amendment to be by majority vote in convention. The distinction between constitutional amendment, ordinary legislation, and specific decree therefore tends to be blurred in such associations, and is not especially clear in some of the others. The common

[28]Constitution of the International Brotherhood of Electrical Workers, Art. 27: 15, 16.

[29]Quoted in Kovner, op. cit., p. 207.

[30]S. M. Lipset, M. Trow, and J. Coleman, *Union Democracy* (Glencoe, Ill.: The Free Press, 1956).

attitude toward constitutional amendment was expressed many years ago by John Mitchell, then president of the United Mine Workers:

The constitution of the trade union, moreover, has been evolved by and through the efforts of workingmen. The trade union is a government of workingmen, by workingmen, for workingmen and the framers of its constitution have been workingmen. Although the supreme law of the union was not formulated by highly paid constitutional lawyers, nevertheless, it represents in a clear and definite manner the ideals, purposes, and aims of the great majority of the members of the organization.

The faithfulness with which trade union constitutions represent trade union sentiment is due to the elasticity of these constitutions. The government of trade unions is loose and flexible and neither constitutions nor by-laws are rigidly fixed and immutable. The object of the leaders, as of the rank and file of trade unionists, has been to preserve the largest possible elasticity and freedom of movement to the ruling majority of the organization. In trade union management, there is no tyranny of the "dead hand." Even the most conservative unions are not bound by a blind, unthinking worship of an outgrown instrument, but adjust their form of government to the changing needs and exigencies of the times.

To a certain extent, therefore, the formal written constitution of a trade union is rather a statement of principles and a formulation of the present policy of the union than a hard and fast determination of its future laws. Trade union constitutions are easily changed.[31]

When all the foregoing features of trade union government are considered they fit into a remarkably consistent pattern. They are all derived from the same central conception of politics, sometimes termed "majoritarian democracy." The term, however, is a somewhat misleading description of the political realities of these associations, for it suggests that a very high place is given to majority rule. In actual practice, something more than mere majority assent is sought. The common stress upon "not washing dirty linen in public" and the frequent decrying of factionalism embody a goal far closer to unanimity than simple majority rule.

Unity is seen as the price of staying organized. The fear of organizational disintegration is recurrently the decisive factor in the framing of governing institutions, and although this fear may often be the immediate motivation, the arrangements that emerge are consistent with a particular conception of democratic rule. Even more important than fear of disintegration, however, is the belief that such devices as checks and balances and constitutional limitations are both unnecessary and improper. The argument may be summarized briefly: If power is good, why limit it? If power is evil, why have it? Since the organization is the total of its membership and since its goals are the common goals of its members, limitation of its power is not only undemocratic but also irrational.

[31] John Mitchell, *Organized Labor* (Philadelphia: American Book and Bible House, 1903), pp. 75, 76.

IV

This conception of government seems to be pervasive throughout the array of American labor organizations, but it is not peculiar to unions. How widespread it is among other types of association is impossible to say in the absence of any thorough study of the multitude of American associations, but even the most casual inspection suggests that it is common to many farm organizations, veterans' organizations, and numerous others. What, then, is its validity?

If such a conception were offered for the government of the United States it is probably safe to say that it would be rejected by most people. It is incompatible with the actual practice of government in any large democratic society we know of. Moreover, many people would also reject the conception even if institutions compatible with it could be put into effect. The question accordingly arises whether there are peculiar characteristics of private associations that justify their accepting it.

There is no simple answer to this question. The unions and other associations are exceedingly varied, but they do have a number of common traits, and it is necessary to examine these traits one by one.

Perhaps first among the general traits of private associations is that emphasized in the word "private." The implications of the concept of privacy have never been thoroughly and systematically explored, but it is safe to say that it is fundamental to Western traditions of government. It is closely tied to the idea of constitutionalism, which implies limitations upon the sphere of public government. Most typically, the distinction between *public* and *private* relates to the state and the individual. In the present discussion, however, the tradition of real corporate personality as developed by a long line of pluralist thinkers from Althusius to the early Laski is involved. Most of the pluralists of earlier times combined a deep concern for individual rights with enthusiasm and concern for the corporate personality of the association. If there is irony in their position, it has become apparent only in fairly recent years.

A second distinctive characteristic of these associations is autonomy. Almost all assert a right to be self-determining and self-governing. This may take the form of an appeal to the historical origin of the association in a spontaneous meeting of like-minded individuals. But it is often asserted where such an origin cannot be claimed. Thus the claim of autonomy is hardly less strong among those unions of the old CIO which were the direct creations of organizing campaigns under leadership provided by older unions. The claim and its presumption of rightfulness within the context of American labor ideology was one of the difficulties the CIO encountered when, some years ago, it "tried" several of its component unions for Communist domination and then attempted to destroy them by establishing new organizations to take possession of the convicted organizations' jurisdictions. Autonomy here seemed to reside in the international union rather than the federation, and it was asserted quite as much against the federation as it recently has been asserted by the Teamsters against both federation and public government.

Traditionally the claim to autonomy has involved a hesitancy to utilize public aid, even where this aid could be demonstrated to offer much to the associations' constituencies. Thus, during the long discussion of the merits of unemployment insurance the official (albeit challenged) position of organized labor was that less social security with autonomy for labor's organizations was better than greater social security provided through the medium of public government. The argument that what government might give, government might also take away, was in part founded on good grounds; it was also a rationalization of the desire for undivided member loyalties. If there was a nice counterpart here to the claims of laissez faire from the business organizations, it was also true that in practice the more conservative and consistent position was that of organized labor. Even organized agriculture, traditionally more willing than either organized business or organized labor to resort to public government, has attempted at various times to act autonomously. The Society of Equity sponsored a plan for farmers to withhold their produce from the market until the Equity-declared prices were met. The National Farm Organization has more recently attempted the same tactic. Here was good, if simple, imitation of business practice. It was also an attempt to maintain autonomy. The farm organizations have sought a similar goal with their cooperatives.

An important corollary of autonomy is the association's claim of the right to formulate its own constituency. Nearly every association lays down conditions for membership, affecting both entrance and continued membership. The conditions of eligibility are usually quite explicit, and oaths or pledges are frequently required of new members. Candidates for membership, even when they are solicited by the organizations, must come as suppliants or at least applicants, the formal decision on acceptance being made by the association.

A third important trait of these associations is limited purpose. They do not purport to concern themselves with all aspects of their members' lives. Sometimes their purpose is stated quite specifically, as for example: "To establish through collective bargaining adequate wage standards, shorter hours of work and improvements in the conditions of employment for the workers in the industry";[32] at other times the object may be quite vague. In either event, it is presumed that the association's objects do not encompass the entire range of the individual constituent's interests or preoccupations. He will have his own privacy, and he will, accordingly, have other loyalties. So a man may be a trade union member of a particular craft; but he may also be a church member, a Legionnaire, and a member of a team in the municipal bowling league, to say nothing of his place within his family or in a political party. The assumption is that no association will encroach on spheres of life other than its own.

A fourth trait, in considerable degree a corollary of some of the characteristics already listed, is homogeneity. Since the autonomous association selects its membership, and since its purposes are limited, within the scope of the association there will be only people of similar characteristics and like minds. Most important, there will be no conflicts of interest or grounds for legitimate conflict within the association; there is thus a presumptive absence of the basic political problem that other democratic societies of larger scope must resolve. If there is no conflict of interest or outlook, the only possible reasons for conflict will be error, personality, or something amounting to treason. The condition of homogeneity is precisely the solution Madison named in his famous argument in the

[32] Second object of the United Steelworkers of America, stated in Article II of its Constitution. The other two stated are to unite all eligible workers and to secure legislation safeguarding the economic security and social welfare of workers in the industry.

Federalist Number 10, but felt compelled to reject as a solution to the problem of faction in the larger society.[33]

A fifth distinguishing characteristic is the voluntary character of the association. So, although the association may determine its own membership, the individual member also makes a decision to join or not. Typically he must actively request admittance. He is not a member automatically—as he is a citizen by birth in a state—but by virtue of positive choice. Initiation and probationary status serve to emphasize the element of individual choice in joining. Equally important is the individual member's right to resign. Resignation is the individual's ultimate recourse and the element that finally distinguishes the private association from the public body.

The voluntary aspect of private associations has repeatedly been held to place them in a very special relationship to democracy, one often so special that it is described as a necessary condition of democracy. Such a view was cogently argued by the pluralists of several decades ago; more recent writers have repeated the argument forcefully. Thus, V. L. Allen has argued that so long as individuals are free to join and to leave societies of their own choice, the essence of democracy is present even if there is no machinery permitting the members to control the societies.[34]

It should be apparent that these different characteristics of the private association to a very large degree overlap and rest upon each other. The meaning of privacy is impaired without autonomy. Homogeneity cannot be achieved without limitation of purposes, and voluntary choice underlies the entire arrangement. These, indeed, are all aspects of a single perception of the private association.

The conclusion at this point, then, must be that insofar as the conditions prescribed in this perception are met, the system of government that has been described earlier is proper and reconcilable with the goals and objectives to which we are committed in the governments of the United States and other liberal democracies.

V

However, a question remains: to what extent are the qualities so described actually found in existing unions and other private associations? How well, for example, have they maintained the distinction between "public" and "private"? Obviously, no precise answer in general terms is possible; it is apparent, nevertheless, that for many associations this particular distinction has been seriously blurred in recent years.

This is most apparent with labor unions. Until 1933, it could reasonably be argued that their private character was relatively unimpaired. The American labor movement had rejected political means of action, that is to say, the use of

[33] This argument has been previously advanced in Lloyd H. Fisher and Grant McConnell, "Labor Union Solidarity," in Kornhauser, Dubin, and Ross, eds., *Industrial Conflict* (New York: McGraw-Hill, 1954).

[34] V. L. Allen, *Power in Trade Unions* (London: Longmans, Green, 1954), p. 10.

public government. Not only had socialism been decisively defeated within the labor movement, but positive legislation, however mild, was mistrusted. This was most striking with regard to social insurance: not until 1932 did the AFL so much as commend unemployment insurance. The only legislation commanding strong official enthusiasm was directed against labor injunctions, that is, it was legislation designed to curb state intervention in labor disputes. Organized labor sought its goals through the medium of its own economic bargaining power. It would be difficult to imagine a more thoroughgoing observance of the distinction between what is private and what is public.

With the passage of the National Industrial Recovery Act and its Section 7-A, however, and more particularly with passage of the Wagner Act and labor's acceptance and utilization of the provisions assisting labor organization, organized labor departed radically from its previous position. This was not just a matter of legal theory. Since the law conferred exclusive bargaining rights upon a union which succeeded in winning a government-supervised election, that union acquired a substantial measure of public power—power that extended to individuals and minorities which had not voted for the union in the election. The process of NLRB-supervised elections has been widely resorted to by American unions. The surrender of privacy so entailed was not fully apparent, however, until the Taft-Hartley Act was passed, and became even more apparent with passage of the Landrum-Griffin Act, which explicitly provided for public intervention in the internal affairs of unions. Although some unions have indicated a willingness to revert to the situation existing before the passage of the Wagner Act, the element of privacy is not likely to be regained.

Different situations prevail with other associations; it is nevertheless apparent that for many a question remains whether their private character has been preserved. Often, for example, the exercise of licensing powers is delegated to "private" associations, even though the coercive power involved is that of a state.[35] In the clearest case of this sort an association receives direct delegation; in other cases professional or trade associations are given the power to nominate personnel, virtually as a form of representation, to official licensing boards (bar associations, for example) and, on occasion, to policy-making boards. This is by no means unusual and is perhaps a growing trend.

A more perplexing question arises when a private association called into being by actions of government officials acquires the power to exert great influence over policy and administration, in the form either of membership on advisory boards of administrative agencies or of any exceedingly influential association's commanding the close attention of powerful congressional committees. Examples here are the American Farm Bureau Federation and the Chamber of Commerce of the United States, both of which had direct governmental encouragement in their formation. Obviously in such situations there is a shadowland between what is public and what is private. The years since the inception of the New Deal have seen much rationalization of this blurring, but clearly it is a concomitant of the growth of associational power during this period; clearly also, the blurring is incompatible with the previous conception of the private association.

[35]Cf. J.A.C. Grant: "The Gild Returns to America," *Journal of Politics,* Vol. 4, pp. 303-36 and 458-77.

These comments apply, too, to the private association's claim of autonomy. Labor unions, in taking an extreme position for laissez faire and freedom from social legislation, were defending their autonomy vis-à-vis government. In defending themselves from their own federations with which they have individually had occasional conflicts, however, the "international" unions are in a sense also defending their privacy. Not that this has been a matter of explicit discussion within the labor movement; but here, as with other matters of policy, labor's highly pragmatic leadership has behaved with a greater consistency than it has always been ready to acknowledge. The consequences of large units of organization do seem to have been visualized, however vaguely. If the locus of power within the labor movement is to be in the federations, the common form of action must be broad in character—almost necessarily a form of political action. Whether this takes the form of pressure for legislation, closely controlled administration, or political strikes, it weakens organized labor's claims to be uninhibited by governmental action. A similar set of considerations applies to the development of the American Farm Bureau Federation. Much of the early controversy about this association centered around the supposed differences between the county farm bureaus and the state and national federations.[36] It is significant that the particular compromise effected also involved a compromise over the distribution of power between the local and federal units of the association. Here, to an even greater degree than later developed in the labor movement, the drift of the gravitational center toward the larger unit inside the association meant a drift toward political action.

As for the third trait of the private association, limited purpose, the practice of some of our more important associations has evidently also departed rather far from the conception sketched above. Some trade unions have sponsored educational plans; others have developed housing and recreational resources for the benefit of their members. The activities of the United Automobile Workers and the International Ladies Garment Workers are leading cases in point. Almost all unions have long-established systems of friendly benefits—pensions, insurance, and so on—which, however advantageous they may be to their members, also serve the purpose of strengthening the members' ties to the organizations. Agricultural organizations have from their very beginnings sought to solve many of the problems of rural life through subsidiary cooperatives. Many associations seek to demonstrate their civic responsibility by resolutions on matters of citizenship, Americanism, and foreign policy, and by gifts to colleges, scholarships, and other means.

The fourth trait of private associations, homogeneity, is in some ways the most important. A membership united in interests, beliefs, and tastes is itself a solution to the most troubling problem of government, and the possibility of achieving such an identity is in some measure the peculiar governmental advantage possessed by private associations. Every such association must and does achieve it in some degree, yet none can achieve it completely. In the concept of homogeneity, in fact, lies a latent inconsistency with the characteristic of limited purpose. A single interest may be shared, but the complexities of human nature are too great for a homogeneity that extends much beyond this. Even where the

[36] See Grant McConnell, *The Decline of Agrarian Democracy* (Berkeley and Los Angeles: University of California Press, 1953), pp. 52-54.

boundaries of the association are fixed to coincide with the number of people sharing the one interest, divergencies of interest will arise and persist within the association. Examples are the differences between young and old in a trade union with a pension system, between employed and unemployed in any union during a depression, between producers of different commodities in a farm organization, between large and small producers in a trade association. There are serious grounds for doubting a claim of extensive homogeneity in any association that rests on the obvious differences in taste, ability, and understanding among men. Associations characteristically exaggerate the homogeneity they achieve.

The fifth trait of associations, their voluntary character, is probably the main justification of their forms of government. Here, it is evident that the penalties for not belonging to an association differ greatly in incidence and degree, and the severity of the penalty is an index of the association's power. The penalty for not belonging to a particular trade union in some communities may be forfeiture of the right to practice a trade; it may be the same with the right to practice medicine.[37] The penalty may be denial of the most effective means of access to publicly offered benefits, for example those administered by the Veterans Administration. When the right of resignation is accompanied by the availability of membership in competing organizations, the right is worth something. However, few trade unions are true rivals in any sense meaningful to their members; "dual unionism," as we have seen, is accounted a cardinal sin within the American labor movement. General farm organizations do compete in this manner, but their respective areas of strength are different. As for trade associations, it is clear that their fundamental rationalizing impulse is hostile to competition. Where their jurisdictions overlap and open warfare cannot quickly settle the boundary, consolidation or demarcation by agreement is soon accomplished. In fact, this pattern seems almost to be a law of behavior among our most significant private associations. The simple fact, then, is that often the private association is not voluntary.

The conclusions emerge that, first, the government of private associations is very commonly founded on a theory of absolute democracy; second, the validity of this theory rests on a series of assumptions about the peculiar characteristics of private associations; and third, these assumptions are seriously at odds with the facts about some of our most important "private" associations.

In assessing the significance of these conclusions it must be kept in mind that there are very great differences among the practices of different associations. These differences may be principally of degree, and yet be of great importance; thus although the governments of the United Mine Workers and, say, the League of Women Voters may have some similarities, to ignore the differences between them would be to produce a very false picture.

But if the existence of large differences of degree among private associations is recognized, how widely shared is the theory of government that has been outlined in the preceding pages? No precise answer to this question is possible, but it does appear probable that the theory is very widely shared. The International Typographical Union is the only association of significance that has been offered

[37]Cf. *Yale Law Journal,* May 1954; Oliver Garceau, *The Political Life of the American Medical Association* (Cambridge, Mass.: Harvard University Press, 1941).

as a great exception to the rule of the "iron law of oligarchy."[38] Virtually all others that have been made the subject of careful study have to some degree substantiated that "law." The examples of trade unions are particularly important, since these profess a special dedication to democratic methods, with institutions very generally framed on a strictly majoritarian pattern.

The reasons for the prevalence of this pattern of government in private associations are not easy to state. The reason most commonly offered is that most associations, certainly most trade unions, are in some degree warring institutions. According to this argument, such an organization needs to present a united front, and must not display internal disagreement, lest advantage be given to its opponents. The argument probably had some effect in persuading potential dissidents not to voice their dissent; it is not altogether obvious, however, that expression of internal opposition necessarily weakens the organization. Generally, trade unions have experienced most internal opposition at times when their most intense battles for organizational survival have been fought. In point of fact the times of peace are those in which tolerance of internal opposition declines.[39] The usual argument seems to rest on an assumption that any internal opposition can end only in complete victory for one of the contending factions, the defeated would-be leaders going over to the external enemy. Actual illustrations of such occurrences can be given, but they hardly support the contention that it is a necessary result.

Strong distaste for anything less than unanimity seems to be one of the principal characteristics of private associations. Perhaps the most common response to disagreement when it does appear is to attempt to suppress it, either by appeals for unity or by more drastic means. Some associations do attempt to confront the problem in a different manner. One of the more interesting devices was the elaborate system of referenda utilized until the late 1950s by the Chamber of Commerce of the United States in formulating its own positions on matters of national policy. On subjects the Board of Directors deemed to be "national in character, timely in importance, and general in application to business and industry," committee reports were sought and presented in pamphlets submitted to the membership. The committee recommendations were balanced by statements drawn up by the Chamber's research department, of reasons opposing the recommended position. The machinery for insuring the integrity of the balloting was elaborate. A two-thirds majority vote was required to commit the organization. The procedure had some large deficiencies as a democratic device, most notably the absence of genuine debate on the measures considered. Nevertheless, it was remarkable how frequently measures were adopted by majority votes of more than 90 percent. This record is reminiscent of plebiscites elsewhere and suggests that the function served by the referenda was to proclaim policy rather than make it. The nature of the referenda themselves and their phrasing, however, indicated that the desire for unanimity had much to do with the results. The positions taken were, by comparison with the

[38] However, it has been claimed that even in the ITU the party system is dying out. See Paul Jacobs, *Old Before Its Time: Collective Bargaining at 28* (Santa Barbara, Calif.: Center for the Study of Democratic Institutions, 1963), p. 28.

[39] For example, the history of the Auto Workers. Cf. Jack Stieber, *Governing the U.A.W.* (New York: John Wiley & Sons, 1962), chap. 5.

positions taken by other business groups on the same subjects, moderate, and the language in which they were stated was moderate.[40] This consequence of the drive for unanimity, however, is not common.

In general, the weight of available evidence on private associations is overwhelmingly on the side of Michels' "law" of oligarchy. Supporters of particular associations quite properly insist that there are significant differences among associations, differences which cannot always be seen merely by looking at constitutional provisions; the spirit and practice of some unions and other organizations are more democratic than their internal law requires. It could well be argued that the differences are more important than any general similarities that may be found among associations; some observers, in fact, seek to dismiss the question of democratic control of union governments as unimportant. It is claimed, for example, that the members of the Carpenters' Union may be quite aware of the undemocratic character of many of their union's practices, but are generally satisfied with the union nonetheless; the economic benefits it confers on its members outweigh any misgivings on other scores.[41] Nevertheless, when all these different arguments have been made, the really general fact is the prevalence of oligarchy in private associations.

In one sense oligarchic rule is what might have been anticipated once private associations were regarded as forms of government, for every government is to a degree an oligarchy. But the difference between public and private government does not lie here. Public governments have a long tradition of grappling with the problem of controlling and limiting power. Few topics have so occupied political philosophers over so many centuries. There have been many attempts to solve the problem by trial and error; consequently, a large variety of devices for checking and limiting power exists in public systems. The entire tradition of constitutionalism is discernible in the governing institutions of any Western nation.

With private associations, however, this tradition has not applied, and there have been few attempts to develop institutional restraints on governmental power or to seek in any way to limit it. There would appear to be no intrinsic reasons why such restraints should not be developed. A few American trade unions (the UAW, the Upholsterers, and the Packinghouse Workers) have instituted a device of independent boards to review cases involving individual members and their unions.[42] Some unions have managed to tolerate very lively factional disputes without major disaster; the Typographical Union, as we have noted, has even had a formal system of parties. Although these are relatively exceptional examples, they are sufficient to illustrate the possibility of constitutionalizing private governments. Experience, nevertheless, does appear to bear out the expectation deriving from the considerations set forth in the

[40] This trait of the referenda was remarked on by Childs in his study of 1929. The point remained valid throughout the period in which the referendum was in use. See Harwood L. Childs, *Labor and Capital in National Politics* (Columbus, O.: Ohio State University Press, 1930), pp. 161-71.

[41] This is the argument of Walter Galenson in the foreword to Morris A. Horowitz, *The Structure and Government of the Carpenters' Union* (New York: John Wiley & Sons, 1962), p. ix.

[42] See Jack Stieber, Walter E. Oberer, and Michael Harrington: "Democracy and Public Review" (Santa Barbara, Calif.: Center for the Study of Democratic Institutions, 1960).

previous chapter that small political bodies limited in diversity of constituency are unlikely to develop constitutional patterns of internal politics.

The remarkable fact about private government, then, is not that it is oligarchic, but that it generally lacks the limitations that guard against tyranny and injustice to minorities and individuals. This lack, in turn, seems to be related to a deep and widespread illusion about the nature of politics in private associations. The illusion is that in any group homogeneity is ever complete or that unanimity is ever possible. Certainly a greater degree of homogeneity is possible in a private association than in a nation. Agreement within a private association can perhaps be more extensive and more concrete. Nevertheless, the difference is one of degree, and the problems of politics, of reconciling differences, and of limiting political power remain. The record of private associations in dealing with these problems gives little justification for the wishful view that the private association is the natural home of democracy.

2

Corporations

Earl Latham

THE BODY POLITIC OF THE CORPORATION

To understand the relationship between public government and the private enterprise system, we need to recognize that the great corporations are themselves "political systems," Earl Latham maintains. Here he examines the analogy between public and private government as it applies to giant firms and points out that they have all the requisite characteristics: legislatures, executives, judicial systems, and political factions.

One of America's most important political problems is a long-needed and now-urgent redefinition of the relation between giant corporations and the commonwealth, for the growth of the corporation has produced a tension of power in which giant enterprises have at points come to rival the sovereignty of the state itself. The great corporations are political systems in which their market, social, and political influence goes far beyond their functional efficiency in the economy. Indeed, in the very culture of the American people, the influence of the larger principalities overflows the banks of their corporate jurisdiction or economic reason. In the name of free enterprise, corporate collectivism has made deep inroads upon the celebrated individualism of the economy, and corporate welfarism has gone an equal distance toward tranquilizing the historic iniative of the individual in a smother of narcotic "togetherness."

It is the purpose of this paper to discuss these corporations as systems of private government.

The Concept of the Corporation

Although the political influence of the corporation on public affairs is widely appreciated, its political nature as a system of private government is not. It is easy to see it as an economic institution, as a complex of legal rights and duties and even as a social system. But the economic and political natures of the corporation do not dwell apart in a Nestorian separation. To go back no further than Hobbes, we find a clear statement that the elements of the corporate nature are welded in a single body; and that the dominant characteristic is the political. In speaking of the infirmities of the commonwealth, of the diseases from which governments might suffer or perish, Hobbes spoke of "the great number of corporations; which are as it were many lesser commonwealths in the bowels of a greater, like worms in the entrails of a man." Although the physiology may be distracting, the political figure is unexceptionable, for, indeed, corporations were "lesser commonwealths," distinguished from Leviathan, according to Hobbes, only in that they are normally less absolute in their dominion

Reprinted by permission of the publishers from Edward S. Mason, ed., *The Corporation in Modern Society*, Cambridge, Mass.: Harvard University Press.

than the state. The identity they share with the state, he said, is their characteristic as *systems,* public systems, and like all public systems they are known as a "body politic." Or, as Arthur Bentley put it twenty-five decades later, "A corporation is government through and through." To be sure, "certain technical methods which political government uses, as, for instance, hanging, are not used by corporations, generally speaking, but that is a detail."

Although the economic aspects of the corporation have received widest notice, the concept of the corporation as a political system is by no means unknown. The work of Walton Hamilton makes free use of the Hobbesian concept that the corporation is a lesser commonwealth, and indeed in some cases not the lesser but the greater. Merriam has spoken of business enterprise as a form of private government and has concluded that sectors of it at times have controlled the public government. C. Wright Mills refers to the corporation as a political institution. A. A. Berle, Jr., also talks of the corporation as a political institution, and thinks that it should be studied as such because this "is the stuff of pure political theory," which stuff is, however, otherwise unidentified. In another flash of fateful precocity, Berle found politics in all manner of organized enterprises besides the corporation, a view he shares with Aristotle and Walton Hamilton.

In the literature on corporations, there are even corporate equivalents of bad German theories of the state. Thus the citizen of the corporate state—the individual stockholder—is made to disappear in the mystic organic unity of the corporate totality in the statement, "It might even be said without much exaggeration that the corporation is really socially and politically a priori whereas the shareholder's position is derivative and exists only in contemplation of law." This is a little like Gierke's belief in the fundamental reality of the Group-person from which so much misfortune has flowed, from concentration camps to the euphoric groupism of the "organization man."

Besides modest recognition of the political concept of the corporation, some small attention has been given to certain institutional aspects of the corporation as a political system. More should be done in this field, since the corporation surrenders a rich yield of political experience and confirmation. Dimock, for example, has said of business firms that they, like governmental organizations, "are inescapably involved in the distribution of power and influence in the society," and his earlier work in the Temporary National Economic Committee did much to demonstrate the essential identity of the problem of bureaucracy in both business enterprises and the public government. A recent work on business leadership in large corporations carries inquiry into the bureaucratic characteristics of the corporation well beyond the point to which the authors of the Temporary National Economic Committee monograph were able to or perhaps cared to carry the analysis.

But the literature lacks full-scale examination of the corporation as a political system, as a lesser commonwealth (to return to Hobbes), and some of the writing that does exist makes faulty analyses. A mature political conception of the corporation must view it as a rationalized system for the accumulation, control, and administration of power. Speculative theories of the corporation, like speculative theories of the state, whether metaphysical or juristic, yield less understanding than do more empirical approaches. The corporation is a body politic which exhibits describable characteristics common to all bodies politic.

In a functional view of all such political systems it can be said that there are five essential elements: (1) an authoritative allocation of principal functions; (2) a symbolic system for the ratification of collective decisions; (3) an operating system of command; (4) a system of rewards and punishments; and (5) institutions for the enforcement of the common rules. A system of organized human behavior which contains these elements is a political system, whether one calls it the state or the corporation. And state and corporation are mature political systems to the degree in which they exhibit all the essential characteristics.

The Authoritative Allocation of Functions

In the state, the constituent power makes an authoritative allocation of governmental powers and functions through a constitution, whether written or unwritten. In the lesser commonwealth of the corporation, this allocation is made through the corporate charter. The earliest corporations were groups of private adventurers, created as bodies politic in order to fulfill some public purpose. The charters of the early corporations were not only instruments to organize the internal government of the corporation. They created what were, in effect, branches of the public government. The companies of the mercantilist period, for example, were "charged with responsibility for commercial regulations and fiscal administration in particular spheres of foreign trade, and were equipped even with military forces and their own courts."

The use of corporations to fulfill political ends and the exercise by corporations of the functions of the public government are illustrated by the colonial charters in America. The first charter of Virginia in 1606 vested in certain "loving and well-disposed Subjects," Knights, and Gentlemen not only the right to take up part of the royal domain in America for a colony but to exercise in it some of the powers of the Crown, including the creation and management of military forces and the coinage of money. In the Second Charter of Virginia, granted in 1609, the company was given "full and absolute Power and Authority to correct, punish, pardon, govern, and rule" all "such Subjects of Us" as might journey to Virginia and come under the jurisdiction of the local company. At the northern end of the Atlantic seaboard, the First Charter of Massachusetts in 1628 created "one body corporate and politique in fact and name" and gave to the "Governor and Company of the Mattachusetts Bay in Newe England" the authority to exercise powers of the public government.

It is clear that these corporations were created for public purposes, indeed, more specifically, to exercise for the state certain functions of the Crown, such as the regulation of the economy and the spread of empire. This is not to say that there were no more narrowly commercial companies than those that established the colonies, for there were such. But of the thirty-four joint stock companies incorporated in England and Scotland before 1700, fourteen were established to perform some peculiarly public function, and of the rest, the principal aim was to introduce some new line or process of manufacture.

In the nineteenth century, the management of the economy passed largely from the state into the hands of private enterprisers. The charters of the seventeenth century were instruments by which private persons served public purposes; the nineteenth-century charters became instruments by which private groups used the state in the enrichment of private interest. Or rather, it may be said that this was the consequence at the end of the century of a process that started rather slowly. In the early years, "it was not considered justifiable to create corporations for any purpose not clearly public in nature; each application was considered by itself, and if favorably was followed by an act of incorporation." The great change in the basic relation of the state and private interest in the control of the economy came with the abandonment of the special act of incorporation and the adoption of general incorporation laws for special classes of corporations. The climax was reached in some states when permission was accorded in advance for incorporation "for any lawful purpose." At the same time the competition of the states with each other for the privilege of giving away privileges to the corporations produced a great relaxation of the safeguards by which the rights and interests of the public were preserved and protected in the earlier limitations. For example, directors were given the authority to reshape the capital structure of the corporation at will, and only a few states enforce the principle of accountability to the state for the manner in which the corporation exercises its franchise.

This trend made it possible for incorporators, not the state, to define the values both of the corporation and the state, and to fix the allocation of fundamental functions in the corporation. The corporation thus acquired the constituent power from the state, and came to share the sovereignty. For constituent power is the power to make the constitution which fixes the basic distribution of powers, rights, and functions in the society. Those who share the constituent power share the sovereignty. The corporations have acquired the power to make their own constitutions.

The formal view is that the corporation is a dependency of the state, owing its existence to the state, and receiving only those rights and privileges which the state chooses to grant, but this overlooks the politics of the relation between the corporation and its legal creator. Can one suppose that the great Dupont empire is a dependent of the state of Delaware, and forced, without influence, to accept the mandate of state functionaries? Or that the political power and influence represented by control of the international oil market, which is in the hands of seven integrated companies, is of equal weight with and may be countervailed by bucolic legislators in provincial states?

Having the constituent power which they preempted from the state, the corporations have designed the basic functions and distributed power within the corporation in a standard structure which violates the prevailing values of the American democracy. Corporation charters permit the disenfranchisement of the qualified through manipulation of the voting rights of owners of various classes of stock, they institutionalize minority rule through the diffusion of stock ownership and the separation of ownership and control, and they deny the principles of due process in the adjudication, within the corporation, of relative rights, such, for example, as those of dealers, minority stockholders, workers, and consumers. More will be said below of the elements of due process in corporate adjudication. As William Graham Sumner said fifty years or more ago, "Industry may be republican; it can never be democratic." In the exercise of their constituent power, the corporations have fashioned massive clusters of antidemocratic force and influence. As another writer has put it, management has "substantially absolute power," and the "only real control which guides or limits their economic and social action is the real, though undefined and tacit, philosophy of the men who compose them."

Symbols and Ratifications

Every political system, whether the state or the corporation, has an apparatus for ratifying and making legitimate the basic choices of the collectivity. It has a ritual for approval of the choices of policy, of the fundamental decisions, of the selections among broad alternatives of action—in short, a legislative system. The corporation has its legislature, and, moreover, it has parties and publics which attempt, respectively, to win the legislative power and to influence its course.

Let us first consider the legislative power. The legal constituency of the corporation is the multitude of owners; it is they who are the citizens of the corporate state. They are the lawful electorate. This electorate, like that of the public at large, holds the franchise which chooses the corporate legislature—the board of directors—and gives it legal authority to legislate. But it is only a mockery of the representative principle to say that the owner-constituency of the corporation elects its representatives in the board of directors who then meet to enact legislation that the president and his officialdom carry out. The constituency is either apathetic, or otherwise normally incapable of exercising its franchise. Over a million stockholders of American Telephone and Telegraph cannot possibly get together to wield the formal authority of the ballot on issues they don't understand for candidates they know nothing about. The managerial class of the corporation has come to diminish the role of the owner-constituent-stockholder-citizen who is usually interested only in a pecuniary result. His normal recourse is to withdraw from the corporate state, if he isn't satisfied, and to take up citizenship in another.

The election of the legislature in the corporate political system is practiced every year, however, with farcical solemnity. The annual stockholders' meeting is held, the managers are bright and brisk with the agenda, the newspapers get the usual laugh out of the usual crank who wants to protest, the business of the meeting is conducted with slick efficiency, and the winning slate wins as predictably as it does in a rigged election in a gangster-ridden union.

The meetings of this legislature, once elected and reelected, are as rigidly ritualized as those of a conclave, a Zuñi ceremony, or a fraternity meeting. Board meetings have a pomp and circumstance appropriate to the occasion and the class. The walnut-paneled rooms, the grey flannel suits, the boned-and-polished shoes, the good cigars, the deep rugs, murmurous acolytes and courtiers—these are some of the appurtenances that legitimize decisions about big money. Crap games have their rituals also, and a special vocabulary, but this is generally a lower-class pursuit favored by soldiers, and the stakes are trifling compared with corporate standards. Imperial decisions are ratified in this regal atmosphere—decisions to divide up the United States, develop Venezuela, support an Arab oligarchy, lengthen cars so that they fit nobody's garage, approve treaties with other satrapies of economic power and influence—in short, *govern* in the name of free enterprise.

This oligarchic regimen is occasionally moderated by the appearance of party factions. In the public government, the party system exists as a regular method by which the government can be changed. It is one of the more important functions of the party that it enables the electorate to line itself up—for and against. Thus the element of party affords the voters the voice that would, unorganized, be a meaningless babble, or mute. But corporation governments can be changed only rarely by the owner-constituencies they presumably represent, because there is no continuous party system to organize their grievances or to test periodically the confidence of the electorate in the corporation government. However, corporate parties do appear often enough to take them out of the statistical limbo of remote contingency. The operation of the party system in the corporate state, as a device for challenging the government of the corporation, is best seen when there is a contest over control of the corporation. In the make-believe democracy of the corporate commonwealth, the stockholders vote by casting ballots, or by giving their proxies to others to cast. This is a refinement of machine politics that no public party organization would dare propose.

Famous fights for control were the successful raid by Robert Young against the management of the New York Central Railroad, and the battles between A. P. Giannini and the Bank of America, Louis Wolfson and Montgomery Ward, and Charles Green and Spyros Skouras in the struggle over 20th Century Fox. Although the rituals of a democratic contest are practiced and the symbols of democracy are brandished, these struggles are usually contests between adversary political machines. All of the rhetoric of a national campaign is employed—the apostrophes to reason and good sense, the celebration of virtues like honesty and loyalty, the promises to reform, the campaign literature in which party leaders are portrayed in flattering hyperbole by their partisans, while the opposition is seared, crimped, and shrunken by caustic reductives. In the meantime, behind the scenes, professional organizations hired for the purpose solicit the proxies of the sovereign owner-electors, much as a city machine quietly organizes the vote while the candidates fill the air and the press with outrageous declamation.

Then the sovereign owner-elector comes into his brief own. The showdown in the New York Central fight took place in the Tenth Regiment Armory in Albany. Public relations men, company employees, and some owner-electors wore buttons for the president of the road, bearing the legend "We Want White"; while the insurgent partisans wore buttons with the caption "Young At Heart." Rival slates of candidates were read off, they made speeches, the balloting took place, and Young was declared the winner by 1,067,273 shares, of which 800,000 were contributed by two members of his alliance from Texas. Although these fights are expensive, there are certain opportunities for the winner to recoup. At the annual meeting of the stockholders of the New York Central in 1954, it was voted to reimburse the Allegheny Corporation, of which Mr. Young was again chairman, in the amount of $1,308,737.71, this for the necessary expenses of the campaign by which Mr. Young secured control of the road.

The two-party system in the corporate commonwealth, however, is not a permanent institution. The corporate state normally is a one-party state, in the hands of the managers. But no oligarchy works in a political vacuum, however much it may be dominated by the management. In the making of the broad choices which represent policy, in the decision-making process, both the symbolic and the operative agencies of choice find their autonomy inhibited by various "publics" with which they must contend. These publics may operate as a moderating influence upon the otherwise unchecked power of the managers, even although stockholders may not be able to supply much restraint through the exercise of their franchise.

In the important field of labor relations, for example, the unions have managed to acquire a share of the former autonomous power of the managers to legislate wages, hours, and other working conditions. Here the existence of strong unions constitutes a two-house structure for the making of decisions that affect workers, and legislation is enacted only by the consent of both houses. The bargaining table is the corporate equivalent of Capitol Hill.

Other publics of the corporations also have from time to time limited the power of managers to legislate the rules that affect those publics. The significance of the mass of regulatory legislation that began to grow in the 1880s is that each Act represents a compromise that corporations had to make with disaffected publics—farmers, shippers, customers, competitors, and so on—who were strong enough to influence the public legislatures to establish protective agencies. The weakness of these compromises is that sometimes they do not continue to be operated in favor of the publics that forced them, because these publics do not represent themselves and are not represented within the management structure of the corporation, but are outside it.

Some of the publics with which corporate legislatures have to deal—like the financiers—have come to represent their own interests very skillfully, occupying inside entries of access, and some—like consumers—have rarely learned to represent themselves at all, and don't do it very well when permitted. As to the financiers, when large corporations depended almost exclusively on the market for their capital requirements, the financiers cut themselves in for important slices of control to protect their investments, and to expand their power. Increasingly, however, corporations have been able to free themselves in considerable part from reliance on the market for capital requirements, and this freedom has removed one form of control from the decisional autonomy they have recovered.

The consumer interest, however, has never been satisfactorily structured nor continuously organized to serve as an internal check to the power of corporation governments. Widespread consumer resistance to the vulgarities of automobile design that the manufacturers said the consumer insisted upon having is thought to have had something to do with the recession of 1958. And the commuters on the New Haven Railroad were able to force the resignation of a president when highhanded inefficiency threatened to collapse the service on the line. But these are peasants' revolts; they do not, and did not, achieve anything like a share in the enactment of corporate legislation. Their historical prototype is Wat Tyler, not the barons at Runnymede. *Piers Plowman,* not Magna Carta, is their text.

Although occasionally moderated by parties and publics, the power to legislate, like the constituent power, is almost absolute in the corporate oligarchy. The growth of virtually unchecked corporate power has drawn some speculation about the course of the future, with many answers of varying kinds. The inner circle of the legislative power of the corporation may be a family, a dynasty, a managerial group, or, as C. Wright Mills has lately suggested, in an elite with some class characteristics, but however animated, the power is formidable. Control of this power by a supposed automatic countervailance in the economy is unlikely, for the countervailance is, for the most part, leverage on the seller's side of the market; and it doesn't work in times of inflation, which has been most of the time in the last two decades. It has been suggested that corporations—anthropomorphic corporations, endowed with intelligence, will, personality, and other human attributes—will develop that final testimonial to St. Augustine and Freud, a conscience, the operation of which will curb and control the excesses of corporate power and establish a benevolent regimen: the new "City of God," no less. But one of the lessons of politics is that it is power that checks and controls power and that this is not done automatically and without human hands. The unions show the way, and the consumers are the example of ineptitude. If the legislative power of the corporation is to be curbed and controlled, the checks will have to be built into the structure of corporate enterprise, and not just merely laid on from without, nor entrusted to the subjective bias of the hierarchs within.

The Corporate Bureaucracy

The third requirement for a political system is an operating structure of command. In the classic definition of bureaucracy, supplied by Max Weber, there must also be added a structure of functions, and methodical provision for the recruitment and replacement of qualified personnel. When these three elements are in conjunction, the resultant organization of the wit and muscle of numbers of people is a bureaucracy; and corporations have bureaucracies, just as does every large rationalized organization, like the Pentagon, the Roman Catholic Church, and United States Steel. Indeed it is hardly necessary to point out that bureaucracy, in this technical meaning, has existed in the business world since long before Frederick Taylor discovered the one best way to do everything; and it was two General Motors executives who wrote books to establish the proposition that the principles of large-scale organization are universal social laws.

There are critics who say that the term "bureaucrat" as applied to the top levels of the business world is as anachronistic, or at least as misleading, as the word "entrepreneur," not because corporations do not exhibit most of the characteristics of large organizations, but because corporate practice violates the third of Weber's qualifications for bureaucracy. C. Wright Mills has said that the "bureaucratic" career in corporations means not only a climb through a hierarchy of offices but "more importantly, it means the setting up of strict and unilateral qualifications for each office occupied." Usually these qualifications involve both specified formal training and qualifying examinations. The bureaucratic career also means that men work for salaried advancement without any expectation of coming to own even a part of the enterprise. But the advancement of corporation executives to the higher levels is "definitely mixed up in a 'political' world of corporate cliques." Choice is in the hands of superiors, "and there are no strict impersonal rules of qualifications or seniority known to all concerned in this process."

Support for this view is provided from an unintended source, the former president of the New Jersey Bell Telephone System, who formulated the functions of the executive in the corporation as three in number: maintaining communications; securing services; and formulating purpose. These were for the most part an arrangement of familiar principles of administration, including the third. But his discussion of informal executive organization, at the time, was fresh. The general method of maintaining an informal executive organization, he wrote, "is so to operate and to select and promote executives that a general condition of compatibility of personnel is maintained." Those are chosen who "fit," and fitness includes "education, experience, sex [it is not clear whether this is compulsory], personal distinctions, prestige, race, nationality, faith, politics, sectional antecedents," and "manners, speech, personal appearance, etc." This informal executive organization is based upon few if any rules, and represents, according to Barnard, the "political aspects of personal relationship in formal organization."

Bureaucracies are systems for the making of decisions; and central to the success of decision-making is leadership. Few will now disagree that the leadership function in corporations has been transferred from owners to salaried managers. And this transfer is properly thought to raise important questions concerning the "distribution of powers within the corporation" and the functioning of the free enterprise economy itself. In the discussion of symbols and ratifications, attention was centered on the gulf that stretches between the owners and the management, and the problem was treated ex hypothesi as though the board of directors were the effective legislature of the corporate commonwealth. Attention here is centered on the decline of this legislature (just as the legislature in the public government has tended to decline in the importance it once had) as an "active and independent decision-making body." The legislature in the public government—the Congress, at least—has developed compensatory institutions for the control of the executive. In this respect, as in other aspects of governance, the corporation is behind the public government.

A great deal of the initiative in the making of corporate decisions comes from the lower ranks, as Gordon has demonstrated and as Barnard earlier stated. The small size of the stockholdings of professional managers frees them from the impulses that generate decisions oriented toward the maximization of profits, impulses that presumably worked for the owner-entrepreneur. Although profits may not be disregarded, since the directors and the stockholders regard the corporation as a revenue-producing agency, the professional managers are free to respond to such considerations as prestige, power, and social welfare. They become private planners.

The hearings of the Senate Subcommittee on Antitrust and Monopoly of the Senate Judiciary Committee gave evidence that much of the administration of General Motors is done through committees, one of which, the price review committee, receives price recommendations from the divisions, and then makes recommendations to the operations policy committee, which usually ratifies the recommendation. In view of the profit of over a billion a year, after taxes, that General Motors has recently been making, interest was expressed in the method by which prices are reached. The theory of pricing requires a standard, which has not changed in twenty years, under which the planned yield is 15 to 20 percent on the net capital employed. That is to say, the leaders of

General Motors plan their pricing as though the corporation were a public utility; and although the return to General Motors from 1948 to 1955 far exceeded the standard, prices were not lowered because, it was said, the volume at some time in the future might decline. In these determinations, which are largely free of market considerations, the General Motors managers closely resemble the top functionaries of the public bureaucracies, and are almost exactly like the managers of socialist enterprises, the difference being that between the public collectivism of the socialist state and the private collectivism of the corporate state. Price rigidity is not the result of factors external to the firm but is in part the result of factors internal to the firm.

Rewards and Punishments

The fourth requirement in a political system, whether that of the corporation or the state, is a system of rewards and punishments. The system is internal—to the ranks under the command of the corporation—and external—to various publics that threaten the security of the corporation. The growth of corporate welfarism and the bureaucratization of benevolence are recent trends in the development of complex reward systems. The execution of sanctions against threatening publics external to the corporation has a range from the violence of a Memorial Day massacre to the Byzantine subtleties of legal sabotage against the antitrust laws.

The bureaucratization of benevolence is a function of the depersonalization of work. Pats on the back by the entrepreneur-owner and an extra day off around the time of the accouchement of the worker's wife were the equivalents of the fringe benefits that are now written with scrupulous and mechanical generosity into union contracts. Bureaucratized benevolence for the lower classes of corporate society is paralleled by the development of corporate welfarism for the middle classes of that society. Millions are bound in a system of tribal dependence through paternalistic personnel policies, conformitarian training programs, tax-deductible expense accounts, an ever-ringing celebration of corporate interest through advertising propaganda, and the growth of the new company towns in suburbia and exurbia. The new middle class of suburban split-level Babbitts, riding the 8:05 into the city and the 5:05 out of it, wearing the status badges that mark their level in the corporate world, more anxious than yearning, looks for solace and safety in the "togetherness" of the corporate collective. For the upper classes of corporate society, bonuses play an important part in the reward system, as do the numerous opportunities for beating the tax laws; and the risk of loss of status is a powerful incentive to conform when the juniors are being looked at closely to see whether they will "fit." For all classes the threat of deprivation of these social sweets is a strong sanction that makes the cruder forms of discipline less necessary.

In the relations between the corporation and its various publics, the political function of crime and punishment is somewhat more difficult to administer because the corporation is unable to control as many of the variables as it does in its internal affairs. An example, however, of the rather full range of sanctions against threatening publics was provided by the Cement Institute, which the

Supreme Court held to be in violation of the antitrust laws in 1948. The Institute was a security system for cement producers in which truckers, dealers, customers, domestic rivals, foreign importers, and Federal and state agencies were subjected to discipline. Punitive taxes, for example, were laid in the form of differential charges on customers who wanted delivery to trucks and not to railroads. When this penalty pricing did not work, members of the combination in many instances refused by flat prohibition to allow delivery by truck. Penalties and prohibitions were also used to prevent dealers from competing in the manufacturers' products at prices lower than those that the manufacturer was charging the customer. Efforts of customers to beat the basing-point system by diversion of traffic were met by the use of no-diversion bills of lading, which the railroads were invited to honor. The companies influenced government procurement officers to buy from dealers at a higher price than the companies could have got from the manufacturers direct. When the TVA threatened to make its own cement to avoid the squeeze of noncompetitive prices, the companies complained about coercion, arbitrary government, and ruthless declarations. The appearance of imported cement in the American market brought upon the dealers who handled it attacks that included espionage, encirclement, systematic price undercutting, boycotts, and reprisals.

The courts themselves may become a form of harassment of rivals. Early in 1953, the organized truckers of Pennsylvania sued the eastern railroads in a United States District Court for $250,000,000 in treble damages. The Pennsylvania Motor Truck Association and thirty-seven trucking firms sought damages because, counsel for this combination said, the railroads had used dishonorable means to restrain commerce illegally. Thirty railroads and the Eastern Railroad Presidents Conference filed a countersuit for $120,000,000 in treble damages. The total damages of $370,000,000 claimed by both sides represented the symbolic stakes in a rivalry that had nothing to do with the damages claimed. The railroad attorney charged that the truckers had filed their suit after the president of the Pennsylvania Railroad had refused to withdraw his objections to the removal of certain truck limitations on the highways. The suit was pressure on the roads, if not reprisal, and the countersuit of the railroads was counterreprisal.

Although the state has a theoretical monopoly of violence, the corporation has command of forces that commit violence when this ultimate resort seems necessary. The history of labor relations in the steel industry through the 1930s provides many examples of naked warfare and death on both sides. Not unusual are company-maintained detective services, constabularies of guards and security forces, police forces in company towns, and access to the state soldiery through the intervention of compliant public officials. These add up to a body of militia of considerable strength. Bentley's remarks about hanging seem particularly apt at this place.

The Judicial Function

The fifth requirement for a political system is a set of institutions for the enforcement of the common rules. We have already seen in the discussion of the previous two sections that corporations have an administrative apparatus and a system of rewards and punishments, and these are part of the machinery for the enforcement of the common rules. But the most mature political systems also provide an objective agency for making judgments about the application of the common rules to individual cases—a judiciary of some kind—and although the judicial function is not as fully developed in the corporation as in the state, it nevertheless exists.

In the hearings on General Motors held in 1956 by the Senate Judiciary Committee Subcommittee on Antitrust and Monopoly, there was evidence that dealers were bound to the company by agreements which gave the company practically unrestricted rights to renew or to cancel. GM lawyers, in the few cases in which dealers sought to enforce their agreements in the courts, argued successfully that the "contracts" were not enforceable. Unenforceable though they were in the public courts, these contracts were nevertheless litigated in a private judiciary maintained by the company. Provision was made for the appeals of dealers from decisions of nonrenewal or termination by division heads, to a court of last resort established in 1939, and staffed with "judges" who were company men. In this corporation court of last resort, over a period of eighteen years, few cases were decided in favor of dealers. The proceedings in this private judiciary lacked the basic elements of due process of law, for only dealers and members of their organizations, without benefit of counsel, were permitted to appeal and appear.

The quality of the justice that was strained through this private judiciary appears in the testimony of a dealer in Lake Orion, Michigan, who had strongly irritated the company officials by provocatively criticizing the company policy that granted to GM employees and executives in his territory the right to buy cars from the manufacturer at the same price he had to pay. The company was competing with one of its dealers. For his protests against the company policy of selling cars at the factory discount in his territory, the dealer was given notice that his franchise would not be renewed. At his hearing before the final court of corporate appeal he was called a "Red" and sneered at by the president of GM, who asked him what Art Summerfield (Postmaster General and a former automobile dealer) was "going to do for [him] now." The dealer was not allowed to take counsel with him, nor was he given a transcript or other record of the proceedings made by General Motors.

Corporations in certain industries like the garment trades made regular use of arbitrators, who comprise a lay court, and the American Arbitration Association is a serviceable private judiciary, from which "judges" may be assigned for specific commercial and labor cases as they arise. Arbitration by private "lay" judges has been a well-known procedure for years in certain areas of labor relation[s]. The procedures used by firms working on government contracts for the discharge of persons thought to be security risks may be scrutinized by the United States courts for compliance with the minimum requirements of due process. It is possible that the public courts may require the private judiciaries within the corporations to conform to the standards of the public judiciary in such cases.

Commonwealths: Greater and Lesser

Hobbes might think that today's corporations were not "lesser commonwealths" embodied in a greater but, in fact, rivals to the formal sovereign both in size and power. The Temporary National Economic Committee reported with awe the existence of billion-dollar corporations. In less than two decades after the TNEC, General Motors produced a billion-dollar profit after taxes. Through the General Motors Acceptance Corporation, GM controls the financing of approximately 50 percent of total car sales. Although the GMAC and GM were found guilty of violating the antitrust laws in 1939, "nothing was done to separate them so as to deprive General Motors of this competitive advantage." They did pay a fine of $20,000. The yearly budget for advertising in GM is around $100,000,000. Although this corporate prodigy is outstanding, it is by no means unique.

The literature of law and economics has tended to discuss corporations and the concentrates into which many have clustered in terms of the legal rules, like the antitrust laws and court decisions, optimum size, economic efficiency, and welfare considerations that touch upon the condition of small business. New concepts of function and control must be devised, and these formulations cannot neglect the basically political character of the corporation.

Antony Jay

THE STATE, THE CORPORATION, AND THE DEVIL

Among themselves, Antony Jay suggests, corporations compete as did sixteenth-century Italian city-states—and like those city-states, they exercise power often far more threatening to members of the firm than that of more distant systems of authority.

In all important ways states and corporations are the same—in particular in the framework they construct within which economic and political necessity interact with the minds and wills of men. States and corporations can be defined in almost exactly the same way: institutions for the effective employment of resources and power through a government (board) to maintain or increase the wealth of the landowning classes (shareholders) and provide safety and prosperity for their citizens (employees). The competition of commercial and industrial rivals, strikes, the problem of getting the most advantageous trading situation with the least possible sacrifice of independence—all these problems are in their essence the same as enemy invasion, civil rebellion, alliances with other states that have a common interest or a common enemy. Cartels and price rings are only a form of treaty, placing a limit on areas of conflict at a time when continued warfare is likely to damage all the combatants more than it can reward them. As one General Electric executive said at the time of the great electrical industry antitrust case of the 1950s: "Sure, collusion was illegal, but it wasn't *unethical*. It wasn't any more unethical than if the companies had a summit conference the way Russia and the West meet."[1]

Of course there are certain superficial differences: In particular, (1) corporations do not meet in military conflict, (2) they do not have absolute authority over a geographical area, and (3) a member of the staff of, say, General Motors does not belong to General Motors in the way a Frenchman belongs to France or an Englishman to England. All these points are worth examining.

Military Conflict

The first transference you have to make when studying political history in management terms is to read "economic conflict" for "military conflict." Corporations compete just as keenly as states, and are impelled by exactly the same human emotions of greed and fear and pride, or self-interest and opportunism and a desire for security, or whatever else you believe to be the root of man's competitiveness with man. Corporations do not exist in a state of constant war, any more than states do; it is when one of them tries to break into an export market previously dominated by a rival, or manufactures a new product cheaper or better than one already marketed by another, that you have a situation comparable to war and invasion. But a great deal of the conflict between corporations, especially as they get larger, is confined to frontier skirmishes or guerilla warfare, where each side tacitly accepts its share of the market (its territorial limits) and is more concerned to safeguard what it has than to make any dramatic advances. Corporations, like states, can exhaust themselves by too much warfare, just as they can become fat and lazy from insufficient exercise. But this transference only points up the comparison: A sales director planning an assault on a rival's market needs exactly the same qualities as a general planning an invasion: not just courage and a steady nerve, but, more precisely, knowledge of the enemy's strength and weakness and how strong his reserves are and how fast he can mobilize them (e.g., has he the capital to step up his advertising, the capacity to step up his production, the margin to cut his price, the sales force free to intensify his selling); what the strength of his own force is and its endurance, how far he can push them, what ground they fight best on (which sort of product they sell best and which worst); where the likely counterattack will come (price cut, advertising, etc.) and how to meet it—these sort of comparisons can go on almost endlessly, since the essentials are identical and only the superficialities are different. The difference between killing and selling may, objectively, be rather more than superficial, but not in the qualities they demand of those planning and executing the campaign.

[1] Richard Austin Smith, *Corporations in Crisis* (New York: Anchor Books, Doubleday and Co., 1966), p. 119.

Authority over a Geographical Area

This difference is even more superficial than the previous one. It is only important if you try to compare corporations with present-day states; but it is not in modern Britain and Russia and America and France that the comparison between corporations and states lies. If it were, it would have been obvious long ago. Modern states incorporate a number of nineteenth-century concepts, like nationalism and universal suffrage, which (at least so far) are not embodied in the great corporations; but if you go back to prenineteenth-century states, the parallels become much clearer, and particularly if you look at the continent of Europe rather than Britain: Britain developed the idea of nationality (and nationalism) much earlier than most of Europe. A sixteenth-century Italian state, or a German city-state of the seventeenth century, is better understood as a tract of land owned by men or families than as the tight, highly organized, and highly governed nation-state of today. And just as modern corporations own their land, their offices and factories and refineries and oil wells, not absolutely, but under a higher authority, so many of those earlier states held their authority under the Pope or the Hapsburgs or the Bourbons; nevertheless it was, for practical purposes, theirs, just as Seattle is, for practical purposes, Boeing's and Wilmington is du Pont's. The interplay between groups of men and tracts of land, according to one of the greatest modern historians, Lewis Namier, is the essence of history. For most of history tracts of land have been the only source of wealth. If by "tracts of land" you can now include factories and refineries as well as mines and oil wells and farmland, and if you can also include sales areas, home and overseas markets, then the essence of history can be distilled from the modern corporation just as it can from the earlier states.

Belonging to the Country

This also depends on comparing corporations with prenineteenth-century states, before the state came to mean the same as the nation and the race, when much of the Polish nation was in Prussia, the Czech in Austria, the Greek in Turkey. A wandering craftsman traveling through Italy in the sixteenth century and spending a year or two in Naples and then in Florence and then in Venice would not feel he was in a new country or a new state in the modern sense; he would be much more like an English research chemist, say, working for British Petroleum for a couple of years, then for the National Coal Board, then for British Nylon Spinners. The research chemist is always primarily a British citizen under the general authority of the British government, though while he is in the different firms they profit from his labor and he takes his salary and keeps to their staff regulations and policy rulings. In the same way the Italian craftsman was under the general authority of the laws of Christendom, and the individual laws of the separate states were much more like company regulations, and while he was there he would keep their laws and pay their taxes but not feel as much of either a citizen or an alien as a modern traveler in different countries. The citizens of those states were much closer to employees of the king (or prince or duke) than to citizens of a modern nation-state. It is not unreasonable to look on their citizenship in terms of a contract of service: They were employed by the king to create wealth for him (taxes) and when necessary give him security (military service) or help him enlarge his territory and dominion. In return he protected them (with an army they might serve in) from the depredations of enemy states, and guaranteed that they would not have their land taken away by the force or fraud of their fellow citizens (legal system). But they had few if any civil rights: If they incurred the king's displeasure then they could be jailed or executed with no trial and no appeal. Their consolation was that they were all full citizens of the kingdom of Christ, that before the throne of God their soul weighed as heavy as the king's and that servitude on earth was a small price to pay if it would buy a ticket to the kingdom of Heaven.

It is at this point that the parallel becomes uncomfortably close. For most of the employees of big corporations, the power of the government to make them happy or miserable is very small: A rise in the bank rate may slightly affect the cost of a mortgage; over a long period the establishment of a health service, the abolition of military service, the building of roads, the preservation of the countryside, and so on may raise the general quality of their lives; but what the government does it does for everybody—they all rise or fall together. The power of the firm over their lives, however, is far greater. They can be told to go and live in another part of the country, or another part of the world, or to desert their wives and children for months or years: they can be publicly exalted in the eyes of all their colleagues, the men whose respect they most prize, or publicly humiliated, passed over in favor of a subordinate; and these are not things which happen to all alike, but specifically and personally to them. Of course they are free to resign, just as the Neapolitan could go and live in Venice; but he might arrive with a record and a reputation, Venice might be no more congenial, and a man has to live somewhere. So the petrochemical expert, the employee of an oil company, has not much alternative but to work for another oil company—and explain why he left the last one; and a man has to work somewhere too.

The government is like Christendom, an overriding system of law which only very marginally affects the actual physical conditions of their lives, but gives them an illusion of equality in that their vote weighs as heavily in the ballot box as the chairman's or the managing director's. In the important part of their lives, their forty years of work, they have none of the freedoms that matter: No political freedom—the corporations rarely have the courage to risk the customer and community antagonisms which might be aroused by an executive who campaigned for a political party or ran for election on a party ticket; no freedom to publish—they cannot write newspaper or magazine articles without clearing them with the corporation, and according to *Industrial Marketing,* "an important part of the company spirit is the forfeiture of the pride of authorship"; no freedom of speech—if they gave their subordinates or the press details on the incompetence of their board they would be liable to be fired, and if this is not the death penalty it can still shatter a man's life as much as banishment; no right of trial, and no judiciary which is independent of the executive—their career can be blighted and promotion stopped for utterly unjust reasons such as the personal whim of a hostile nobleman (director); and they have no sort of representation in the councils which decide how the firm shall be run, no say in its government, however much the decisions may affect their lives. The twentieth-century junior manager in Standard Oil or Ford lives in a state of voteless dependence on the favor of the great just like the sixteenth-century Italian.

A corporation, in fact, is not something different from a state with some interesting similarities: It *is* a state, with a few unimportant differences. A corporation has its king and its barons, its courtiers and ambassadors, its loyalists and its dissident elements, its allies and its enemies. What is important to our understanding is not the superficial differences but the underlying unity.

Richard Eells

CONSTITUTIONAL CRISIS IN THE CORPORATION

Because the giant corporation is not simply a vehicle for economic enterprise but a "decisional center in a pluralistic society," Richard Eells contends that it faces inescapable political issues. The responsibilities of corporate managers to their various constituencies need to be spelled out, and better ways must be found to hold them accountable for their decisions. Until these problems are resolved, the modern corporation cannot avoid a "constitutional crisis."

Many observers deny that the business corporation today has any "constitutional" structure. Others who concede the existence of a corporate constitution refuse to recognize that it differs today or will differ tomorrow from that of the traditional corporation. Yet closer students of the modern corporation express profound interest in the problem, and it is not too much to say that in the decades ahead corporate constitutionalism will become one of the major issues confronting corporate executives and public policy-makers.

The idea of the modern corporation as merely the enlarged figure of the classical owner-enterpriser no longer suffices for the making of either corporate or public policy. The authority of executive managers of great collectivities is not in practice the translation of the property rights of stockholders into the "right to manage" large enterprise on behalf of absentee owners. So to regard managerial authority is to miss the significance of recent changes in the nature of property and changes in the concept of authority itself.

Even in the administration of a business enterprise below the board level, the question of corporate governance raises real problems of power and authority which one can usefully attack with techniques of analysis drawn from political science. But when one widens the scope of the inquiry and takes into account not only the board of directors but also the stockholders and the array of external groups with which a corporation carries on relations of many kinds, then one gets far beyond the mere administering of the enterprise through the organization of executives, managers, and individual contributors.

When one begins to ask about the influence of boards, stockholders, customers, the public, and—not least—the unions in the shaping of a company's objectives and even in the day-by-day running of the business, one gets into problems of authority and responsibility. When they occur *within* the organization structure below the board level, these problems are usually discussed in terms of "scientific management," business administration, and so on. But beyond these considerations there exists also the question of adapting and assimilating the corporation as a private government into the general social picture.

Let us consider for a moment some issues which are of universal concern to both businessmen and the public generally: Who really controls a company? What power does it exercise? To whom should the power-wielders be accountable, and how? Is the company a "self-perpetuating oligarchy," as some have charged, or is it a type of republic? And if one or the other, what difference does it make, so far as the public is concerned? What is the role of the large corporation in the total power structure of the nation? Is it an important element in the balance of social powers? Does a "free society" depend heavily upon the kind of pluralism we have in our economic and other sectors, with the private business corporation playing a significant part in sustaining a healthy distribution of power throughout society as a whole; or would we do better without it?

These are all questions that pertain to the government of society and of its integral parts. They are questions that inevitably draw the inquirer into the deeper issues of political science and political ethics—with respect not only to *public* government but also to *private* governments. The failure to acknowledge this omnipresent problem of government, especially as it arises in economic organizations like the corporation, is a dangerous oversight. The problem is there and cannot be escaped. So far, few answers have been given and those which have been suggested have originated outside, rather than inside, the corporate community.

The man in business is, quite naturally, so engaged in minding his business that he has little time to speculate about its nature. To get the enterprise going and to keep it going take all his ingenuity and energy. Like the medieval mystic who remarked that it is better to feel compunction than to know how to define it, the businessman is usually better at doing his job than at thinking about the governmental processes inherent in it.

Yet, with the growth of giant economic organization it becomes plain that underlying the superstructure of administration there is the substance of visible and not so visible private government. Students of the subject discern an evolutionary process imperceptible to those who see in the business corporation a clear and fixed pattern of authority relationships among stockholders, directors, executive managers, and employees at lower operating levels. Stereotypes of the corporation, provided by received legal doctrine and economic theory, have succeeded in obscuring its nature further. We are inclined to see the social institutions around us not as they really are, but in accordance with preconceived notions handed down to us by our predecessors.

The business corporation, like all social institutions, has such an image in our minds, but it has also an objective reality which may or may not correspond to the image. In static periods the lack of harmony between image and reality can to some extent be safely ignored. In a dynamic age the distortion creates dangers. A common-sense view of the corporation, based on the wisdom of the past and respectable dogma, would suffice were it not for the fact that political, economic, and social change has moved it so rapidly away from this base.

Evidence of Tension

The growing divergence of the corporate image from corporate realities has led to an accumulation of unresolved tensions. One example is the debate about the respective positions of share-owners and managers in the control of large enterprises where stockholding is widely dispersed: the so-called separation of ownership and control. Another example is the touchy question of social responsibility—the problem of the general public's share in the authority structure of large enterprises, since obviously responsibility and authority must somehow be linked together. A further example is the unresolved problem of union power vis-à-vis corporate managers: the encroachment of organized workers on managerial authority and the drive by labor unions to enjoy a "fair share" of the fruits of enterprise. Then there are the growing concerns about human relations in industry, the sensitivity of managers to the personality requirements of people in the work force, the nature of authority at the workplace, and the right to discipline. At the outer reaches of the constellation of interests that make up a large corporate enterprise we find the pension and investment trusts of a "paraproprietal society." These trust funds are institutionalized share-owners who are far removed from the going concern; but by the traditional canons of corporate theory they are the ultimate sovereigns as they accumulate large blocs of stock in a concern.

All of these examples provide evidence that the traditional view of basic authority relationships in large enterprises is an unstable compound of hypotheses about relationships among the primary interests and the direct contributor-claimants of the going concern. The instability of this outmoded compound of received doctrines becomes evident in relatively minor explosions here and there: the recurrent struggles over collective bargaining, the intervention of legislators to protect first the creditors and then the share-owners against abuses of managerial authority, the revisions by general incorporation laws accompanied by acute conflicts of opinion about the theory that should underlie them, and the struggles for "control" in certain large companies.

Taken separately, these are but dramatic episodes in the long evolution of new constitutional theory for corporate enterprise. These episodes must be seen comparatively and historically in order to get the proper perspective for the evolutionary lines of development. The changes that are occurring in basic corporation theory are most clearly observable only over a considerable time span and after comparative analysis of many situations.

The Constitutional Pattern

As a point of departure one can begin with the traditional pattern of corporate constitutions, as expounded in the standard treatises and as they are generally understood by businessmen and lawyers. This constitutional pattern, it must be emphasized at the start, does not emerge clearly unless a distinction is made between the corporation as an economic unit and the corporation as a *decisional center* in a pluralistic society. We need to see it as a decision-making center with an impact on the larger society where many authority centers exist, and as a complex of forces seeking places at the table of power within the corporation itself.

As an economic unit, the corporation is a producer and distributor, a buyer and a seller, of economic goods. From the point of view of the economist it is an entrepreneurial unit; but our focus here is upon the corporation as an instrument of power and authority, an institution with its own constitutional structure, maintaining a system of organization, discipline, and morale within its own ranks as well as influential external relations with other authority centers public and private.

Thus, a corporation, like any other organization, exhibits certain more or less well-defined patterns of leadership, subordination, superordination, and coordination within the boundaries of the firm, and patterns of authority relationships with other organizations and persons beyond its corporate frontiers. All organizations require some basic constitutional pattern of authority relationships, internal and external, to achieve unity of effort with a diversity of human resources. They all have common purposes defined by written or unwritten rules, expressed or implied by their basic charters. Though their objectives differ, all make more or less successful attempts to pattern the organizational structure in a functional way; the authority structure is presumably a reflection of the organizational goals.

One of the most important problems confronting the managers of the modern corporation is whether the basic pattern of authority relationships—internal and external to the organization—is functionally appropriate in view of contemporary corporate objectives and the organizational requirements for achieving these objectives. The issue has become highly debatable today. Conflict of opinion on the point is one cause of the contemporary crisis in corporate constitutionalism. This is in fact a crisis of larger dimensions. Similar issues arise with respect to all large organizations and not least those public organizations which we designate as nation-states. The structure of authority is changing the world over, and we do not know what the future holds. The nation-state system, which reached maturity in the early modern period, is under heavy stress and may not survive such polarizing influences as international communism and Western constitutionalism, the "revolution of rising expectations" in the less developed regions of the world, and the phenomenal technological developments of the nuclear and space age. In the evolution of new patterns of authority, however, it is not improbable that the business corporation will play a telling part, perhaps as a catalyst, or perhaps as the forerunner of some new and still inchoate type of governmental pattern.

The tensions that are building up in economic organization are thus traceable to external as well as internal forces. Inside the company the stockholder-manager-employee complex reveals the tug and pull of certain easily definable forces. But outside, in the immediate neighborhood, there are the forces of labor unionism and plant-community interests; and in the farther reaches of the environment, the rising fiscal and other demands of public governmental agencies, the still quiescent but looming power of pension and investment trusts, the ever-changing market picture at home and abroad, and epoch-making changes in the global patterns of political authority.

Control of Corporate Power

The resulting constitutional crisis in the corporation derives from the extension of the authority relationships both within and beyond the firm. The major issues in corporate constitutionalism—as in traditional constitutionalism—center on the scope and legitimacy of power and the means of controlling it. Of these two major problems, the emphasis in contemporary writing on the corporation is given to the problem of control. A relatively undeveloped theoretical field is the question of adequate power in corporate governments to perform their legitimate tasks.

There are two major possibilities for the control of corporate power: controls of managerial power by external agencies; and internal controls through institutionalized devices within the firm, designed to secure responsible corporate government. Mixtures of these remedies for abuse of corporate power are likely, but here we are concerned mainly with the question of internal controls. What likelihood is there that such institutionalization will resolve the problem of corporate constitutionalism?

According to Carl Kaysen, "the development of mechanisms which will change the internal organization of the corporation, and define more closely and represent more presently the interests to which corporate management should respond and the goals toward which they should strive is yet to begin, if it is to come at all." Yet the fact is that the trend in this direction is already well started, though the evidence is not to be found in too narrowly defined organizational terms within the formal structure of the firm. The evidence is to be gathered rather in such peripheral developments as collective bargaining and the attendant growth of the idea of the work force as a corporate constituency, the newer relations between franchised dealers and manufacturing companies, the rise of pension trusts with their yet unrealized potential as corporate policy-determiners, and the gradual internalizing of cultural mores in the form of "social responsibility of the businessman" and what Berle calls the "corporate conscience."

In comparison with these developments, the attempts on the part of the "corporate democrats" to activate shareholder control of management have had insignificant results. Nor has the legislation, stemming from the 1930s, which seeks to protect stockholders from managerial abuse of power, effected any revolutionary changes in the corporate constitutional system. The legislation of the thirties on securities marketing, on the contrary, seems to have been based on a theory of corporate governance in which the stockholders were the sole relevant constituency. But this theory is hardly reflected in corporate practice. It is significant that in recent decades most critics of corporate governance have concentrated their fire on the separation of management authority from stockholder control. Only within the past few years has any systematic attention been given to the impact of other developments on corporate constitutionalism. And a great void is left—even by the latter-day critics—in the relatively untouched area of the nature and scope of corporate authority.

Adequacy of Corporate Power

As we have suggested earlier, the issue of control of power is logically subordinate to (though not necessarily of less practical importance than) this question of legitimate power. The standards of justice to be applied in corporate constitutionalism will depend upon what we expect corporate power to accomplish. Because their aims are different, one has to be cautious in making simple analogies between the state and the corporation. Even in states, different systems of value are discernible, as was evident in the varying sorts of meritorious conduct esteemed in the classical Aristotelian classification of states. Democracy esteemed freedom; the quality of being a free man was the measure of control of power in a democratic state. Oligarchies esteemed wealth or noble birth, while aristocracies esteemed virtue or honor. The nature and scope of governmental power in these cases stemmed from different standards of value.

What standards of performance do we expect of a business corporation, and will these standards supply the key to the scope of its powers? At first blush the Aristotelian oligarchy, with emphasis on wealth, would seem to provide the key. If one assumes that the business corporation is some kind of self-contained society with its own full-blown concepts of internal corporate citizenship—a *koinonia* or fellowship standing alone, with consonant principles of the good life to guide its members—one might conclude that creation of wealth is the source of its standard of performance. But, while the production of goods for profit is undoubtedly the major business of the corporation, this is hardly the *sole* concern of its members, who are, after all, bound by ties to societies other than the corporate institution.

This multiplicity of ties is certain to modify the otherwise clear-cut purpose of a business corporation, and the modification is in the direction not of a narrowing but rather a widening of the scope of corporate authority. This is so in part because the pursuit of profit (wealth, by analogy, in the Aristotelian oligarchy) has to be conducted in terms of the dominant standards of justice in the greater society. But the enlargement of corporate objectives also arises from the fact that its people must commit much of their time and energy to its affairs. Nor is this involvement necessarily a function of organizational size; it happens in small as well as large businesses.

Given the fact that people "in trade" must invest so much of their time and energy in the particular business in which they are engaged, the organization inevitably assumes kinds and degrees of control over their lives that are not describable in purely economic terms. *Any* organization—whether it be political, economic, religious, educational, or scientific—involves some degree of teamwork in which controls only peripherally related to the primary function of the organization have to be set up and exercised by governing authorities.

Quite aside from the powers of officials in any organization, arising logically from its specialized purpose, there are always other powers growing out of organizational necessities of a more general kind. There are at least minimal disciplines to be enforced to build up and maintain an esprit de corps and to preserve unity of effort in the face of internal disintegrating forces as well as external threats to the common enterprise.

Emphasis is necessary on this point, particularly with respect to the business corporation as a going concern, because of the renewed emphasis on the value of human freedom, a value of high priority in our society. We do face, however, in today's struggle for power in the international arena, extraordinary pressures that enhance the countervalue of solidarity—a solidarity not only in the direct instrumentalities of national defense but also in the less direct. The large business enterprise is such an indirect instrument; and when we speak of the global struggle we need not confine our attention solely to its military aspects. Certainly in the economic and social phases of our global efforts the role of business and other nonmilitary organizations is vital.

To put the matter in another way: the *powers* required to sustain a viable corporate constitutional structure, especially in the larger business organizations, must be adequate at least to control the entropic tendencies in any organizational effort. So viewed, the mustering of corporate authority may in some cases leave something to be desired. A putative enemy could wish for no greater boon than the disintegration of civil organizations in the logistic lines of his adversary, and of course it is reasonable to assume that this method of undermining the foundations of national power is systematically pursued.

The problem of corporate power in these terms has hardly been faced squarely, nor is it an agreeable field of controversy. One too readily encourages the exorbitant claims of the authoritarians who would—in the name of national emergency—invoke the harshest forms of industrial discipline without sufficient proof of their necessity. Yet the potentialities of crippling blows to our social fabric by "the enemy within" have been dangerously evident in more than one area of industry and commerce. A serious crisis could very quickly impel national leaders to invoke legislation already on the books, and to enact even more stringent controls, all of which might make the older insistence on "managerial prerogative" look like the golden age of freedom by comparison.

Pluralistic Implications of Corporate Power

We tend to assume—perhaps too optimistically—that the pluralism of our relatively competitive economy is in itself an immeasurable source of strength for the nation as a whole. Undoubtedly there is much truth in this claim; yet the other side of the coin bears scrutiny—namely, the *adequacy of decisional authority in the dispersed centers of privately organized power.* If the authority is to be widely dispersed in the interests of liberty and freer choice, it must not be forgotten that choice in itself means decision-making, and decision is the most important component of power. The decision centers, in other words, are *power* centers; and in an increasingly *organizational* economy these *power* centers are found not entirely or even mainly in the individual human units of a completely atomized society but increasingly in the artificial units of capital aggregates.

This means that, under the impact of the organizational revolution, a pluralistic society is not a society of individual free men who release bits of their primitive freedom of choice to public government alone, retaining all other decision-making power to themselves as private persons. Rather it is a society in which decision-making is transferred to a variety of public and private governments—that is, to various public and private officials who hold more or less extensive authority to act for otherwise free men on numerous issues that affect the lives and property of these individuals.

This transfer of decisional authority goes far beyond anything contemplated in the received doctrines of democracy and constitutionalism. It has long been a popular pastime to bridle at the extent of this transfer of authority to public government's decision-makers, but only in recent years has systematic attention been given to the extent of the transfer to the officials of private governments. In both cases there is a retransfer: in the case of public government, for example, the delegation of powers by legislative assemblies to administrative agencies with "quasi-judicial" and "quasi-legislative" authority; and in the case of private corporate governments the delegation of decisional authority by boards to operating managers, on the one hand, and by shareholders, incipiently, to trust and pension funds, on the other.

In this process of transfer of decisional authority from the primitive units of a democracy of free men to the public and private governments of a pluralistic society the accretions of power by these governments are responses to the need (or at least the felt need) for collective action. The debate about shrinkage of individual freedom of choice, as this transfer proceeds apace, is not mainly a debate about the individual *versus* the state; it is a debate about the *kinds* of organization that ought to have the power to govern men, and about the distribution of powers among these public and private organizations.

It is from this point of view that one has to approach the normative question of power-mustering (that is, decisional authority) in the business corporation. What power has to be transferred to the private government of the corporation if it is to perform the tasks assigned to it? And how can one define those tasks in such a way as to make a rational distribution of decisional authority as between this particular kind of private government and other kinds of public and private government?

As a purely scientific problem—quite aside from one's preferences in the matter—one must also ask how in practice the muster of power in corporate governments has been effected. What, in other words, are the written and unwritten basic principles that spell out the nature and scope of corporate powers? For it must be conceded that in private as well as in public polities based on the traditions of constitutionalism, a constitution is an instrument of government as well as a symbol of liberty. The rule of law, as against the dominance of arbitrary will, implies rule as well as limitations on the rulers.

In very large corporations, moreover, the authority of corporate governments at the top must be adequate to meet the demands made upon them by outsiders. While a considerable delegation of authority is indispensable for extensive and diversified operations, the reservations of authority at the center must necessarily be substantial. This necessity was pointed up on the recent antitrust cases against the electrical companies. Decentralization obviously has certain limits; it can go very far with respect to some matters, but will be quite impractical in others. The distribution or allocation of powers within a firm to various divisions, committees, departments, branches, and individuals is not simply a question of power distribution for the purpose of checking the exercise of power. It is also a question of preventing the dispersal of power to that point beyond which the governing board and executive managers lose control over matters for which they will be held accountable.

In sum, then, we can observe a constitutional crisis in the modern corporation which raises two equally important questions: the adequacy of power in corporate governments, and the control of that power.

Eugene V. Rostow

THE CASE AGAINST CORPORATE "DEMOCRACY"

Is corporate "democracy" the answer to the constitutional crisis of the corporation? Eugene V. Rostow doubts that it would be a good idea; "shareholder democracy" is impractical and is no total solution even in theory. The best way to hold corporate managers responsible, in his opinion, is to restrict their functions to profit-maximization in the interest of the shareholders; he implies that representation of employees should be left to unions and protection of the public interest should be left to governments.

The critics of managerial autonomy have long preached democracy as the manifest remedy for feudalism: if only stockholders could be more fully informed, protected by better proxy rules, and given cumulative voting and easier access to stockholders' lists, they urge, the stockholders' annual meeting would become a meaningful source of authority for the directors, and a meaningful procedure for reviewing their stewardship.

It is becoming clear that such hopes for corporate "democracy" are bound to be disappointed in the case of many, perhaps most, of the endocratic enterprises which have become so important a feature of the economic scene. They are not addressed to prevailing reality. In comparatively few large publicly held corporations, managerial control is in fact exercised by or for considerable stockholding interests—as in the familiar instances of corporations where Ford, Rockefeller, Mellon, or duPont investments are dominant. In such companies,

Excerpted by permission of the publishers from Eugene V. Rostow, "To Whom and for What Ends Is Corporate Management Responsible?" in Edward S. Mason, ed., *The Corporation in Modern Society,* Cambridge, Mass.: Harvard University Press. pp. 53-71.

practice corresponds to the legal forms, as it does, by and large, in the case of smaller, closely held companies: responsible ownership, using the voting powers of the common stock, provides a classically legitimate base for the power of the directorate. But cases of this kind are growing rarer every year. The estate tax, the antitrust laws, the process of dilution through growth—these and other forces tend to disperse large stockholdings formerly held by individuals, groups, or families who were willing to participate in management, or take responsibility for selecting it, in order to protect their investment. The current prototype, increasingly, is that of a corporation with stock widely scattered among individuals, investment trusts, or institutional investors, who faithfully vote for the incumbent management, and resolutely refuse to participate in its concerns. In such companies, the stockholders obey the management, not the management the stockholders. Most stockholders of this class are interested in their stock only as investments. The prevalence of this view makes it almost hopeless to expect that the electoral process can ever become anything more significant than an empty ritual. The reforms of the Roosevelt era accomplished much, in requiring financial and corporate disclosure and in establishing procedures for enforcing these requirements. But no amount of disclosure can make corporate democracy effective where the corporate vote belongs to weak, scattered individual investors or to institutional investors who cannot or will not take an effective part in the corporate electoral process.

Many believe that the prevailing state of gloom about corporate democracy may have gone too far. After all, they point out, political elections often fall far short of the ideal, both in the motivation of voters, and in the level of discourse at which their franchise is solicited. Shortcomings of this order, if not too widespread, do not gravely impair the usefulness of the institution.

But for the endocratic corporations, the corporate election is frequently not a partial but a total farce. Well-informed investors, analyzing the company's documents, often prefer to sell their stock, despite the tax and other costs of such sales, rather than to engage in lengthy and dubious battles for remedying managerial shortcomings. It is better business for them, they conclude, to shift capital to a profitable company than to conduct a quixotic struggle against the inherently powerful and entrenched position of the management. Thus far, investment trusts, welfare funds, and institutional stockholders have by and large refused to cross the line which in their view divides investment from management. The few exceptions, like the Atlas Corporation, underscore the generality of the rule.

Various proposals have been put forward, intended to make corporate democracy more effective.

Mr. Justice Douglas, while he was a member and later Chairman of the Securities and Exchange Commission, urged the development of a new profession —that of full-time directors. Vigorous and well-paid directors, he thought, purged of all conflicting interests, would provide sustained supervision over the work of management, and protect the interests of those orphans of the business system, the scattered small stockholders, now doomed to impotence in most corporate environments. "The paid director," he wrote, "would revive and strengthen the tradition of trusteeship. His job would not be to represent the management or to represent himself. It would be primarily to represent the stockholder—to return to the stockholder the protection which today's stockholder has too frequently lost." Unfortunately, the Commissioner did not indicate how most corporation presidents could be persuaded to elect, and then to reelect, directors who would make their lives more difficult, perhaps even actually dangerous, or how paid directors could avoid becoming identified with the management which paid them.

Other critics have urged the formation of Small Stockholders' Protective Committees or Councils, to pool their voting strength, and to obtain representation on boards in behalf of their members. The analogy of the Foreign Bondholders' Protective Council is sometimes invoked, as a private device for encouraging or accomplishing this end.

Some reformers look to salvation through the development of new attitudes by investment trusts and other large fiduciary investors. The astronomic growth of welfare funds, they point out, will soon compel the managers of such portfolios to assume a responsibility for corporate management which they have so far largely shunned. Then we should face a situation to arouse Professor Mills' ire—one group of professional managers supervising another, in an atmosphere, as he would view it, of tacit conspiracy among the members of the Establishment against the rest of us.

Writers like Scott Buchanan go even further. They would accept the de facto autonomy which economic and legal history has conferred upon the management of the endocratic corporations, but they would seek to make its internal procedures more democratic. Solutions of this type, like those espoused in earlier periods by syndicalists, cooperators, and Guild Socialists, would seemingly enfranchise not only stockholders, but also workers and perhaps bondholders, who would then determine corporate policy through "republican" forms of government. While Mr. Buchanan's prescriptions are vague, and difficult to isolate, he would apparently hope to cure the present shortcomings of corporate democracy in endocratic corporations by adding new groups of apathetic and disinterested voters to the masses of stockholders who now fail to exercise their franchise intelligently.

Such approaches would deny the possibility of public oversight for endocracies. After all, the endocratic corporation is an institution which deeply affects the public interest in many ways—not only as a potential monopolist or collaborator in monopoly arrangements, but as a reservoir of savings and a combination of men and skills, which for many purposes should be subject to publicly established rules governing the use of money, the modalities of finance, and even the pattern of business policy. General Electric and General Motors are private companies in form. They are also indispensable parts of the national defense establishment. Accepting the autonomy of the endocratic corporation would remit its government more and more completely to groups which have strong financial interests in certain lines of policy. These policies may, or may not, also serve the public interest.

There is, on the other hand, a considerable opinion about modern corporations which welcomes the idea of self-perpetuating management, not genuinely based on the will of substantial stockholders' votes. Men of this persuasion question the relevance of the democratic model to the problem of organizing and conducting a business corporation or, for that matter, a trade union. And they find much to applaud in what they regard as a more civilized concept of corporate responsibility, which they detect emerging as the professional manager supplants the old-style owner-manager in one business situation after another. Dean Mason has recently characterized this literature as the "apologetics of managerialism." While there is variety in detail among the prescriptions of those who have contributed to this general view, they share certain attitudes.

First, they believe that something should be done to provide a substitute for or, more often, a supplement to, the fading dream of corporate democracy in the large, publicly held endocracy. As Professor Berle has said,

Whenever there is a question of power there is a question of legitimacy. As things stand now, these instrumentalities of tremendous power have the slenderest claim of legitimacy. This is probably a transitory period. They must find some claim of legitimacy, which also means finding a field of responsibility and a field of accountability. Legitimacy, responsibility and accountability are essential to any power system if it is to endure. They correspond to a deep human instinct. A man desires beyond anything else to have someone give him the accolade of "Well done, thou good and faithful servant," thereby risking the condemnation of "You have been no good–get out." If he has to say it to himself, or hear it from a string of people whom he himself has hired or controls, he is apt to die a cynical and embittered man.[1]

But no member of this school of thought would accept the proposals of the British Labour Party, that the government purchase shares of such companies, to achieve both legitimacy and accountability through socialism. Nor would many of them view with favor the postwar German practice of having workers' representatives on boards of directors, which Mr. Scott Buchanan seems to have had in mind in his recent pamphlet on the subject. Most such reformers seem to be groping for a private device, or a device of state law rather than of federal law, which could give the managers a more tangible source of authority than the accident of their own possession of the seats of power, and a more serious and official procedure of accountability than the empty histrionics of the usual annual meeting.

Professor Manning has sketched the outlines of an idea which has intriguing implications and merits further exploration. His suggestion is addressed primarily to the issue of accountability, rather than to the problem of providing corporate boards with a more tangible mandate. His article proposes to consider the large, publicly held corporation as if it were in law what it often is in fact, a kind of voting trust, where the stockholder delegates all his rights save that of collecting his dividend to the directors–that is, to the management. Viewing the corporation in the light of this theory of itself, he points out, immediately brings certain problems into the foreground, and indicates certain possibilities for remedial action. In order to establish more effective procedures for visitation and control, he has in mind the development of a new device, public or private, which could carry out certain functions presently neglected, or relatively neglected. He seems to visualize this device as preferably private, and as a kind of "second chamber," distinct from the board of directors, and with more limited powers. This "extrinsic" body would presumably review decisions of the board where

[1]Adolf A. Berle, *Economic Power and the Free Society* (New York: The Fund for the Republic, 1957), p. 16.

conflicts of interest arise, particularly with regard to the compensation of officers; it could also pass on other board and managerial decisions, notably where corporate funds are spent for charitable contributions not directly related to the company's business. It might well have broader powers, in enforcing a full disclosure of the corporation's financial and business affairs, for example. In a corporate world organized in this way, the stockholder would hold in effect certificates in a voting trust. He would "own" his stock, and not the equity of the corporation, save for such problems as the determination of creditors' rights, where Professor Manning would not alter the existing law of contractual priority.

Professor Manning's proposal is in its preliminary stages, and it is not now without ambiguities. He seems, for example, to contemplate the continuance of the present stockholder voting machinery, and even the occasional catharsis of a good proxy fight.

This original line of thought might well offer much to protect the corporation, in that important group of cases where stockholders as a class are unable to function in accordance with the expectations of legal theory. The development of the idea might be most fruitful if it clearly separated the directors' function from that of monitoring their work, and provided a device which excluded management from any role in the selection of the "Second Chamber" —perhaps by delegation to a trustee under an indenture.

Professor Manning's proposal does not solve the problem of managerial legitimacy in large endocratic enterprises, as he frankly recognizes: "Although the proxy system of electing directors is largely an engine of, rather than for, management control, someone has to select directors, and there would be no advantage in permitting them overtly to choose their own successors."

Perhaps we can do no better, in a system of private property, where the claimants to the residual equity insist on delegating their interests to the managers. One can, however, visualize more constructive solutions. Building on a long if checkered experience with corporate trustees under bondholders' indentures, could we not consider requiring the issuance of stock in endocratic corporations in a form which gave small stockholders the option of delegating their voting rights to a trustee, who would act for them more effectively than they can ever hope to act for themselves?

In reviewing the literature about the current development of endocratic corporations, and about possible programs for their reform, one is struck by the atmosphere of relative peace. There seems to be no general conviction abroad that reform is needed. The vehement feelings of the early thirties, expressing a sense of betrayal and frustration at a depression blamed on twelve years of business leadership, are almost entirely absent. Ideas for reforming endocracy are not supported by anything like the sense of purpose which sustains the antitrust laws and the income tax.

I suspect that enlightened lay opinion could be summarized in these terms:

"Yes, there are paradoxes and anomalies in the way boards of directors are elected in some large, publicly held companies. But what of it? There are irrational moments in most of our legal arrangements, some more illogical than this one. The disclosure requirements of the Securities Act and the Securities

Exchange Act do a lot of good. And most boards of directors are not so bad. Business seems energetic. There's a good deal of competition—not enough, but still a good deal. Corporate executives are overpaid, but the income tax must take quite a lot of their excessive salaries. All in all, the system may be illogical, but it works. And besides, any serious reform would have to bring government agencies more directly into the internal affairs of corporations, and that would be worse."

So long as the problem of corporate responsibility is viewed in this pragmatic light, change will come only from within the system, in response to moves which corporate management may consider prudential and protective in the long run. Many such moves have characterized the development of the corporation during the postwar period, most notably the spread of the idea of "public directors," and the flowering of the view that the primary duty of the corporation is not to make as much money as possible for its stockholders, but to advance the public interest in some alternative sense.

Many have proclaimed this doctrine as the dawn of a better day, in which the outworn maxims of Adam Smith have yielded at last to the higher virtue of responsible citizenship. Corporations have "souls" and "consciences," we are told. They no longer take a "narrow," "selfish" view of policy, but what passes for a more statesmanlike attitude towards their problems.

* *

From the point of view of legal and economic orthodoxy, the New Capitalism is all bewildering balderdash. The law books have always said that the board of directors owes a single-minded duty of unswerving loyalty to the stockholders, and only to the stockholders. The economist has demonstrated with all the apparent precision of plane geometry and the calculus that the quest for maximum revenue in a competitive market leads to a system of prices, and an allocation of resources and rewards, superior to any alternative, in its contributions to the economic welfare of the community as a whole. To the orthodox mind, it is therefore unsettling, to say the least, to have the respected head of the Standard Oil Company of New Jersey equating the management's duty to stockholders with its obligation to employees, customers, suppliers, and the public at large.

The stubborn relics of an analytical tradition have difficulty translating the soothing formulas of managerialism into terms they can understand. And perhaps the task is impossible. In sectors of the economy more or less effectively insulated from direct dependence upon market pressures, as the economists have long known, the negotiated solutions of multilateral oligopoly, or even of bilateral monopoly, are neither so uniform nor so predictable as those of the straightforward competitive model. In such situations, it has been customary to conclude, there is no equilibrium position towards which the market tends to move, but rather a zone of possible solutions within which ignorance, accident, or other bargaining factors yield an oscillating and unstable result, explicable only in the tenuous terms of game theory.

Accepting this reservation, however, what does the "new" concept of corporate responsibility imply? Does it mean that the management of a great corporation should not bargain very hard in negotiations over wages or the prices paid to suppliers? Does it mean that a statesmanlike and well-run company should charge less for its product than the market would bear, less than the prices which would maximize its short-term revenues, or what it conceives to be its long-term profits? Should it regard its residual profits, not as "belonging to" its stockholders in some ultimate sense, but as a pool of funds to be devoted in considerable part to the public interest, as the directors conceive it—to hospitals, parks, and charities in the neighborhood of its plants; to the local symphony or the art museum; to scholarships for the children of employees, or to other forms of support for the educational system of the nation at large? If what is good for the country is good for General Motors, as is indeed the case, does this view of managerial responsibility set any limit upon the directors' discretion in spending corporate funds for what they decide is the public good?

* *

The political and legal aspects of corporate statesmanship present vistas which are quite as disturbing as its economics. The endocratic corporations are accepted as powerful and effective instruments for carrying on the business of society. If their directors begin to act as if they really were general trustees for the public at large, they may well imperil their present freedom. Corporations are not accepted in public opinion as institutions through which society makes its educational policy, its foreign policy, or its political policy. Programs which would give reality to the idea of spending corporate funds to advance the general welfare, as the directors visualize it, will sooner or later invite the critical attention of legislators, governors, and presidents, who consider that they have been elected by the people to advance the general welfare, and know more about it than the directors of endocratic corporations. As Professor Ben W. Lewis has recently said, commenting on the thesis that "the corporation, almost against its will, has been compelled to assume in appreciable part the role of conscience-carrier of twentieth-century American society":

It is not going to happen; if it did happen it would not work; and if it did work it would still be intolerable to free men. I am willing to dream, perhaps selfishly, of a society of selfless men. Certainly, if those who direct our corporate concentrates are to be free from regulation either by competition or government, I can only hope that they will be conscientious, responsible, and kindly men; and I am prepared to be grateful if this proves to be the case. But, I shall still be uneasy and a little ashamed, with others who are ashamed, to be living my economic life within the limits set by the gracious bounty of the precious few. If we are to have rulers, let them be men of good will; but above all, let us join in choosing our rulers—and in ruling them.[2]

The responsibility of corporate directors requires redefinition. It may give us a warm and comfortable feeling to say that the director is a trustee for the community, rather than for his stockholders; that he is a semipublic official, or a quasi-public official, or some other kind of hyphenated public officer. It would be more constructive, however, to seek redefinition in another sense: to restate the law of corporate trusteeship in terms which take full account of the social advances of this century, but which direct the directors more sharply

[2] Ben W. Lewis, "Economics by Admonition," *American Economic Review* (Supplement 49, 1959), pp. 384-85.

to concentrate their efforts on discharging their historic economic duties to their stockholders. The economic job of directors and management is quite difficult enough to absorb the full time of first-rate minds, in an economy of changing technology, significant general instability, and considerable competition, both from rival firms in the same industry and from those which steadily offer rival products.

Similarly, watching the investment of trade union funds in a variety of banks and other business enterprises, one wonders whether the public interest is really served by their present freedom. Is it sound public policy to allow unions to accumulate funds not required by their primary needs, and to invest those funds at will, in ways which often lead to grave conflicts of interest?

Would such a redefinition of goals for large endocratic business units and trade unions serve any useful purpose? How could such rules be enforced? Could they have any impact on the flow of events? Is "the long-run economic interest of stockholders" any more meaningful, as a standard to guide the deliberation of directors, or the decisions of courts or other public bodies reviewing what the directors have done, than "the interests of the enterprise as a whole," or "the interests of the community"? Such a "rule" would comfort the few remaining adherents of the older orthodoxy. What else would it accomplish?

* *

The function of rules of law is both descriptive and normative. Such rules reflect the pattern of accepted behavior and the standards which the community seeks to have upheld in the daily conduct of business affairs. They are at best hypotheses, articulated to guide and explain the wayward course of events. As an abstract statement of the social duty of business enterprise in the middle of the twentieth century, I believe the "rule" I have suggested—that of long-term profit maximization—conforms more concretely than any alternative both to the image of preferred reality for business behavior in public opinion, at this state in the evolution of our legal and economic order, and to the ends business enterprise is expected to fulfill as part of the nation's system of law for governing the economy.

But how can such policies be enforced? Are the votes of stockholders, or of some agent for stockholders in endocratic corporations, such as the optional voting trustee suggested earlier, a better guide to the long-term economic interests of stockholders than the business judgment of directors? Are minority stockholders' suits, even if brought by a public officer in the name of the inherent visitorial powers of the state, a suitable or sufficient remedy? Such devices, backed by strong policies of required disclosure, may help curb overreaching, the wrongful taking of corporate opportunity, excessive managerial compensation, trading on inside information, and other abuses. Professor Manning's "second chamber" is a provocative thought which deserves extended consideration in this connection. It can hardly be assumed, however, that any of these procedures, or all of them in combination, would provide a better basis than the directors' judgment for determining the long-term *economic* interest of the stockholders.

The voting of active stockholders, or, in the case of endocratic corporations, voting by an independent trustee for stockholders, would have one advantage over the present rule of untrammeled managerial discretion: it would provide a less dubious base for the authority of directors and officers of great enterprises, now almost cut off from their source of power.

On the other hand, a clear acceptance of profit maximization as a legal principle might well do something, perhaps a good deal, to order the pattern of corporate policy. Legal rules are not always fully self-enforcing, of course. But they do exert an influence, even though procedures of enforcement are not comprehensive. Adequate means for surveillance and accounting can and should be developed, to minimize abuses of corporate power. The more important problem, however, is the orientation of legitimate business policy: Should it be essentially economic in purpose, or should it become an ambiguous amalgam of economic and noneconomic themes? I, for one, conclude that a clear-cut economic directive should help directors to discriminate more effectively among competing claims upon them, in carrying out their public trusteeship for the economic system as a whole.

Timothy K. Barnekov and Daniel Rich

THE CORPORATION AS A SOCIAL WELFARE INSTITUTION

Should large corporations confine themselves to profit-making and leave social reform to others? They can make an important contribution to the solution of the problems of the poor, Barnekov and Rich argue, but only if the concept of corporate accountability is redefined.

Controversy about the meaning and implications of "corporate social responsibility" has recently focused upon the role of corporations as social welfare institutions; specifically as organizations which can contribute to the solution of the problems of the ghetto and of the poor. Advocates of "corporate social responsibility" believe that mobilization of the power, wealth, and managerial skills of American corporations can help to overcome domestic welfare problems. In addition, corporate involvement in social welfare is viewed as having potential benefits for the corporation itself; it is expected to provide a source of direct profit and contribute to a public image of the corporation as a socially valuable institution.

Objections to corporate involvement in social welfare have been based on pragmatic and ideological arguments. Some critics believe that expectations for

Authors' note: We are grateful to Andrew Stewart for his assistance in collecting background materials for this article.

"The Corporation as a Social Welfare Institution" by Timothy K. Barnekov and Daniel Rich is reprinted from *American Behavioral Scientist,* Vol. 15, no. 5 (May/June 1972), pp. 749-763, by permission of the Publisher, Sage Publications, Inc.

adequate performance of social welfare functions by the private sector are economically unrealistic. Investment in the ghetto is viewed as a bad business risk—unattractive to profit-seeking institutions without government subsidies or safeguards. Others argue that the poor are unlikely to be the beneficiaries of corporate involvement, and that involvement may lead to the extension of a colonial relationship between the ghetto and the larger society.

Our purpose in this paper is to identify the conditions under which the corporation can perform social welfare activities in a manner beneficial to the poor. We believe that the corporation can be an effective social welfare institution, but this outcome is predicated upon changes in the nature of corporate accountability and in the relationship of the poor to the corporation.

The Corporation as an Instrument of Change

Some government leaders and often the victims of poverty have looked upon the corporation as an agent of social change and as an instrument of social welfare. Frequently, the problems of the ghetto and of its inhabitants have been perceived so that their solutions involve mobilization of the managerial and technical skills of American corporations. The causes of poverty are identified with the characteristics of the poor (their lack of education and skills, their lower-class culture) or with the environmental inadequacies of impoverished areas (lack of jobs, poor housing, inefficient transportation, and the like). The ghetto and its inhabitants are regarded as objects of social welfare. By locating in the ghetto, by providing jobs and training, by fostering entrepreneurial skills and motivations, and by providing health, education, and transportation services, the corporation is expected to contribute to the rehabilitation of the poor and the revitalization of depressed areas. Thus, it has been argued that:

It is primarily up to private enterprise, and not to the government, to upgrade the disadvantaged, to provide training for the unemployed, to break down the complexities of job components, to employ the willing, to make them able, to push for social betterment, to dissolve the ghettos, to break through the vicious cycle of welfarism, to integrate the poor into an affluent economy, and to rebuild the cities [Cervantes, 1967: 56].

These arguments give rise to a belief that it is industry that must provide the creative leadership and resource potential necessary to help the poor. But why should industry be expected to respond? Involvement of this nature appears to be a poor investment; the ghetto has little to offer the corporation. The corporation's role as a social welfare institution may be viewed as incompatible with the profit motive; insofar as that role is taken seriously, it will have a fundamentally subversive impact upon a system of private property.

Economist Milton Friedman (1970) believes that the very idea of "corporate social responsibility" is a myth and a delusion; if it is not pure rhetoric, it must mean that corporate management is to act in some way that is not in the interest of its employers. This amounts to managerial irresponsibility since, in a private property system, management's only responsibility is to its employers.

That responsibility is to conduct the business in accordance with their desires, which generally will be to make as much money as possible while conforming to the basic rules of the society, both those embodied in law and those embodied in ethical custom [Friedman, 1970: 32].

Friedman's concerns appear to be at least partially unfounded. There is no evidence that corporate willingness to become involved in social welfare reflects a lessening of self-interested motivation and a lack of desire for profits. Indeed, Jules Cohn's (1970) survey of 247 major corporations participating in urban problem-solving indicates that without exception these efforts are viewed by corporate leaders as consistent with the profit motive. Enlightened self-interest is the principal motive offered by the top executives of the corporations surveyed. Thus, David Rockefeller said: "We believe that our urban affairs work is good for Chase Manhattan in a strictly business sense" (Cohn, 1970: 70).[1]

Involvement in social welfare may be incompatible with corporate profit-making if profit is defined simplistically in terms of immediate economic returns. However, welfare expenditures are often undertaken because they are "profitable" in the long run. As Michael Reagan (1963: 136-137) points out:

Many actions taken on behalf of long run profitability have no provable effect on the balance sheet . . . . Some observers have suggested that, because the connection cannot be proved, such actions constitute a shift away from the profit motive. This judgment seems unwarranted. The managers believe and hope that their good-will expenditures will enhance profits, and so long as they are operating on this premise, profit is still the motive.

Future returns from current expenditures in social welfare enter into corporate managements' calculus of profit. The reasons for the adoption of a more comprehensive conception of profit have been outlined in a recent statement by the Committee on Economic Development (1971: 22), a group composed of major corporate leaders:

The large corporation is developing long-term goals such as survival, growth, and increasing respect and acceptance by the public. Current profitability, once regarded as the dominant if not exclusive objective, is now often seen more as a vital means and powerful motivating force for achieving broader ends, rather than as an end in itself. Thus, modern managers are prepared to trade off short-run profits to achieve qualitative improvements in the institution which can be expected to contribute to the long-run profitable growth of the corporation.

These perceptions are shared by some economists and social scientists; the modern corporation is viewed as no less self-interested than its historical counterparts, but corporate self-interest is regarded as less narrowly defined. As a permanent institution in society, the corporation may be expected to look upon long-term security and stable growth as more important than immediate economic returns. It is no surprise, therefore, that the rhetoric of modern

[1]Other motives involved corporate reputation for equal opportunity in employment and in the awarding of contracts, insurance against boycotts, violence, and other threats to company well-being, and explicit efforts at profit-making, including the opening up of new markets, the attraction of new customers, and the sale of services as trainees or consultants to government or other companies (Cohn, 1970: 70).

corporate management emphasizes the compatibility of social responsibility and "enlightened self-interest."

The Limits of Corporate Success

Nevertheless, some government and corporate leaders believe that enlightened self-interest alone will not be a sufficient incentive for corporate involvement in social welfare. What is advocated is an alliance of government and private enterprise whereby government provides tax credits, contract incentives, and location subsidies to mobilize corporate skills and resources for the solution of social welfare problems. Such an alliance has been viewed as offering "a new means for developing the innate capabilities of a . . . political-economic system capable of managing social and technical change in the interest of a better social order" (CED, 1971: 59). In the context of social welfare this alliance represents what the late Senator Robert Kennedy proposed in 1967 as a new partnership against poverty (see Congressional Record, 1967).

Can such a partnership benefit the poor? Michael Harrington (1968: 6) believes that federal subsidies may succeed in prodding industry into the ghetto but at the cost of excluding all the poor and the majority of Negroes from the benefits. Thus, federal subsidy to private builders results in the construction of housing beyond the economic means of the very poor, amounting to what Harrington describes as a public subsidy of private profit. Similarly, William Tabb (1969: 399) an economist, doubts whether the use of government incentives to attract industry to locate in urban poverty areas is really worthwhile.

To the extent that industrial location drives real estate prices up, adds to traffic congestion, uproots people from their homes and brings industry into residential areas, the program may have distinctly harmful effects on the neighborhood which may not be offset by the advantage of the additional employment opportunities in the urban poverty areas.

Proposals for a government-private-enterprise alliance often have taken as their justification the past contributions of this alliance in other public policy areas; specifically, in the area of national defense. Just as a mobilization of scientific, technical, and managerial skills through an alliance of government and industry has provided for defense against external threats by making possible the development of sophisticated weapons systems, now it is expected that this alliance can help win the domestic wars: "the war on poverty, the war on crime, and the war on blight" (Sapolsky, 1969: 2). These expectations have been characterized by Harvey M. Sapolsky as the "ballistic missile solution to the urban crisis."

Sapolsky contends that the solution is unrealistic. The success of a government-private-sector alliance in national security affairs has resulted from systematic mobilization of scientific and technical skills to achieve goals designated by a centralized authority. However, there is no agreement as to the nature of the problems of the city, much less the goals of urban public policy, nor is there a legitimized domestic equivalent of the Department of Defense to provide overall direction. Moreover, as Sapolsky points out, the problems that seem most susceptible to solution by the mobilization of managerial and technical skills—water pollution, air pollution, transportation—are essentially middle-class concerns. They "are high on the agenda of the people that live in the suburbs but low on the agenda of the core city poor, black or white" (Sapolsky, 1969: 10).

Some critics believe that corporate involvement in social welfare will be detrimental to the interests of the poor. Richard Cloward and Francis Piven (1967) contend that corporations entering the ghetto as government subsidiaries cannot function in ways that benefit the poor; indeed, such involvement will lead to "corporate imperialism for the poor." Corporations will become "new managers" of the ghetto, exploiting opportunities for subsidized profit while remaining insulated from effective political control. Inhabitants of the ghetto, they believe, will be absorbed within the corporate enterprise—co-opted through token participation in corporate decision-making—and, as a result, will become instruments of national corporate power.

According to these authors, the long-term economic prospects for the poor depend upon their potential political power. While the short-term economic conditions of the ghetto may be improved by corporate involvement, long-term prospects will be endangered. Corporate involvement will prevent ghetto populations from developing a power base in local government by diminishing the importance of the political process and limiting the ability of local government to control the distribution of rewards and services.

Also, the view that the problems of the poor must be resolved by political decisions calling for a strong governmental role is advocated by Michael Harrington (1968: 6). He believes that the basic decisions needed "are not susceptible to business priorities." Corporate involvement, unless it is subordinate to public decisions, cannot help the poor because it is precisely the pursuit of profit "that has exacerbated our crisis and can hardly solve it" (1968: 5). What is needed to solve the problems of the ghetto, according to Harrington, is "an 'uneconomic' investment of public funds motivated by considerations of social and aesthetic values rather than by a calculus of private profit" (1968: 6).

Because profit-making is regarded as the principal motivation for corporate involvement, Harrington, as well as do Cloward and Piven, believes that the corporation should be excluded from the ghetto, or at least that its presence should be rigorously controlled by public authority. Despite ideological differences, these authors appear to agree with Milton Friedman's assertion that the objectives of the corporation are inconsistent with "social responsibility." On the one hand, there is fear that involvement will be detrimental to the interests of the poor; on the other hand, there is concern that it will undermine the free enterprise system.

Corporate Power and Accountability

We share the concerns of those who believe that corporate involvement in social welfare will result in an extension of corporate power. Yet we do not believe that the exclusion of the corporation from the ghetto will mitigate the effects of corporate power on the poor or that it will ensure that an economic calculus of value will not prevail in decisions affecting the poor.

Implicit in the assertion that decisions affecting the ghetto and the poor ought to be made independent of a calculus of private profit is the assumption that a strict separation of public and private power can be achieved in America. In fact, a number of scholars have pointed out that a dominant characteristic of American society is the increasing fusion of economic and political power. It has become difficult to identify the boundaries between the public and private sectors.

In the conventional wisdom of laissez faire, according to Michael Reagan (1963: 129), "the corporation had no political responsibilities, nor even a rationale for any interest in political affairs so long as government did not 'intervene' in private business." The separation of public and private decision-making was conceived of as both feasible and desirable.

This conventional wisdom is no longer, if it ever was, a useful guide to the political status of the corporation. As Reagan points out (1963: 129-130), "corporations are not only much concerned to protect their own immediate legislative interests, but are reaching out in an attempt to create a business-oriented political and social framework within which all public decision-making would be constrained." Clearly, it is unreasonable to assume that decisions made by "public authorities" affecting the poor and the ghetto will be insulated from corporate power and an economic calculus of value. Indeed, Morton Baratz (1956: 413) contends that "public policy necessarily tends to be oriented in the direction which is fundamentally in line with the interests of giant corporate enterprises."

Even apart from their impact on the decisions of public government, the decisions made by corporations affect to a considerable degree, important social values of a large number of persons (Bachrach, 1967). Corporations constitute a political elite precisely because they significantly influence the authoritative allocation of values in American society. There is no reason to expect that their absence from the ghetto will reduce the impact of corporate power on the poor. Moreover, the increasing fusion of public and private power suggests that the status of the corporation as a political elite will not be diminished in the future. The underlying problem posed by the extension of corporate political power is that it has not been matched by equivalent accountability. Adolph Berle (1954: 105) has pointed out that "American political thought has been frightened, and corporations themselves have been frightened, at any suggestion that they might emerge as political institutions in their own and separate right." The basis for this fear is the expectation that recognition of political status will ultimately lead to demands for political accountability.

The power of American corporations and the skill and wealth underlying that power can be utilized to improve the conditions of the ghetto and its inhabitants if the corporation does not remain insulated from accountability to those affected by its actions. By itself, neither the introduction of the corporation into the ghetto as an instrument of change nor its exclusion as an obstacle to change will significantly affect the conditions of the poor. The corporation will operate effectively as a social welfare institution when the status of corporations as a political elite is accepted in American political culture and the corporation becomes, as a result, an object of change. There are some signs that this change in American political culture is already under way. Indeed, managerial rhetoric emphasizing the importance of corporate social responsibility may be viewed as an adaptation to changing public attitudes toward the corporation and as an attempt to forestall direct public accountability.

The Corporation as an Object of Change

There is no reason to view the corporation as a static institution. The modern corporation already represents a significant departure from the classic model of the corporation as a private-property institution with accountability extending only to the stockholders. In fact, as Daniel Bell (1971: 28) has argued, the corporation has "lost many of the historic features of traditional capitalism, yet it has, for lack of a new rationale, retained the old ideology—and finds itself trapped by it." Ownership is largely a legal fiction because "given the pattern of stock ownership today—particularly with the growth of mutual funds, pension funds and trust funds—the stockholder is often an 'in-and-out' person with little continuing interest in the enterprise" (Bell, 1971: 29). Thus, Bell, recalling the Berle-Means thesis of separation of ownership from control, maintains that "the corporation may be a private-enterprise institution, but it is not really a private-property institution."

It is no longer reasonable to take as given what the corporation should do and whom it should serve. Contemporary corporations continue to operate in a "profit-seeking" and "self-interested" manner, but the meaning of profit and self-interest has become ambiguous. Indeed, what Richard Eells (1962) has identified as the "constitutional crisis of the corporation" implies recognition of the legitimacy of claims beyond the stockholders. This recognition represents a more realistic assessment of the current status of corporate enterprise. Contrary to Milton Friedman's view, the corporate executive already responds to a larger constituency:

As a business institution, the 'corporation' is the management and the board of directors, operating as trustees for members of the enterprise as a whole—not just stockholders, but workers and consumers too—and with due regard to the interests of society as a whole. But if this view is accepted, there is a significant logical corollary—that the constituencies which make up the corporation themselves have to be represented within the board of corporate power. Without that, there is no effective countervailing power to that of executive management. More important, without such representation, there would be a serious question about the 'legitimacy' of managerial power [Bell, 1971: 30].

While corporate management continues to fear direct political accountability, there are some indications of a growing awareness that, if the corporation is to survive and prosper, it must respond to a broader constituency. Indeed, it may be the fear of direct political accountability that has fostered this awareness. Thus, the Committee on Economic Development (1971: 16) proclaims that:

Today it is clear that the terms of the contract between society and business are, in fact, changing in substantial and important ways . . . . Inasmuch as business exists to serve society, its future will depend on the quality of management's response to the changing expectations of the public.[2]

[2]The recognition that business depends on public consent may contribute to the acceptance of a broader constituency. CED (1971: 21) suggests that "the great growth of corporations in size, market power, and impact on society has naturally brought with it a commensurate growth in responsibilities; in a democratic society, power sooner or later

For the most part, however, demands for accountability must come from groups outside the corporate leadership. Recently, several organized efforts have manifested a concern for ensuring corporate accountability. "Campaign GM" and the recent study of DuPont's influence in Delaware, both products of Ralph Nader's organization, had greater corporate accountability as their goal. The corporation has also experienced pressure from a variety of consumer protection and environmental groups. More broadly, there is evidence of support for changes in the corporation. A 1970 study by the Opinion Research Corporation indicates that "a clear majority of the public thinks corporations have not been sufficiently concerned about the problems facing our society. Two-thirds believe that business now has a moral obligation to help other major institutions to achieve social progress, even at the expense of profitability" (CED, 1971: 15).

Public government as well has initiated efforts to ensure corporate accountability, particularly in the areas of consumer protection and environmental quality, but often these initiatives have been undertaken only in response to claims made by private groups (as in the case of automobile safety standards). Indeed, if the labor movement in America is to be taken as an indicator, government's role is likely to be legitimization of claims made upon the corporation by other groups.

If the poor are to benefit from corporate involvement in the ghetto, then the corporation must be accountable to those affected by its performance of social welfare functions. The poor by themselves cannot ensure such accountability. Even the achievement of formal representation for the poor in corporate decision-making may make little difference in accountability. Indeed, it is likely that demand for representation of the poor will result in co-optation rather than corporate accountability. Cloward and Piven (1967: 367) warn that:

Advocates of "participatory democracy," "decentralization" and "black control of black affairs" will find these themes turned against them as they are invited to endorse and participate in the new corporate subsidiaries . . . . Once absorbed in local corporate subsidiaries . . . blacks will become instruments of national corporate power.

Demands by the poor for corporate accountability can help create pressures for the corporation to change, but by themselves the poor cannot ensure accountability. The poor have been and continue to be a politically impotent minority which has not had the means to effectively confront political elites—corporate or governmental. Corporate accountability can be achieved only if the cumulative pressure of many groups—consumers, environmental protectionists, community representatives, as well as the poor—can establish the legitimacy of a redefinition of the corporate constituency. The process of legitimation should be expected to culminate in changes in public law, but government is more likely to respond to rather than initiate pressures for change.

begets equivalent accountability." Furthermore, there is some reason to believe that future corporate leaders may be more receptive to a broader conception of corporate accountability. A recent study indicates that some young executives are pressuring present corporate leaders to include social as well as economic values in the corporate decision calculus (Athos, 1970).

Conclusions

Only when corporate accountability is established as a basic tenet of American political culture will it become possible for the poor to demand and receive recognition as a group whose interests and welfare are affected by corporate activity. But changes in American political culture will not guarantee that corporate performance of social welfare activities will benefit the poor. As part of a new corporate constituency, the poor will enjoy the same rights and authority as other constituent groups. At the same time, the poor will be faced with the same dilemmas that they face in relation to public government. In a pluralistic political process, the needs of an unorganized minority frequently are subordinated to other demands. Thus, the need is as great for the poor to organize for political power in corporate government as in public government. In the short run, such efforts can help develop the legitimacy of corporate accountability; in the long run, they can ensure participation in the process of accountability.

It might be argued that focusing on the corporation as an object of change will divert attention from more immediate improvements in the conditions of the poor, that the best strategy for change lies in the direction of increasing pressure on public government. In our view, this argument assumes an independence of public authority from private power. We believe that it is necessary to think of government as a continuum from public to private, to conceive of changes in public government as being linked to changes in corporate government (Lakoff, 1969).

While we have made a case for corporate political accountability, we have not specified the structure of that accountability. We have not identified the form of a new corporate government which is consistent with the development of a broader corporate constituency. We must admit to our own uncertainty about the meaning of political accountability in private institutions, an uncertainty which results in part from the failure of American political thought to address itself to the building of a political theory of private government.

Although the mandate for political science is clear, the nature of corporate political accountability will not be settled by political scientists. It will result only from the mobilization of groups claiming representation within the new corporate constituency and from the resolution of competing claims. Because of the status of the corporation in American society—its possession of critical resources, skills, and wealth—it stands as both a major obstacle to improving the social welfare of the poor and as a necessary instrument for the accomplishment of social change. If the corporation is to be an effective social welfare institution, then it must be politically accountable to those affected by its performance.

References

ALLEN, L. L. (1969) "Making capitalism work in the ghettos." *Harvard Business Rev.* 47 (May/June): 83-92.

ATHOS, A. G. (1970) "Is the corporation the next to fall?" *Harvard Business Rev.* 48 (January/February): 49-61.

BACHRACH, P. (1967) *The Theory of Democratic Elitism.* Boston: Little, Brown and Company.

BARATZ, M. (1956) "Corporate giants and the power structure." *Western Pol. Q.* 9 (June): 406-15.

BELL, D. (1971) "The corporation and society in the 1970's." *Public Interest* (Summer): 5-32.

BERLE, A. (1954) *The 20th Century Capitalist Revolution.* New York: Harcourt Brace Jovanovich, Inc.

CERVANTES, A. J. (1967) "To prevent a chain of super-Watts." *Harvard Business Rev.* 45 (September/October): 55-56.

CHEIT, E. F. (1964) "Why managers cultivate social responsibility." *California Management Rev.* (Fall): 3-22.

CLOWARD, R. A. and F. F. PIVEN (1967) "Corporate imperialism for the poor." *Nation* 205 (October 16): 365-67.

COHN, J. (1970) "Is business meeting the challenge of urban affairs?" *Harvard Business Rev.* 48 (March/April): 68-82.

Committee on Economic Development (1971) *Social Responsibilities of Business Corporations.* New York.

Congressional Record (1967) "Some remarks introducing a bill for industrial investment in poverty areas." Volume 113 (July 12): 18443-48.

COOK, J. W. (1969) "Why a company gets involved." *Bell Telephone Magazine* (March/April): 9-13.

DEMAREE, A. T. (1969) "Business picks up the urban challenge." *Fortune* 79 (April): 103-84.

EELLS, R. (1962) *The Government of Corporations.* New York: The Free Press.

FRIEDMAN, M. (1970) "The social responsibility of business is to increase its profits." *New York Times Magazine* (September 13): 32+.

HARRINGTON, M. (1968) "Can private industry abolish slums?" *Dissent* 15 (January/February): 4-6.

LAKOFF, S. A. (1969) "Private government in the managed society," pp. 170-201 in R. Pennock and J. Chapman, eds. *Voluntary Associations.* New York: Atherton Press.

McKERSIE, R. B. (1968) "Vitalize black enterprise." *Harvard Business Rev.* 46 (September/October): 88-99.

REAGAN, M. (1963) *The Managed Economy.* New York: Oxford Univ. Press.

SAPOLSKY, H. M. (1969) "On the ballistic missile solution to the urban crisis." (unpublished)

TABB, W. K. (1970) *The Political Economy of the Black Ghetto.* New York: W. W. Norton & Company.

——— (1969) "Government incentives to private industry to locate in urban poverty areas." *Land Economics* 45 (November): 392-99.

3

Trade Unions

Seymour Martin Lipset

THE LAW AND TRADE UNION DEMOCRACY†

As trade unions have become larger and more powerful, the issue of their internal government has evoked concern both inside and outside the labor movement. Can public laws protect union democracy? Seymour Martin Lipset suggests that while they are no real guarantee where conditions are not congenial, they can and do set an influential standard.

Concern with internal government of the trade union is probably as old as the institution itself. Nineteenth-century labor history is filled with discussions of constitutional structure. When unions became powerful and received recognition as legitimate institutions in the mid-twentieth century, experimentation with different forms of union government declined and a new period emerged —a period marked by a growth in *realpolitik,* and by the incorporation of the ideology of business unionism. Attachment to idealistic doctrines declined and, although constitutions continued to differ among various unions, the nature of union government settled down to what has been described as a one-party oligarchy. With few exceptions the national administrations became political machines, remaining permanently in power and co-opting their new members.[1]

In most unions the characteristic road to high office is to be designated as a successor by a higher-up or previous incumbent. The death or retirement of a dominant leader occasionally brings about a succession battle, such as that among the Steelworkers following the death of Philip Murray, but a much more characteristic pattern is the promotion of the man next in line for the office. Although the inheritance of the leadership of the Carpenters Union by Maurice Hutchinson, the son of the previous president, is an atypical exhibition of nepotism, its occurrence in one of the AFL's most important affiliates is an indication of how dominant an administration group can be. So common is one-party oligarchy that the major remaining defender of the Soviet Union within the labor movement has attempted to justify Communist totalitarianism by pointing to its parallels with the government of American unions:

What is totalitarianism? A country that has a totalitarian government operates

†This article has been written as part of a general investigation of the condition of the American labor movement being conducted by the Trade Union Committee of the Fund for the Republic in conjunction with the Institute of Industrial Relations of the University of California, Berkeley. It was presented, in slightly different form, to the 1960 meeting of the American Political Science Association. The author would like to express his appreciation to the Fund and the Institute for their support of this work, and to acknowledge a debt of gratitude to Faith Denitch for research assistance, and to Laurel Fujishige and Daniel Bell for editorial advice.

[1] For a balanced, recent analysis of trade union government, see Leiserson, *American Trade Union Democracy* (1959). See also Taft, *The Structure and Government of Labor Unions* (1954).

Reprinted with permission from *Virginia Law Review,* Vol. 47, no. 1 (January 1961), pp. 1-47.

like our union operates. There are no political parties. People are elected to govern the country based upon their records . . . . That is totalitarianism. If we started to divide up and run a Republican set of officers, a Democratic set, a Communist set and something else we would have a hell of a time.[2]

Though the fact of union oligarchy has occasioned little concern within the ranks of union politicians, who see it as necessary and even proper, the same has not been true for friends and enemies of labor outside union ranks. Increasingly, as trade unions have become accepted as key power groups in the larger society, the question of how representative and democratic they are internally has become a matter of public inquiry and controversy. The recent investigations by the McClellan committee, followed by the passage of the Labor-Management Reporting and Disclosure Act (LMRDA) of 1959,[3] obviously have made the question of union government a legitimate issue for general concern. In a certain sense, the unions themselves must acknowledge some responsibility for this development, since they welcomed and supported government intervention on their behalf as collective bargaining agencies when they supported the Wagner Act in the mid-thirties.

This article is designed as a contribution to that discussion. It deals with a number of topics: the sources of the current interest in union government, the conditions accounting for the dominant pattern of union government in America, various past efforts to change union practices by legislation, some of the possible effects of the LMRDA and reform legislation in general, the nature of and potential for internal opposition, and possible activities for concerned outsiders.

The Concern for Union Democracy

With the shift in our national ideological cycle from the leftism or liberalism characterizing the period from 1930 to 1950 to the dominant conservatism of the 1950's has come a complementary shift in the kind of institution vulnerable to attack. Although a variety of factors are involved, this has been a major one in the focus on union democracy and the rights of union members. Paralleling the larger political trend there has been a drastic change in the social and political situation of the union movement. The relatively weak movement of the early thirties became the large, established, sixteen-million member AFL-CIO of the fifties. By then, every major industry, with the exception of chemicals and textiles, had accepted unions as the legitimate representatives of their employees, the government had guaranteed the right to organize and to bargain collectively, and the unions had strong ties to, and influence with, the Democratic party.

Perhaps as important as the shift in the power position of unions has been the change in the relative income position of the different occupational classes.

[2] Address by Harry Bridges, April 7-11, 1947, in ILWU, *Proceedings of the Seventh Biennial Convention* 178 (1947).

[3] 73 Stat. 519 (1959) (codified in scattered sections of 29 *U.S.C.*, Supp. 1, 1959) [hereinafter cited as LMRDA].

During the thirties and early forties, white collar and professional employees were much better off both in terms of salary and job security than manual workers. Unemployment was considerably lower among white collar workers of all varieties than among wage earners, and large sections of the former possessed various special privileges such as regular vacations and participation in pension programs. These traditional advantages of white collar workers and salaried professionals have gradually declined under the impact of full employment, inflation, and growing unionization among manual workers. The increase in the income and fringe benefits of manual workers has far surpassed that of the nonmanual groups, and many of the latter have, in fact, experienced a decline in real income. This change in relative economic situation may have contributed to a loss of sympathy among the employed middle classes, both for the manual worker and for unions in general.

But if a change in the larger social, political, and economic climate helps to account for the fact that it is now labor rather than business which faces attack from congressional committees, journalists, and academicians, it does not explain why so much of this criticism should have taken the form of a moral crusade against violations of internal union democracy. There are many American institutions, such as the American Medical Association, the American Legion, and the National Association of Manufacturers, whose practices are as undemocratic as those of trade unions, but which have not been subject to the same severe criticism. Most nominally democratic private associations in America can properly be described as governed by one-party, self-perpetuating, and self-recruiting oligarchies. Why, then, pick on unions?

The concern for union democracy emanates from several sources: the image which unions perpetuate of themselves as champions of the underprivileged, the view of many intellectuals that unions are or should be agents in the building of a better society, the belief in the need of a counterbalance to the employer's power, and the view that an institution to which is delegated some of the authority of a democratic state has a special obligation to be democratic in the exercise of this authority. In addition, in the United States at least, the trade union movement has demanded and secured a high degree of control over representation rights for all workers in given companies, as well as power over hiring and firing within an industry.

There are two sides of the trade union movement which are emphasized by participants and observers at different times and in different contexts. Daniel Bell has called them the "market unionism" and the "social movement" aspects of trade unionism.[4] On the one hand, unions are narrowly concerned with the economic interests of their members, and will use any method to advance their specific objectives, even to the point of making arrangements which may adversely affect the interests of other workers employed by the same companies. On the other hand, unions, from their beginnings, have perceived themselves and have been perceived by others—particularly by left-intellectuals and liberal politicians—as the most important part of the social reform movement concerned with redistributing income, status, and power. Although American unions have been more or less explicit advocates of business, as contrasted with ideological unionism, they have always had a general political program which touched upon

[4] Bell, *The End of Ideology* 208-21 (1960).

many nonlabor matters. Currently, for example, the unions have policies with regard to civil liberties and civil rights, medical care for the aged, expenditures for schools, and foreign policy. On the whole, these policies have consistently followed those advocated by liberal political forces. The very rhetoric used by labor leaders to describe their objectives and social role usually has reflected this general identification with the values of a more inclusive democracy, of increased rights for all, and particularly for the various depressed sectors of the population.

During the organization drives of the 1930's, many intellectuals dedicated to larger movements for social reform or for socialism did a great deal directly and indirectly to win public acceptance of unionism.[5] But because these helpful intellectuals have rarely been interested in business unionism, the trade union movement has frequently been subject to serious criticism from its friends for failing to live up to the intellectuals' idealistic image of a reformist and democratic union movement.[6]

Other critics have argued that there is a conflict between socially oriented unionism and union democracy. For example, Paul Jacobs has suggested that highly democratic unions, as a *consequence* of being concerned with membership wishes, are narrowly devoted to the interests of their craft, to the detriment of the public or the interests of the union movement as a whole. To support this thesis, he points to the International Typographical Union which has both an unusually high degree of internal democracy and a variety of collective bargaining policies not consonant with public morality, nor in the interest of the labor movement. Thus, the union requires that matrices be reset each time they are to be used for different publications simply to make work, and it opposed permanent election registration laws in New York because annual registration meant more work for printers. On the other hand, Jacobs indicates that an autocratically-led union like the International Ladies Garment Workers Union has long been known for its broad and liberal social policies.[7]

Still others have argued that union democracy is one of the causes of irresponsible bargaining demands and unnecessary strikes, because those union leaders who face the possibility of deposition in a succeeding election seek to

[5] See Lipset, *Political Man* 313-23 (1960).

[6] Many labor leaders have voiced their annoyance at such criticism. For example, the President of the International Association of Machinists, replying to Clark Kerr's analysis of deficiencies in union democracy, said:

> [The intellectuals] became disenchanted with organized labor when the skirmishes of the 1930's were past. They look nostalgically at the good old days of mass organization, sit-down strikes and Memorial Day massacres, and conclude that, since such things are past, labor no longer has any cause and the [sic] labor's prime concern now must be one of internal administration and conformity to the pattern of society at large.

Hayes, "Union Leaders of Their Own Choosing"—A Review, 3 AFL-CIO *Education News and Views* 1 (1958). Kerr's original analysis is in Kerr, *Unions and Union Leaders of Their Own Choosing* (1957).

[7] See Jacobs, "Union Democracy and the Public Good—Do They Necessarily Coincide?" 25 *Commentary* 68-74 (1958). The ITU leaders finally persuaded an international convention to repeal the union law requiring that type be set in each shop that uses a matrix. The membership by a vote of 41,090 to 30,863 *refused* to ratify this change although their national leaders strongly urged them to do so on the grounds that the practice was regarded as "featherbedding" and hurt the union. See *N.Y. Times* (Nov. 2, 1960), p. 39, cols. 2-3.

justify their incumbency by a show of extreme militancy in advocating major contract improvements.

Apparently no one has as yet made systematic comparisons to determine whether democratic unions are in fact more irresponsible in their economic demands and social policies than dictatorial ones. Although the ITU's practice of retaining so-called bogus work is often used as an extreme illustration of featherbedding supported by democratic unions, many of the railroad brotherhoods, which are much less democratic, similarly retain historic policies which keep more workers than are necessary on the job. The highly dictatorial United Mine Workers ran more strikes during wartime than any other union. Currently, the labor organization whose behavior is most often cited as an example both of disrespect for the norms of the larger polity and of aggressive bargaining tactics is the oligarchic Teamsters Union.

There is little evidence that an autocratic union leadership will actually behave more in accord with the public interest than one which is democratically controlled. But whatever relationship may actually exist between forms of union government and collective bargaining tactics, there can be little doubt that corruption, racketeering, and other practices detrimental to the public interest are much more likely to flourish in dictatorial unions than in those subject to membership control.[8] Of course, autocratic unions may fulfill basic functions, but they lose much of their ideological justification.[9]

A different argument for union democracy raised by politicians and lawyers more than by academic intellectuals concerns the status of American unions under law. As Archibald Cox observes:

[L]abor unions occupy their present position largely by force of law. Under the National Labor Relations Act a union which acts as the bargaining representative has power, in conjunction with the employer, to fix a man's wages, hours, and other conditions of employment without his assent. The individual employee may not lawfully negotiate with his employer. He is bound by the union contract. As a matter of practice, if not in legal theory, the union also controls the grievance procedure through which a man's contract rights are enforced. The government which gives unions this power has the concomitant obligation

8 It is argued that decisions required in collective bargaining are not appropriate for the democratic process. In part this rests on the fear that if bargaining is constantly subjected to political pressures, union officers in the grasping for votes will make unrealistic demands, and process worthless grievances . . . . Perhaps union leaders who were not answerable to the members could be more responsible to the public but the critical question is whether they would. Is there really good reason to believe that a union leader who came to power in an undemocratic union, and who was answerable only to the entrenched group through whom he gained power, will in fact demonstrate more social responsibility than the leader who is answerable to his whole membership? Democracy does not guarantee responsible leadership, but an authoritarian system promises even less.

Summers, *The Public Responsibility of Unions in Internal Union Affairs* 8-9 (dittoed 1960).

9 An autocratic union may serve the material demands of its members by bargaining effectively for higher wages and increased benefits. It may establish a measure of job security. None except a democratic union, however, can achieve the idealistic aspirations that justify labor organizations.

Cox, *Law and the National Labor Policy* 94 (1960).

to provide safeguards against abuse. The most effective safeguard is legal assurance that unions will be responsive to the desires of the men and women whom they represent.[10]

This argument, of course, runs counter to the traditional view of the trade union as a voluntary association. Because they maintained the latter view, the courts for many years were reluctant to intervene in disputes between unions and their members; but even then, before the government became a protector of union rights to organize and bargain, it was urged that if the ability to earn a livelihood depends upon membership in a voluntary organization, the courts should grant relief in expulsion cases.[11]

Although most American discussions concerning the role of union democracy stress the consequences of diverse forms of union government on collective bargaining, there is good reason to relate this concern to the political role of labor. American and British economists are tending to agree that unions have little enduring or major effect on the distribution of industrial income, or on the real wages of workers.[12] If this conclusion, still much debated among economists, is valid, it would seem that the "social movement" aspect of the role of unions is more important both for their members and for society as a whole. One leading labor economist has in fact maintained that unions have two primary functions, to "protect the worker against arbitrary employer action . . . [and to] provide an effective means of stabilizing the political power of low income groups."[13] If this is true and unions operate as the counter-lobby to that of business, then it is more important than ever to have democratic unions which actually speak for their members.[14]

The question as to whether a trade union leadership actually reflects the opinion of its membership has most frequently occasioned comment and action by those who disagree with the politics of the leadership. In a number of countries, the problem of representativeness has been perceived as most crucial when Communists have gained control of unions and attempted to use them for political purposes. For instance, it is estimated that at the height of their power in the forties, the American Communists controlled unions with between one-

[10]Cox, "The Role of Law in Preserving Union Democracy," 72 *Harv. L. Rev.* 609, 610-11 (1959). See also Roberts, *Unions in America: A British View* 47-9 (1959); Hanslowe, "Individual Rights in Collective Labor Relations," 45 *Cornell L.Q.* 25, 52-55 (1959).

[11]See Chafee, "The Internal Affairs of Associations Not for Profit," 43 *Harv. L. Rev.* 993 (1930).

[12]See Dunlop, *Wage Determination Under Trade Unions* (1944); *The Theory of Wage Determination* (Dunlop, ed., 1957).

In a detailed summary of research on the subject, Clark Kerr concludes that there is no evidence that collective bargaining has increased labor's share of the national income in the United States, and further that there is no significant relationship between the degree of unionization and labor's share, industry group by industry group. See Kerr, "Trade Unionism and Distributive Shares," 44 *Am. Econ. Rev.* 291 (1954). Contra, Ozanne, "Impact of Unions on Wage Levels and Income Distribution," 73 *Q.J. Econ.* 177 (1959). A new study of trade unionism in Britain concludes: "[I]n the long term there is no concrete evidence that unions have raised the wages of any workers significantly above the market rate." Cyriax & Oakeshott, *The Bargainers: A Survey of Modern Trade Unionism* (1960).

[13]Reder, "Job Security and the Nature of Union Power," 13 *Ind. & Lab. Rel. Rev.* 349-62 (1960).

[14]See Summers, op. cit. supra note 8, at 11-12.

quarter and one-third of the membership of the CIO. This control was not questioned by the leaders of the other CIO unions so long as the Communist line was congruent with the policies of the rest of the federation. But the Cold War and the Communists' effort to build the Wallace Progressive party in 1948 created a basic split between them and the rest of the CIO leadership. The result was the expulsion of those unions which followed the Communist party line.[15] Similarly, in Australia Communist domination of labor continued until the combination of new legislation requiring honest, secret elections and the formation of formal opposition groups contesting elections enabled the members to vote Communist trade union machines out of office.[16]

While the unrepresentative character of Communist union leaders is evident in countries in which the Party is weak, non-Communist leaders often are equally unrepresentative in their political attitudes. A striking example of this occurred in 1940, when despite John L. Lewis' endorsement of Wendell Wilkie for President, a study of miners' voting behavior revealed that the large majority of them continued to back Roosevelt.[17] A like situation exists in Britain, where reliable public opinion surveys indicate that at the time of the 1960 Trades Union Congress and Labor Party conferences, only a small minority of the union members supported their leaders who cast majorities at both conventions for unilateral nuclear disarmament.[18]

The three major American apparel unions, whose strength was based for many years on the Jewish garment workers of New York, provide an interesting illustration of the way in which leaders of comparable organizations formed of members with similar backgrounds may differ widely in political tactics. The Furriers Union, led by Ben Gold, was a mainstay of the Communist party for many decades, while the International Ladies Garment Workers Union under the leadership of David Dubinsky fought the Communists in every way possible. Sidney Hillman as leader of the Amalgamated Clothing Workers Union pursued a political path which sometimes meant alliances with the Communists, and on other occasions meant fighting them. Because of the rivalry between Hillman and Dubinsky, the two large Jewish-dominated garment unions were rarely within the same political camp, each leader having his own "third party" in New York State for a while.

Within the labor movement when men forcefully oppose the political tactics of a given group of leaders their concern is almost always with the policies of a specific oligarchy, not with the phenomenon of oligarchy itself. On several occasions factional groups have succeeded in overthrowing a union's leadership, and in the context of the struggle have charged the incumbents with denial

[15] For a detailed discussion of the role of the Communists in the American labor movement see Kampelman, *The Communist Party vs. the CIO: A Study in Power Politics* (1957); Saposs, *Communism in American Unions* (1959).

[16] Weiner, "The Reduction of Communist Power in the Australian Trade Unions: A Case Study," 69 *Pol. Sci. Q.* 390, 397 (1954).

[17] See Bernstein, "John L. Lewis and the Voting Behavior of the CIO," 5 *Public Opinion Q.* 233 (1941).

[18] See Research Division, Odham's Press, *Report on a Survey of Opinions Concerning Nuclear Disarmament* (1960) (sixteen percent supported leaders' position on foreign policy); cf. 9 *Gallup Political Index Rep.* (1960) (British Gallup Poll showing twenty-four percent support of union leaders' policy by Labor voters).

of basic democratic freedoms. Almost invariably such groups have then retained the antidemocratic mechanisms which they criticized. The principal Communist trade union strategist, William Z. Foster, was one of the first to attempt to apply Robert Michels' analysis of the sources of oligarchy within the German labor movement to American unions, and he clearly was concerned not with establishing democratic procedures, but with using Michels' points as a political weapon.[19]

The Conditions of Union Government

Union leaders are no more impervious to public opinion than are the leaders of other institutions in American society. Why then, in view of the widespread expectation that unions be democratic, do they not conform more to democratic practice? Although there have been many articles and books which have examined the sources of union oligarchy in detail,[20] some of the main points are summarized here.

The complexity of the American economy, the centralization of industry, and the power of the corporate employers all have contributed to the need for efficient, technically competent administration in unions, and to the centralization of union power in the national union.[21] It is inevitable that the important decisions are increasingly made at a level quite remote from rank-and-file control and that even matters of vital concern to the rank and file, such as the union contract, are negotiated by experts, and simply ratified by the membership. The demands of local unions are systematically subordinated to the prevailing system of national pattern bargaining.

The internal structure of American unions maximizes the bureaucratic

[19] See Foster, *Misleaders of Labor* (1927); Sylvia Kopald in an even earlier book glorifying left-wing union upheavals and condemning the AFL hierarchy brought Michels' "iron law of oligarchy" to bear on an analysis of American labor. See Kopald, *Rebellion in Labor Unions* (1924).

[20] See Hoxie, *Trade Unionism in the United States* 177-87 (1926); Kerr, op. cit. supra note 6; Leiserson, op. cit. supra note 1; Lipset, "The Political Process in Trade Unions: A Theoretical Statement," in *Labor and Trade Unionism: An Interdisciplinary Reader* (Galenson & Lipset eds. 1960); Lipset, Trow & Coleman, *Union Democracy* 9-13, 393-418 (1956); Pearlin & Richards, "Equity: A Study of Union Democracy," in *Labor and the Political Process in Trade Unionism: An Interdisciplinary Reader* (Galenson & Lipset eds. 1960); Roberts, op. cit. supra note 10, at 33-35; Seidman, *The Worker Views His Union* 164-241 (1958); Taft, op. cit. supra note 1; Coleman, "The Compulsive Pressures of Democracy in Unionism," 61 *American J. of Sociology* 519 (1956); Strauss, "Control by the Membership in Building Trades Unions," 61 *American J. of Sociology* 527 (1956); Tagliacozzo & Seidman, "A Typology of Rank-and-File Union Members," 61 *American J. of Sociology* 546 (1956); Tannenbaum, "Control Structure and Union Functions," 61 *American J. of Sociology* 536 (1956).

For detailed bibliographies see Haslet, "Bibliography: Internal Affairs of Labor Unions: Administration and Regulation," in *Government Regulation of Internal Union Affairs Affecting the Rights of Members, Selected Readings* 292 (1958); Tagliacozzo, "Trade Union Government: Its Nature and Its Problems–A Bibliographic Review," 1945-55, 61 *American J. of Sociology* 554 (1956).

[21] The view that oligarchy is inherent in large-scale organizations is applied to trade unions in Herberg, "Bureaucracy and Democracy in Labor Unions," 3 *Antioch Rev.* 405 (1943).

tendency to unresponsiveness. Because of its ultimate character as a combat organization whose usefulness to its members lies in its collective strength in relation to management, the trade union has demanded more control over its individual members than do most types of associations.[22] This requirement reinforces the advantages for the perpetuation of administration power which are inherent in the nature of large-scale organization.

The administration already controls the organization's finances, the paid staff, and the internal communications system of the union (which is usually the only source of information about internal union affairs). The full-time officials are the authorized interpreters of the union constitution and of union regulations; they have the power to discipline locals and individual members, and the right to hear appeals. Most of the time, the paid officials work together in a strictly hierarchic and smoothly functioning political machine, and are likely to regard any opposition to their policies as a form of treason to the union itself.

When the membership is scattered, or when the officials have complete control over jobs in the trade through the hiring hall or the shape-up, the full-time functionary is in an almost unassailable position. Control by the officers is, in turn, made easier by rank-and-file apathy, which itself is partly a result of the fact that the local handles less and less of the important business of the union, and few members see why they should be interested in routine and petty business matters.[23]

Since most union officials have risen from the ranks of industrial workers to prestigious positions allowing them to enjoy many middle class comforts, the full-time union functionary is powerfully motivated to maintain himself in office. Defeat in a union election usually means having to return to a relativel low-status, low-paying occupation. Many union officials are thus led by self-interest to circumvent efforts at greater membership control and democratic rights.

The weakness of democratic procedures within American unions is particularly noteworthy today since the individual worker has no effective external organizational alternative if he is dissatisfied with union policy and practices. While there are many arguments against dual unionism, and particularly against the maintenance of the [former] AFL and CIO rivalry, it remains true that the existence of two unions with similar jurisdictions serves to make each of them more responsive to membership wishes. In this sense the worker in America is handicapped in a way that his counterpart in a number of European countries is not. Walter Galenson suggests that in countries where unions have a stable and legitimate position, such as Belgium and the Netherlands, dual unionism contributes to both the democratic character and the solidarity of the different union movements.[24] In Great Britain, officially, "in many industries workers

[22] For a discussion of the problem of discipline versus democracy see Seidman, "Democracy in the Labor Movement," 39 *N.Y. State School of Industrial & Labor Relations Bull.* 4-8 (1958).

[23] See id. at 21-25.

[24] Galenson, *Trade Union Democracy in Western Europe* 112-14 (mimeographed 1960). Whether rival unionism will have positive or negative effects on union democracy and eco-

may choose between several unions when they join, and they may leave one union and join another."[25] There are, however, various agreements among the members of the TUC to prevent widescale raiding of each others' members. Although some observers would disagree it seems true that in general the British worker "has no say in deciding which particular union he will join."[26]

Corruption and Aggressiveness as Aspects of the American Way

While corruption and oligarchy within unions are closely related, since corrupt union officials are even more powerfully motivated than honest ones to circumvent democratic procedures and remain in office, it is important to recognize that they are distinct phenomena. On the whole, as various students of European labor movements have pointed out, most European trade unions are effectively dominated by a self-co-optating oligarchy. What is relatively unique about American labor government, as compared with that of northern Europe and Great Britain, is the problem of corruption, racketeering, and conflict of interest.

Perhaps even more surprising to European observers is the evidence that the rank and file sometimes voluntarily accept such practices. All the exposures concerning corruption inside the International Longshoremen's Association did not prevent that union from winning two government-conducted, secret ballot elections in contests with an AFL-CIO rival.[27] The Teamsters Union is one of the very few major unions which has been gaining rather than losing members in the past few years.[28] Such results, of course, have had numerous equivalents in the American political arena. Many urban political machines, exposed as corrupt and crime-ridden, still have been able to retain large majorities in the poorer sections of the city. James Curley was elected Mayor of Boston with heavy majorities in lower strata districts while under indictment for fraud

nomic strength depends greatly upon other factors in the situation, especially the general acceptance of trade unionism in the country under consideration.

> The French and Italian experience illustrates clearly how dangerous internal division can be to a labor movement which has not gained general acceptance. When trade unions are still in their fighting stage, when collective bargaining is impossible because of gross inequalities in bargaining power, and when industrial enterprises are run as autocracies, concepts of trade union democracy and membership rights have little meaning. Id. at 112.
>
> . . .
>
> In the Low Countries, in Scandinavia, Austria, and Great Britain, trade unions have gained an unassailable position . . . . In these circumstances, competition among unions has an altogether different significance. Here it may act as a powerful lever for the furtherance of internal union democracy. Id. at 114.

[25] Roberts, *Trade Union Government and Administration in Great Britain* 51 (1956). See Grunfeld, "Trade Unions and the Individual: A Study of Recent Developments in England," 7 *J. Pub. L.* 319 (1958).

[26] "A Code for Trade Unions," 186 *The Economist* 640, 642 (1958).

[27] See Bell, "The Racket-Ridden Longshoremen: A Functional Analysis of Crime," in *Labor and Trade Unionism: An Interdisciplinary Reader* 257-59 (Galenson & Lipset, eds. 1960).

[28] See "What's Behind the News and What's Ahead–Labor," 61 *Fortune* 233 (1960).

with regard to alleged soliciting of war contracts, of which he was subsequently convicted.[29]

Like the society of which it is a part, the American labor movement has adopted a strong emphasis upon achievement, on "getting ahead"—the belief that everyone should try to be a "success" regardless of his background. Paradoxically, the achievement norm is closely related to that other key value of America, equality: success should be the goal of *all,* without reference to accidents of birth, class, or color.[30] The stress on these values means that Americans are likely to be concerned with the achievement of approved *ends*—particularly pecuniary success—rather than with the use of appropriate *means*—the behavior considered appropriate to a given position or status. Unlike in Great Britain, which is more particularistic and aristocratic in its values, and where a worker or poor person is less inclined to see himself as a failure, the unsuccessful are under strong pressure to violate conventional morality, to use whatever means they can find to gain recognition.[31]

Moreover, the emphasis on ends, on pecuniary success, combined with an absence of the kind of class consciousness characteristic of more ascriptive societies, has served to motivate workers to use the labor movement itself as an avenue to pecuniary and status gain. Union leadership is regarded as achieved success, not as a sacred trust or way of life; the union leader is considered to be entitled to get as much as he can for himself and his family, as long as he does not injure his members' interests. American union officials receive the highest salaries for union officials anywhere, and American workers accept this fact, even as they accept the right of union officials to be private businessmen, or employers.

The ends-orientation of America as contrasted to the means-orientation of an aristocratic society also manifests itself in the objectives and tactics of American trade unions. Ideologically conservative and narrowly self-interested, the American labor movement has been, in some ways, more violent and militant than the politically more radical European unions. American unions, oriented toward the economic advancement of those in their particular union or trade rather than toward changes in the social system for the benefit of the wider society, have not been loathe to employ physical violence, even dynamiting

[29] A public opinion survey revealed that Curley secured 66% of the vote among [the] "below average" income group, 46% in the "average" income class, and 24% among the "above average" classification. The survey indicated that most of those voting for Curley were aware of the charges of dishonesty, but again and again respondents and informants echoed the phrase, "Curley may steal from the rich, if you want to call it that, but he gives to the poor." Besides the Robin Hood legend, there was the general belief among his supporters that he "gets things done." These two aspects of the Curley legend can be found in the images of a number of seemingly corrupt or dictatorial labor leaders. See Bruner & Korchin, "The Boss and the Vote: Case Study in City Politics," 10 *Public Opinion Q.* 1 (1946).

[30] Toqueville clearly noted that American equalitarianism maximizes competitiveness: "They have swept away the privileges of some of their fellow creatures which stood in their way, but they have opened the door to universal competition." Tocqueville, 2 *Democracy in America* 146 (Vintage Books, ed., 1959). Most Europeans traveling in America during the nineteenth century concurred. Smuts, *European Impressions of the American Worker* 13 (1953).

[31] See Bell, *The End of Ideology* 115-16 (1960); Roberts, op. cit. supra note 10, at 59-73.

buildings, to achieve those ends.[32] They have utilized mobsters in labor disputes (as have employers) and have been more free with the use of the strike weapon than any other labor movement in the highly industrialized, stable, western democracies.[33] Like American industry, and perhaps for the same reasons, American labor has been brutally aggressive in attempting to achieve its goals.

Efforts at Correction

On the whole, labor spokesmen do not contest the argument presented here, particularly after the recent Congressional exposés and the expulsion by the AFL-CIO of its largest affiliate.[34] Rather, they will urge that the labor movement is no worse than other institutions, such as business or government,[35] and that, in any case, problems of internal democracy or corruption are relatively minor when compared with the positive contribution unions make as collective bargaining agencies. If unions are accepted as the defenders of workers' interests, it is argued, *self-regulation* is much more in the public interest than any type of government or judicial intervention. This argument will be elaborated later in this article with reference to the hostile treatment that the union as an anti-

[32] See Adamic, *Dynamite: The Story of Class Violence in America* (rev. ed., 1934). Trade unionism is a feature of every industrialized country in the world, but in no other country has the battle to obtain legal and social status been so bloody and so bitter. Roberts, op. cit. supra note 10, at 49.

[33] See Ross & Hartman, *Changing Patterns of Industrial Conflict* 19 (1960). Some of the unstable usually less industrialized democracies like France have higher strike rates reflecting their failure to institutionalize management-labor relations. Ibid.

[34] In commenting on the congressional exposés in a speech to the AFL-CIO Industrial Union Department, George Meany, the President of the AFL-CIO, indicated his surprise at the extent of such practices:

> We thought we knew a few things about trade union corruption, but we didn't know the half of it, one tenth of it, or the one-hundredth part of it.
>
> We didn't know, for instance, that we had unions where a criminal record was almost a prerequisite to holding office under the national union.
>
> We didn't know that we had top trade union leaders who made it a practice to secretly borrow the funds of their union.
>
> We didn't know that there were top trade union leaders who used the funds for phony real estate deals in which the victims of the fraud were their own members.
>
> And we didn't know that there were trade union leaders who charged to the union treasury such items as speed boats, perfume, silk stockings, brassieres, color TV, refrigerators, and everything else under the sun.

N. Y. Times (Nov. 2, 1957), pp. 1, 9. See generally Lens, *The Crisis of American Labor* (1959); Petro, *Power Unlimited–The Corruption of Union Leadership* (1959).

[35] For example, the President of the International Association of Machinists and Chairman of the AFL-CIO Ethical Practices Committee, A. J. Hayes, said of the recent Congressional investigations of trade unions:

> I wonder if any other group in American life, whether they be doctors, lawyers, businessmen, or newspapermen, could have come out with a better record after 5 years of intensive investigation of their morals and practices? I think not . . . if Congress were to investigate business, industry, the professions, politics or journalism with as much energy as it has investigated organized labor, the percentage of wrongdoing uncovered would undoubtedly be substantially higher.

Haynes, "A Time Bomb for All Our Liberties," *The Machinist* (Nov. 28, 1957), p. 8.

business organization can expect to receive from the courts or conservative politicians.

The examination of the basic structural tendencies within unions in America today strongly suggests, however, that there are severe limitations on what unions can do for themselves. Impartial review boards and/or enforced formal rights of opposition and due process exist in those unions that need them least, such as the United Automobile Workers, the Upholsterers International Union, the International Typographical Union, or the American Newspaper Guild. The unions which most need elaborate and realistic safeguards protecting basic rights are least likely to establish them. The general rule that those who hold power are not likely to consciously undermine their own position applies to union leaders as much as to any other group. What then, realistically, can be done to reduce oligarchy and corruption?

There is general agreement among students of the subject that the ordinary procedures of the law, which rely heavily on complaints to the courts or law enforcement agencies by individuals who have grievances, have not served to protect union members and other workers whose rights were denied. The courts are unable to afford adequate relief in many cases because they either lack consistent and explicit standards and are not familiar with union practices, or because most union members are reluctant to use the courts or cannot bear the costs of litigation.[36]

The NLRB and the Railway Labor Boards have been equally inadequate in protecting individual rights against certified unions, especially in the area of discrimination and admission policies. Neither the NLRA nor the Railway Labor Act attempted to regulate the internal affairs of unions. Furthermore, the federal agencies established by these acts, in cases where they might have done so, did not try to change discriminatory union policies, partly because success in their major functions was dependent upon the cooperation of the unions with which they had to deal.[37]

Because of the exposures of corruption and of the denial of democratic rights, the inadequacy of the courts and federal agencies, and the inability of the labor movement itself to act with sufficient vigor, many informed people who are not unsympathetic to unionism now feel that legislation dealing directly with internal union affairs is necessary. Before discussing the most recent effort at such legislation, the Labor-Management Reporting and Disclosure Act of 1959, a look at some of the sources for the failure of earlier legislative attempts to deal with union democracy may contribute to a better understanding of the limits and problems of government intervention in general.

The Taft-Hartley Act[38] represented the first attempt by Congress to legislate,

[36] Strauss & Willner, "Government Regulation of Local Union Democracy," 4 *Lab. L.J.* 519, 531 (1953).

> A study of the case law shows that the courts have been willing to prevent substantial violations in decision-making. But due to the trouble involved in going to the courts, and the courts' own difficulties in affording adequate relief, judicial intervention has not provided effective protection for [union] member rights. Ibid.

[37] Aaron & Komaroff, "Statutory Regulation of Internal Union Affairs"–I, 44 *Ill. L. Rev.* 425, 438, 445 (1949).

[38] Labor-Management Relations Act, 1947, 61 Stat. 136 (codified in scattered sections of 18, 29 and 50 *U.S.C.* [hereinafter cited as LMRA]).

even indirectly, on internal union affairs. Intended to maximize the freedom of those who do *not* want to belong to unions, the act is based on the assumption that there are large numbers of such workers who need government protection so that they can refrain from union activities without losing their job under a union shop agreement. Despite its purpose, however, the Taft-Hartley Act has had almost no effect in promoting individual workers' rights. There have been few individuals who have taken advantage of the rights provided by the act to keep their jobs under valid union shop agreements without lending any support to the union other than payment of dues and membership fees.[39] The opportunity which the act gives workers to decertify their collective bargaining representatives[40] also has had little effect, since relatively few workers covered under union contract have been involved in any such elections since the bill's passage.[41] The section of the act providing for union shop deauthorization polls[42] has been even less effective. During the first ten year history of Taft-Hartley less than 10,000 workers in the entire country have been involved in elections seeking to drop a union shop.[43] Congress was clearly wrong in believing that the act would liberate workers who were being represented by unions they did not want, or who were covered by union shop agreements which they opposed.

Another section of the Taft-Hartley Act, since repealed, which provided that unions not complying with the non-Communist affidavit requirements would be denied the use of the NLRB,[44] was not only ineffective but violated a basic assumption of jurisprudence that "enforcement measures should be directed against those personally responsible and should be corrective rather than punitive."[45] Guilty individuals, not organizations, should be punished. The tendency to mete out economic punishment to a whole union for the behavior of one or two of its leaders would appear to be derived from a lack of sympathy with the legitimate objectives of unions.

Like the Taft-Hartley Act, state right-to-work laws have sought to protect the rights of that very small minority of employees who do not want to belong to a union. As of 1959, nineteen states had enacted provisions outlawing the requirement of union membership as a condition of hiring or continued em-

[39] LMRA Sec. 7 (29 *U.S.C.* Sec. 157 (1958)) giving the right to refuse to engage in union activities, is qualified by Sec. 8(a) (3) (29 *U.S.C.* Sec. 158(a) (3) (1958)) permitting enforcement of union shop agreements if certain requirements are met. Under the proviso in the latter section, an employer may not justify discrimination for nonmembership in a labor organization.

> (A) if he has reasonable grounds for believing that such membership was not available to the employee on the same terms and conditions generally applicable to other members, or
> (B) if he has reasonable grounds for believing that membership was denied or terminated for reasons other than the failure of the employee to tender the periodic dues and the initiation fees uniformly required as a condition of acquiring or retaining membership . . . .

[40] LMRA Sec. 9(c) (1) (A) (ii) (29 *U. S. C.* Sec. 159(a) (1) (A) (ii) (1958)).

[41] Krislov, "Union Decertification," 9 *Ind. & Lab. Rel. Rev.* 589 (1956).

[42] LMRA Sec. 9(e) (1) (29 *U.S.C.* Sec. 159(a) (1) (1958)).

[43] Morgan, "The Union Shop Deauthorization Poll," 12 *Ind. & Lab. Rel. Rev.* 79 (1958).

[44] LMRA Sec. 9(h), repealed by LMRDA Sec. 201(d), 73 Stat. 525 (1959).

[45] Statement of Clyde W. Summers Before the Subcommittee on Labor and Public Welfare, Washington, D.C., at 6 (mimeographed 1958).

ployment. An analysis of the situation in Texas, the most highly industrialized state to have had long experience under such legislation, indicates that like the federal law, state right-to-work laws have not resulted in freeing workers from compulsory unionism, nor have they greatly hindered organization, as the unions feared they would. It appears that:

In the traditional areas of the closed shop, particularly the construction industry, the old practices remain in force and violate not simply the state law but federal legislation as well. In the industries in which the union shop is the normal mode of operation, the law does not directly inhibit new organization since it only becomes operative after recognition is gained. However, there is no doubt that the statute has had an indirect effect here because it has so changed the climate of organization in some marginal situations that campaigns which would under other conditions have been won have been lost.[46]

The law has not completely eliminated compulsion even of that small number of workers who object to union membership. "Loyal members of strong unions have expressed their resentment against 'free riders' in ways at least as objectionable morally, and nearly as effective, as if union membership were necessary for employment."[47]

The experience with right-to-work legislation in Texas, like that with the Taft-Hartley Act on a national scale, shows that legislation which is premised on the belief that there is a large number of union members held within unions against their will, necessarily has little effect. All the available evidence indicates that there are few such workers, and, to the contrary, that the bulk of union members accept such practices as closed and union shops as necessary for their welfare. Still, there is evidence suggesting that such laws strengthen the position of irresponsible union *minorities* who are in a position to "blackmail" officials to press the case of special interests, and thus produce both greater irresponsibility in labor relations, and less responsiveness to the needs of the majority of the membership.[48] Where the decision of a polity is not binding on all members, extremists within it are given an undue share of power.[49]

The failure of the Taft-Hartley Act to accomplish its major objectives demonstrates the limitations of legislation regulating internal union affairs, and gives an indication of the type of statute which might be effective. Legislation

[46] Meyers, *"Right-to-Work" in Practice* 40 (Fund for the Republic Report, 1959).
[47] Id. at 41.
[48] Right-to-work in Texas:

> has made the unions not more responsible but more responsive to the demands of a tiny vocal minority of the membership. It has consequently caused issues to be pressed through the grievance machinery which, under conditions of union security, would not and should not have been taken up. The union leader without security is often most responsive not to the majority of loyal union members who will remain, but to the small minority, often irresponsible, whose continued membership is doubtful. Ibid.

[49]

> [In Texas,] the absence of union security has forced unions into bargaining positions conditioned by minorities and indefensible on any grounds other than the necessity of survival. Rather than freeing managements of 'excessive' demands and policies, as the preamble to the statute foresaw, it probably faced some managements, both in grievance procedures and over the bargaining table, with more objectionable demands than would have been the case if a union shop had prevailed. Ibid.

affecting internal union affairs should not further the advantages of democracy at the cost of reducing the effective bargaining strength of unions.[50] The framers of the Taft-Hartley Act were both hostile to, and ignorant of, trade unionism as such, and hence could not help but deal inadequately with problems of internal union matters. Union members as well as union leaders viewed the act as punitive legislation. The consequence was the unenforceability and inadequacy previously described.

Discrimination in Admission to Union Membership

Although Congress and important business groups have shown repeated concern for the apparently nonexistent group of entrapped union members, they have shown little interest in what is actually a more prevalent and more important problem—the plight of those workers who cannot join unions of their choosing and who, as a result, may be limited in their employment opportunities. The undemocratic consequences of such restrictions have been frequently noted:

> *Union practices pertaining to the admission and expulsion of members are the threshold to democracy in the government of labor organizations. An employee in a bargaining unit who is unfairly excluded from the union which represents the unit or who is unjustly expelled from membership has no opportunity to participate in fixing the terms and conditions of his employment. He is bound by the action of an organization in whose councils he has no voice. In his case it is a fraud to call collective bargaining an instrument of industrial democracy.*[51]

It is in the area of admissions that the courts and government agencies have made the least progress. The democratizing role that unions have to play in industrial life is greatly limited as long as they bar Negroes from membership, although the unions, by law, are supposed to represent them. In 1944 the Supreme Court, in *Steele v. Louisville & N.R.R.*,[52] concluded that a union which enjoyed exclusive bargaining rights under the law had a corresponding obligation not to discriminate unfairly among the workers it was supposed to represent, particularly on the "irrelevant and invidious" basis of race. However, the Court failed to insist that Negroes be admitted to membership in the union that was supposed to represent them. And it should be obvious that a union cannot and usually will not adequately represent nonmembers.[53]

At the same time that Negroes were excluded from membership in the railway unions, and consequently suffered the loss of their jobs and seniority rights,

[50] See Cox, *Law and the National Labor Policy* 87 (1960).

> Public policy should minimize the danger [of autocratic control] without disabling the unions from performing their beneficient functions. The ability of labor organizations to bargain effectively with employers should not be impaired, for the unions' ability to advance the welfare of their members depends more upon effective bargaining than upon the conduct of union affairs. Ibid.

[51] Cox, *Law and the National Labor Policy* 95 (1960). See also Givens, "The Enfranchisement of Employees Arbitrarily Rejected for Union Membership," 11 *Lab. L.J.* 809 (1960).

[52] 323 U.S. 192 (1944).

[53] Aaron & Komaroff, supra note 37, at 435-36.

their attempts at forming their own organizations were stifled by the National Mediation Board policy of maintaining the "customary grouping of employees into crafts and classes as it has been established by accepted practice over a period of years . . . ."[54] Pointing out that the 1941 Southeastern Conference Carriers Agreement, whereby the railroads and the Brotherhood of Locomotive Firemen and Enginemen excluded Negro firemen from many jobs, and which was outlawed in the *Steele* case, was actually mediated and countersigned by the Board, one commentator has concluded that it is not unfair to say that the Board "has generally been on the side of discrimination and exclusion."[55] The National Labor Relations Board has been similarly deficient.[56]

Nor have the courts provided an adequate remedy. With regard to admission policies, they continue to adhere to the "voluntary association" conception of trade unionism. Archibald Cox has observed:

It is a black-letter rule that no one has a legally protected right to become a member of a voluntary association. Consequently, a union may exclude an applicant for any reason, good or bad, or for no reason . . . .

Until recently, there was reason to hope that the courts might gradually change the rule applicable to labor unions . . . . Unfortunately, the decision in Ross v. Ebert *and the Supreme Court's refusal to review the* Oliphant *case have discouraged, if not permanently foreclosed, this avenue of progress.*[57]

Moreover, decisions in favor of Negro rights have usually been ignored except insofar as they affected the immediate parties. Negroes have won every one of the cases dealing with union membership and employment as firemen on the railroads since World War II, and yet the percentage of Negroes employed in firemen's jobs has declined greatly.

The voluntary efforts of the labor movement to eliminate discrimination in its midst have been distressingly slow and inadequate, as the Labor Secretary of the NAACP has pointed out repeatedly. Here too, the leaders of the AFL-CIO who are committed to progress in this area are prevented from taking action by the balance of forces and sentiments within the federation, and frequently within their own unions.

Despite the obvious need for federal legislation on admissions, and despite a willingness to legislate elaborately on other aspects of internal union government, all legislation, including the Labor-Management Reporting and Disclosure Act of 1959, is totally silent on the subject. "Congress . . . failed to provide new substantive law in the one field in which it was urgently needed—the admission of members."[58] The omission was not, certainly, a simple oversight. However, there is little likelihood that Congress will deal with the issue since the trade unions oppose such measures out of their general objection to government regulation of their affairs, and southern congressmen justifiably regard any attempt to ensure nondiscriminatory admission to unions as a direct invitation to federal fair employment practices legislation. It would be patently unreason-

[54] Id. at 431, quoting 1 *National Mediation Board Ann. Rep.* 21 (1953).
[55] Rauh, "Civil Rights and Liberties and Labor Unions," 8 *Lab. L.J.* 874, 876-77 (1957).
[56] Id. at 877.
[57] Cox, op. cit. supra note 51, at 98-99 (footnotes omitted from quoted passage).
[58] Id. at 98.

able (and ineffective) to insist that unions admit members without bias, without applying the same rule to employers in hiring practices.

The struggle to eliminate racial or other forms of discrimination in union admission remains substantially in the hands of the Negroes and other supporters of civil rights. The recent organization by A. Philip Randolph of a nation-wide Negro trade union committee represents the Negro recognition that they will have to force open the doors of the recalcitrant section of the labor movement.[59]

The Labor-Management Reporting and Disclosure Act of 1959

Perhaps the first legislative effort to directly affect the prospects for union democracy is the Labor-Management Reporting and Disclosure Act of 1959, written after extensive hearings by the McClellan committee. While the act has not been in effect long enough to permit an empirical analysis of its consequences for internal union government, something can be said about the likely consequences of the act by analyzing its provisions in light of what we already know about the functioning of unions and the possibilities of legislation in this area.[60]

A. Election Procedures

Fair and properly conducted elections are, of course, a fundamental aspect of democracy in any polity. An important part of the LMRDA is designed to encourage honest elections in which all points of view have an opportunity to campaign for office, and all members have the right to vote freely. Section 101 (a) (1) of the new act, which provides that every member shall have an equal right to vote,[61] is intended to eliminate second-class memberships without voting rights such as a number of unions have, and also to allow other often disenfranchised groups such as apprentices and employer-members to vote.

[59] A detailed documented report of the grievances of the Negroes against white workers *and* organized labor may be found in an article by the Labor Secretary of the NAACP. See Hill, "Labor Unions and the Negro," 28 *Commentary* 479 (1959). This brought a retort from the Director of the National Labor Service. See Fleischman, "Labor and the Civil Rights Revolution," *The New Leader* (April 18, 1960), p. 30. See also Letter From Harry Fleischman to Editor, *The New Leader* (Aug. 15, 1960), p. 30; Letter From Herbert Hill to Editor, *The New Leader* (June 20, 1960), p. 30.

[60] The LMRDA was signed into law by President Eisenhower on September 14, 1959. Ten days later, Secretary of Labor Mitchell officially established the Bureau of Labor-Management Reports. This bureau subsequently distributed to union organizations the forms by which they were required to file the information demanded by the LMRDA. By June 30, 1960, 52,278 labor organizations had submitted the initial reports required by the law; 2041 alleged violations had been investigated or were in the process of being investigated; and a number of court cases had been decided under the LMRDA, or had involved one or more of its provisions. See U.S. Dept. of Labor, *A Report of the Bureau of Labor-Management Reports: Fiscal Year 1960,* apps. A-B (1960); "Making Landrum-Griffin Work," *Fortune* (Dec. 1960), p. 220.

[61] 29 *U.S.C.* Sec. 411(a) (1) (Supp. I, 1959). For a detailed analysis of the LMRDA, see Smith, "The Labor-Management Reporting and Disclosure Act of 1959," 46 *Va. L. Rev.* 195 (1960).

Title IV sets maximum terms of office for international (five years), local (three years), and intermediate bodies (four years).[62] It also provides for the secret ballot in the election of all officers,[63] for proper notice to members before elections,[64] for the rights of all members to campaign for candidates and to be eligible to run for office.[65] The rights of formal opposition are further protected by clauses which provide that unions *must* mail any candidate's campaign literature, at his request and expense, to the entire membership, and that any candidate has the right to inspect the union's mailing list before the election.[66] The advantages to incumbents of having control of the organization are further restricted by the provision that no union funds derived from dues or assessments may be used to promote the candidacy of any nominee for office.[67]

In seeking to promote democratic procedures, the authors of the act also provided guarantees to members and potential opposition groups to engage in political activity outside the formal context of an election campaign.[68] In so doing, they presumably recognized that an incumbent administration always operates, to some extent, as a political party, and that the formal guarantees of freedom at election time have little meaning unless opposition groups have the right to continuous existence. In effect, the act seems to encourage factions. The guarantees in the section on free speech and assembly are limited, however, by the proviso that the union may adopt "reasonable rules as to the responsibility of every member toward the organization as an institution . . . ,"[69] presumably designed to enable unions to protect themselves against crackpots or truly disloyal oppositions.

In a number of places the act recognizes the need for proper disciplinary procedures, but it seeks to prevent such discipline being meted out arbitrarily to members for exercise of their proper rights by outlawing disciplinary action that is in any way based on a union member's activities as a witness, as a political citizen communicating with government officials or legislators, or as a plaintiff who brings suit against the union.[70] It should prevent any future efforts to formally penalize union members for supporting measures opposed by unions,

[62] LMRDA Secs. 401(a), (b), (d) (29 *U.S.C.* Secs. 481(a), (b), (d) (Supp. 1, 1959)).
[63] Ibid.
[64] LMRDA Sec. 401(e) (29 *U.S.C.* Sec. 481(e) (Supp. 1, 1959)).
[65] Ibid.
[66] LMRDA Sec. 401(c) (29 *U.S.C.* Sec. 481(c) (Supp. 1, 1959)).
[67] LMRDA Sec. 401(g) (29 *U.S.C.* Sec. 481(g) (Supp. 1, 1959)).
[68] LMRDA Sec. 101(a) (2) (29 *U.S.C.* Sec. 411(a) (2) (Supp. 1, 1959)). Cox says:

> [This section] carries the legal protection a step further by guaranteeing freedom of speech inside and outside union meetings, and also by securing the critics an opportunity to meet for the purpose of organizing their opposition. The latter privilege would seem essential to effective minorities even though it flies in the face of traditional trade union opposition to any form of caucus or separate assemblage. However, dissent in a union, like treason within a nation, can be lawfully suppressed if the purpose is to destroy the union or encourage a rival.

Cox, op. cit. supra note 51, at 103.
[69] LMRDA Sec. 101(a) (2) (29 *U.S.C.* Sec. 411(a) (2) (Supp. 1, 1959)).
[70] LMRDA Sec. 101(a) (4) (29 *U.S.C.* Sec. 411 (a) (4) (Supp. 1, 1959)).

such as right-to-work legislation.[71] With regard to due process in disciplinary procedures, the LMRDA contains the following provisions:

No member of any labor organization may be fined, suspended, expelled, or otherwise disciplined except for nonpayment of dues by such organization or by any officer thereof unless such member has been (A) served with written specific charges; (B) given a reasonable time to prepare his defense; (C) afforded a full and fair hearing.[72]

In addition to these, a number of other clauses bear closely on the problem of union democracy. The power of international unions to place locals under trusteeship, a power which has sometimes been used arbitrarily to prevent opposition, is extensively regulated.[73] The sections which require unions to make detailed reports to the Secretary of Labor of their administrative regulations, contracts and financial records, including all sums paid to individuals, as well as those which require union leaders to report all sources of income, union or other,[74] may be very helpful in enabling union members or opposition factions to watch more closely what their representatives are doing.

Many observers of the labor movement who agree that the objectives of the act are worthy still question the extent to which it will actually change the decisive character of the labor movement as a one-party oligarchy, or even the extent to which it will improve the actual rights of the vast majority of union members who do not have special access to means of securing these rights. The main advantages available to incumbent union officers, enabling them to retain office indefinitely and set policy as they see fit, are not greatly restricted by sections of this or any other legislation, though the LMRDA may help prevent outrageous behavior. Certainly, the administration of section 401(g), which prohibits the use of union funds to promote the candidacy of any person, will require "delicate judgments."[75] As one veteran of many labor wars, internal and external, has observed:

It is the crippling weakness of the new labor law that, while prescribing free traffic for dissenting opinion, it does not provide the means for advancing the views or interests of a dissenting member or group. There is a drastic disparity between the material and other resources at the disposal of an officer defending himself–and the union–and the sinews of war available to the individual

[71] See Aaron, "The Labor-Management Reporting and Disclosure Act of 1959," 73 *Harv. L. Rev.* 851, 871 (1960). In California in 1958, the International Association of Machinists expelled two members for supporting the right-to-work referendum proposal, and the courts upheld the right of the union to take such action. Cox, op. cit. supra note 51, at 109.

[72] LMRDA Sec. 101(a) (5) (29 *U.S.C.* Sec. 411(a) (5) (Supp. 1, 1959)).

[73] See LMRDA Secs. 301-04 (29 *U.S.C.* Secs. 461-64 (Supp. 1, 1959)). The passage of the law seems to have had a considerable effect on the practice of putting locals under trusteeships. Of the 592 trusteeships reported to the Bureau through June 30, 1960, only 72 were reported as established since the effective date of the Act, as compared to to 285 which were dissolved during that time. U.S. Dept. of Labor, op. cit. supra note 60, at 32.

[74] LMRDA Secs. 201(a)-(b), 202(a) (29 *U.S.C.* Secs. 431(a)-(b), 432(a) (Supp. 1, 1959)).

[75] Cox, op. cit. supra note 51, at 109. Section 401(g) of LMRDA is codified in 29 *U.S.C.* Sec. 481(g) (Supp. I, 1959).

member. The authors of LMRDA, nearly all lawyers, might have given this some thought, but they did not. . . .[76]

Although gross abuses may be controlled, the advantages that *honest* incumbents of union offices enjoy in elections cannot be eliminated by law. Indeed, most union leaders do not have to resort to stealing elections or other raw practices. In addition to all the assets inherent in the control of the organization machinery itself, the union leader "can rely on membership apathy or on more subtle political maneuvering."[77] The law may well protect the union member against arbitrary power and violence, but cannot avail against the inherent strengths of a bureaucracy.

B. The Problem of Enforcement

The failure of the law to face the facts of organizational life is revealed most clearly in its enforcement provisions,[78] which are especially important in legislation affecting a generally underprivileged, uneducated, and exploitable group such as the blue-collar workers who form the bulk of union membership. With regard to the section designed to protect union members against unjust expulsion,[79] it has been said that there are already numerous applicable common law safeguards. "The need was for a more practical remedy than suit by an individual employee. Congress failed to provide one."[80] After all, another commentator has asked, what rank-and-file member can readily avail himself of the "costly, cumbersome action which the law provides . . . ."[81]

Since the problem of enforcement is so crucial to any evaluation of the potentials of this or any other law to affect union democracy and internal due process, it seems appropriate to look more closely into the reasons why reliance on lawsuits is an inadequate method of dealing with union affairs.

(1) "Workers are unfamiliar with the law and hesitate to become involved in legal proceedings."[82] This can be traced to certain characteristics of the working class generally: they have less education than middle and upper class people and their norms include avoiding involvement with community authorities in general and with the law in particular.

It is well accepted that better educated people are more likely to be aware of their rights under the law, and, more important perhaps, either to know lawyers personally or to know where they can get a reliable lawyer. It is difficult to secure legal protection for the less fortunate classes because of the distrust and hostility with which they are prone to regard agencies that are established and operated by people with different backgrounds and values from their own. Even agencies expressly devoted to the protection of poorer and less educated people are often ineffective because of the suspicions and fears of those whom

[76] Hardman, "Labor Courts for Labor Democracy," *The New Leader* (Jan. 25, 1960), pp. 20, 21.

[77] Strauss & Willner, supra note 36, at 522.

[78] LMRDA Secs. 209-10, 304, 402 (29 *U.S.C.* Secs. 439-40, 464, 482 (Supp. 1, 1959)).

[79] LMRDA Sec. 609 (29 *U.S.C.* Sec. 529 (Supp. 1, 1959)).

[80] Cox, op. cit. supra note 51, at 98.

[81] Hardman, supra note 76, at 20.

[82] Cox, op. cit. supra note 51, at 105.

they seek to help.[83] It is true that the fault often lies in the agencies themselves, whose penchant for red tape thwarts their intended purposes, since the lower social strata are unaccustomed to fulfilling the seemingly meaningless formalities of bureaucracies. Perhaps even more important in accounting for the failure of the lower strata to claim their rights is the fact that they are more likely to have been victims of injustice and exploitation, and hence less prone to become incensed about violations of rights as quickly as those in the middle class. The identical enforcement clauses which might be quite effective in legislation dealing with the rights of stockholders, who have ready access to legal advice, might be very ineffective as part of legislation enacted to protect union members.

(2) Litigation is expensive. Court costs and lawyer's fees in a protracted suit can be enormous, and most union members cannot afford to go to court even if they are willing. For example:

The plaintiff's counsel fees in Weber v. Marine Cooks and Stewards *were set by the court at $7,500 for the trial and one appeal, and there is no reason to believe that these were excessive. In that case, the court ordered the fees to be paid out of the union treasury, but usually the expense must be borne by the anti-administration plaintiffs themselves. Although information is not available as to counsel fees in the* Hod Carrier *cases, it is known that they were only finally paid ten years after the start of the litigation.*[84]

The few lawyers who feel morally obligated to take on rank-and-file labor cases free of charge cannot themselves afford to handle very many at a time or in succession. The American Civil Liberties Union tends to be more interested in constitutional issues than in mundane trade union cases.[85]

Another adverse consideration is that the substantial costs involved in bringing a suit to court can rarely be recovered through litigation. Most internal union issues do not involve that kind of money. Strauss and Willner point out that there are few "individual plaintiffs" who are not backed by a strong faction which has raised money from its members over a long period of time.

[E]ven then, unless the recovery of a large sum of money or the definite control of the union goes to the winner, a faction will hesitate to enter into litigation. It is a rare group of men that will undertake the many pressures and difficulties mentioned, merely to establish the principle of union democracy.[86]

One section of LMRDA makes a step toward resolving this problem, authorizing any union member to bring a suit whenever his union refuses to sue an officer or employee alleged to be guilty of a breach of fiduciary obligations.[87] The trial judge may allot part of any sums recovered for counsel fees and expenses.[88] Cox indicates that these provisions are potentially among the most important in the

[83] See Whyte, *Street Corner Society* (1943), for an analysis of the way in which settlement houses in poor neighborhoods have faced hostility because they are viewed as middle class agencies. An excellent discussion of the general hostility of workers to authority wielded by the middle class world may be found in Archibald, *Wartime Shipyard* 162-70 (1947).

[84] Strauss & Willner, supra note 36, at 530.

[85] Benson, "Intellectuals and the Lonely Union Reformer," *Liberation* (April 1960), p. 15.

[86] Strauss & Willner, supra note 36, at 530.

[87] LMRDA Sec. 501(b) (29 *U.S.C.* Sec. 501(b) (Supp. 1, 1959)).

[88] Ibid.

act. "If individual members have the initiative and interest to bring suit, the Becks, Hoffas, and Webers may be required to account not only for any misappropriations but also for all the profits which they have made by virtue of their offices."[89]

Obviously, this will still be an effective incentive only if considerable sums are involved. In Australia after World War II concern arose within both conservative and labor circles about the unscrupulous tactics used by the Communist party to maintain its control of the majority of the trade union movement. The Labor government at this time faced up to the problem of court costs by amending the Federal Arbitration Act to provide for judicial inquiry where there appears to be a reasonable question of irregularity in union elections, and if an irregularity has occurred, permitting the Attorney General to authorize reimbursement by the government of the person who requested the inquiry for all or part of the costs. Even if no irregularity is found, the government may pay the costs if the court certifies that the person seeking the inquiry acted reasonably in so doing.[90]

(3) In spite of developing standards, the courts (*i.e.,* the judges) are not sufficiently familiar with union affairs to be able to make necessary distinctions between actions which do violate union democracy and those which do not. In the settlement of internal union disputes the courts rely heavily on the terms of the union constitution, the protection of procedural due process, the preservation of democratic process within the union, and "the personal virtuousness of the parties."[91] The union constitution, however, is likely to be vague and contradictory; the standard of procedural due process, though impersonal and fair, is often imprecise; and the standards of democratic procedure, though just, are indefinite in practice. The personal virtue or political purity criterion is largely negative in its effects.[92]

(4) "There is difficulty in obtaining adequate relief from the courts. Courts rarely give positive instructions but only negative commands which are easily by-passed."[93] The result is that court action may be entirely ineffective in a given case, or that essentially the same case may be brought into court repeatedly at considerable cost and inconvenience, still with no assurance of a satisfactory solution.

Thus, in Weber v. Marine Cooks and Stewards, *after the court had set aside the new constitution on the grounds that it was adopted in the wrong way, the*

[89] Cox, op. cit. supra note 51, at 92.

[90] McClelland, "Experiences of the Australian Labor Movement Under Governmental Control," in *Labor in a Free Society* 152-53 (Harrington & Jacobs eds. 1959). It should be noted that this legislation grew out of a situation in 1949 when a prominent defector from the Communist party "told of widespread election frauds, and misuse of office and funds in Communist-run trade unions. An inquiry by a Royal Commission in Victoria led to further revelations of Communist party trade union relations, fraud and corruption." Weiner, "The Reduction of Communist Power in Australian Trade Unions: A Case Study," 69 *Pol. Sci. Q.* 390, 404-05 (1954). See generally Portus, *The Development of Australian Trade Union Law* 182-202 (1958).

[91] Summers, "Judicial Settlement of Internal Union Disputes," 7 *Buffalo L. Rev.* 405, 420 (1958).

[92] Id. at 411-20.

[93] Strauss & Willner, "Government Regulation of Local Union Democracy," 4 *Lab. L.J.* 519, 531 (1953).

union majority then proceeded to adopt the new constitution in the right way, and the bitter and expensive litigation was in that case a complete waste. Injunctions must necessarily be limited in scope. They cannot cover all future violations that may be anticipated . . . . For the courts to make certain that their decisions are effective could involve visitorial powers on a scale quite incompatible with any present ideas of free unionism.[94]

This limitation of the courts represents an enormous problem for the legal protection of union democracy. In a country such as England, a single court decision is sufficient to establish the basis for appropriate future action. In this country, where there is relatively little respect for the law, clear-cut court decisions are not always honored as precedents for future action by persons outside of the specific suit.

(5) The exhaustion-of-remedies doctrine, a necessary rule perhaps, can often mean that a case takes three or four years.[95] This delay can be extended when a judgment is challenged several times, which frequently occurs. Cost and delay are on the side of the wealthier party, so that individual union members are at a sharp disadvantage in suing to protect their rights.[96] However, the courts have developed numerous exceptions to the exhaustion-of-remedies rule,[97] and the LMRDA provisions setting limits on the time a union member must spend in internal appeals[98] will probably serve to minimize the delays imposed by the courts.

Two of the titles in the new law, those concerning trusteeships and elections,[99] are enforceable by the Secretary of Labor upon complaint of a union member. If the Secretary upon investigation determines that a violation has occurred, he is to bring civil action on behalf of the plaintiff in the district court. If the court declares an election invalid, the Secretary must supervise a new election. Obviously, these enforcement provisions go a long way toward eliminating the kinds of objections discussed above. However, the "Bill of Rights

[94] Ibid.

[95] Id. at 530.

[96] Cox, "The Role of Law in Preserving Union Democracy," 72 *Harv. L. Rev.* 609, 615 (1959).

[97] See Summers, supra note 91, at 409-10.

[98] LMRDA Secs. 101(a) (4), 402(a) (2) (29 *U.S.C.* Secs. 411(a) (4), 482(a) (2) (Supp. 1, 1959)). The cases brought before the courts under these provisions have not been in accord:

> One case holds that where a union's constitution and bylaws provide reasonable hearing procedures for violation of union laws, allegations—by a member beginning a court action before exhausting such procedure—that resort thereto would be futile does not satisfy the jurisdictional requirement to exhaust such procedure. The court observed that under such circumstances the member should have demonstrated futility by first resorting to such procedures.
>
> Another case holds that such exhaustion is not necessary where it would be unreasonably burdensome.

U.S. Dept. of Labor, op. cit. supra note 60, at 69.

[99] LMRDA Secs. 301-06, 401-03 (29 *U.S.C.* Secs. 461-66, 481-83 (Supp. 1, 1959)). The holdings of the courts concerning these provisions have also not been in accord. The relevant sections of the Act provide that both union members and the Secretary of Labor may institute corrective litigation. Some courts have held that these are two coordinate alternative remedies, while other courts have held that they are not. U.S. Dept. of Labor, op. cit. supra note 60, at 69-70.

for Union Members"[100] in the LMRDA, designed to protect the rights of opposition groups, still is enforceable only by the courts.[101]

The concentration of enforcement power in the hands of the Secretary of Labor has some important liabilities. Benjamin Aaron has pointed out that under the new law the Secretary of Labor is given considerable discretion as to the selection of the complaints he will pursue. Because he is susceptible to various political pressures, including those from officials of large and important unions whose cooperation he needs, the result may be that the complaints against some unions will not be processed vigorously and complaints against others will be given more serious attention. As Aaron notes:

[T]he general suppression of grass roots democracy may come from the outside. The LMRDA invests tremendous authority over the conduct of internal union affairs in the Secretary of Labor. No countervailing power is directly opposed to many of the decisions he may be called upon to make. It seems likely that the most critical of these will concern not individuals, but factions, not one or two men against "the machine," but the "outs" against the "ins." The considerations affecting such decisions, as well as the decisions themselves, will involve more than simple determination of facts; the Secretary will be compelled, indirectly if not directly, to decide far broader issues than those ostensibly presented for resolution.[102]

The first suit filed by the Secretary of Labor to void an election suggested to many that these fears were warranted.[103] The suit was directed against a small unaffiliated union, the Independent Petroleum Workers Union of Bayway which represents employees at one Esso Standard Oil Refinery. It charged possible misuse of the integrity of the ballot box by the administration which, among other things, had access to the ballots "before the arrival of rival observers of the losing candidates and prior to the agreed time for the collection of ballots."[104] Government action against a small independent union that is sometimes charged with being a "company union" by its AFL-CIO rival clearly will not outrage AFL-CIO leadership. On the other hand, shortly before the United States presidential election, the Labor Department filed suit to invalidate the election of seventy-five officers of the National Maritime Union, one of the smaller affiliates of the AFL-CIO.[105] It is alleged that the union failed to provide a secret ballot, that it disqualified opposition candidates illegally, that union funds were spent to support administration candidates, and that opposition candidates were denied equal treatment in the union's paper. If pressed by the next administration of the department, this suit should help in formulating basic policies and precedents with regard to the effectiveness of the act.[106]

[100] LMRDA Sec. 101 (29 *U.S.C.* Sec. 411 (Supp. 1, 1959)).
[101] LMRDA Sec. 102 (29 *U.S.C.* Sec. 412 (Supp. 1, 1959)).
[102] Aaron, supra note 71, at 907.
[103] *N. Y. Times,* July 29, 1960, p. 5, col. 8.
[104] Ibid.
[105] *N. Y. Times* (Oct. 9, 1960), p. 18, col. 1.
[106] It is unfortunately true that the political complexion of an administration affects the decisions as to which groups will be prosecuted. "In the period from 1945 to 1952 only five cases involving union officials and corruption were filed by the Department of Justice. From

Potential Effects of Legislation

What have been the observable repercussions of the new labor law? It is too early to report any reliable conclusions as to whether the act will have any important effects on the nature of union government. The impressions of labor journalists in touch with the situation in different parts of the country suggest that the LMRDA has not affected the tenure of union officers either on the local or national level. Some people closely connected with the collective bargaining process, particularly arbitrators, have expressed fears that the union leadership's increased responsiveness to members' demands, brought about by the new law, will result in greater union irresponsibility and intransigence at the bargaining table. Benjamin Aaron has predicted that the LMRDA will cause "vigorous pursuit of collective bargaining demands formulated by local majorities, without regard to the broader aims of their national organization."[107] And on the basis of his experience regarding the impact of the bill of rights provisions of the new law, the executive officer of one local employers' association reports:

Individual union members feel more free to criticize their leaders and are doing so. We know that local union leaders are being much more careful in their handling of union affairs and in their conduct of meetings. This has had its consequences for our bargaining. Union bargaining demands are more lengthy and more detailed. There is something for everyone in the list of proposals today. Union officials do more consulting with their membership during the bargaining, and they have less freedom and less leeway for compromise with the employer. Union representatives who are not secure in their jobs and who do not enjoy strong support of their membership are often reluctant to take the responsibility for agreeing to anything less than the original demands. There is much referring of counter-proposals to the membership for action. There is a greater use of union committees to spread the risk of unfavorable reaction by rank and file to counter-proposals and to a final settlement which is short of the original demands.

Where there is a lack of strong and secure union leadership backed by the rank and file, the employer finds his bargaining much more difficult and time-consuming. With lack of leadership and responsibility for reaching a reasonable compromise, unions find themselves involved now more often in strike situations than before . . . .[108]

But while there can be little doubt that the new law and the current climate of opinion may have some effect in making unions more responsive to the wishes of their membership, and hence perhaps more belligerent in their bargaining tactics, it must be repeated that there is no reliable evidence that the tactics of oligarchic unions are preferable from the point of view of the larger polity. In a recent review of the causes of the growth of a "certain degree of rebelliousness and nonconformity within the labor movement that we did not see even as

1952 to 1955 the number was seventy, involving 149 individuals." Roberts, *Unions in America: A British View* 65 (1959).

107 Aaron, supra note 71, at 906.

108 Smith, "Current Trends in Collective Bargaining," in *Current Trends in Collective Bargaining* 18 (1960).

recently as five years ago," David Cole, perhaps the leading labor mediator in the United States, attributes the growing number of incidents in which local unions or rank-and-file members drastically repudiated agreements made or advocated by their international leaders to "a form of anticolonialism." He points out that with the inevitable development of industry-wide bargaining "the local people . . . play a lesser and lesser part" in the affairs of the union. And this decline in function leads to a "feeling of frustration" and a consequent readiness to "latch on to causes in order to use this power which they have." In other words, it is the decline in democracy—a decline which Mr. Cole thinks was necessary and inevitable—that has resulted in a decrease in union responsibility.[109]

Though legislation and juridically protected guarantees may seem relatively ineffective in enhancing the prospects for real union democracy, their importance should not be underestimated. The significance of a law does not necessarily lie in the extent to which it is obeyed: one of its major functions is to set a moral code or standard which society considers proper, but whose parts can be violated within certain limits. If some people commit adultery occasionally—as Kinsey has indicated they do—this does not have much effect on family stability; but if everyone felt free to commit adultery whenever he wished, the family system as we know it would not exist. This restraint function is demonstrated in the area of race relations where even the passage of inadequate fair employment practices acts, with weak enforcement provisions, does reduce discriminatory practices and does force those who violate the law in secret to announce their conformity in public. People may engage in illegal or immoral actions, but the fact that they know these actions are illegal reduces the extent to which they occur, even if violators are rarely prosecuted.

It is important to recognize, therefore, that the function of labor legislation may not be as much to create viable laws that can be used "against" unions, as to set moral standards in an area of institutional behavior that previously was outside the realm of *explicit* moral standards. The exposés of various odious practices within unions and the laws enacted by different legislative bodies have undoubtedly affected the behavior of union leaders. A dictatorial leader is now less likely to take punitive actions against his internal political opposition. He probably will become more sensitive to membership opinions in the many areas in which better service to membership demands is easy to supply and does not interfere with any of his basic concerns. The fact that men know the law is on their side will give courage to some who previously felt inhibited in standing up for their rights. The "good" unions may also feel safe and concerned enough over the general reputation of the movement to enlarge the scope of internal review boards, and thus further due process.

The Role of Opposition

Historically, the most important factor in the achievement and defense of individual rights and democracy has been the existence of organized groups

[109] Cole, "Where We Are and Where We Are Going in Collective Bargaining," in *Current Trends in Collective Bargaining* 2-3 (1960).

that actively demand representation in government and greater equality in society. In most cases, legislation protecting the rights of individuals and extending their freedom would not have been passed except for the continual activities of organized groups representing those interests. Public opinion, in part, is *formed* through the activities and propaganda of such groups, as well as by the resultant legislation. Even after appropriate protective laws have been passed, an organized force is necessary to provide moral support for those individuals whose legal rights have been transgressed and to pay the costs of litigation. The area of civil rights serves as an example: fair employment practices and other civil rights legislation were passed only after years of intense effort by voluntary groups concerned with improving the position of Negroes in society. In the states where such legislation is in effect, these groups now bear the burden of seeing that adherence to the law is maintained.

Within the larger polity unions have formed a "second party" opposing the party of industry to secure various rights for workers. Through their collective strength, unions wrested from employers such employee rights as job security and control over working conditions. Simultaneously, the unions appealed to and formulated public opinion concerning the need to protect workers from the arbitrary power of employers. This culminated in legislation which assured the unions a legitimate and established place as the opposition within industry.

The general rule that the rights of the members of a polity are only safeguarded in the context of a struggle among diverse organized groups holds true within unions as well as within industry and society as a whole. Whether or not opposition candidates are actually elected to union office, the very existence of an organized opposition exerts pressure upon the incumbents to be more responsive to the membership. This is not to say that a union administration does not have formidable weapons against such opposition aggregations—it does; but without such groups, however weak their position within the union, civil liberties within unions remain precarious and the rights of individual members lack their most effective source of defense.

Many students of the labor movement have effectively argued that unions may be considered democratic institutions, that is, organizations which accurately represent the interests of their members and maintain the basic political freedoms internally, without the presence of formal internal opposition. But there can be little question that such a situation necessarily means that these rights are unstable, that they may be undermined and ignored in situations of crisis. Hugh Clegg, who strongly urges that unions without opposition groups may maintain "freedom of speech and association, freedom from arbitrary decisions, and so on," recognizes that he is promulgating a "paradox . . . of authoritarian policy decisions together with the protection of members' rights within the union . . . . a paradox of rights without parties . . . ."[110]

Clegg says that in his native England these rights are protected by two main factors: first, specific British union political institutions, particularly the lay executive committees, composed of men who work full time at their trade. Though weak as compared with the full-time officers, these committees and similar forces play an important role in protecting liberties within the union.

[110] Clegg, "The Rights of British Trade-Union Members," in *Labor in a Free Society* 136-38 (Harrington & Jacobs, eds., 1960).

Secondly, there are "the traditions of public life in Britain [which] reduce the likelihood of gross corruption and misuse of power in British trade unions."[111] Another British authority on trade unions, V. L. Allen, who agrees with Clegg that the existence of opposition is not a basic criterion of union democracy, suggests, however, that democratic rights will endure only when the "penalty for inefficiency, the misuse of resources or the abuse of power is severe." He regards such a penalty as inherent in the voluntary nature of trade unions. The union leader, who is in continual fear of losing his members, will perforce make stringent efforts to satisfy their wants.[112] Clark Kerr, writing about American unions, takes the position that one-party unions "may be and are 'democratic,'" but suggests that in the long run they will retain their democratic character only if they are "under the proper pressures."[113] These pressures, according to Kerr, have historically had four sources: voluntary membership; dual unionism; a "more or less permanent faction, stopping short of a second party but hovering in the wings ready to rush out on any inappropriate occasion . . . ." such as was once provided by the Socialists; and employers who have been willing to challenge the union's basic policies.[114]

It would be difficult to challenge the thesis that an organization may be democratic, that its members may have access to the decision-making process, even without institutionalized opposition and competitive elections. But conversely, it is equally difficult to deny that concentration of power without opposition always carries with it the potential for serious abuse. And since trade unions have more power over their members than most other private governments, and less-educated, lower-status individuals are much less prone to exercise their political rights than the more privileged strata, the fact of the absence of opposition cannot be lightly dismissed. The institutions, values, and practices which Clegg, Allen, and Kerr see as protecting democratic rights in Britain, or in the past in American unions, do not exist for most American unions today. Kerr explicitly notes that his four conditions have almost completely vanished.[115] There is clearly some need to at least guarantee the "right of rebellion" within one-party unions, or as Kerr calls it the "right of competitive discharge," so that when leaders abuse power or otherwise manifestly fail in their leadership role, a "minimum of democratic machinery is available" to replace them.[116] Efforts to enhance the democratic potential of union government, therefore, must be consciously concerned with protecting the rights of potential opposition groupings.

Because the backing for American legislation affecting internal union affairs has generally come from people with an individualistic, if not an antiunion bias, it has never even been attempted to deal directly with the rights of such

[111] Id. at 135-38.

[112] Allen, *Power in Trade Unions* 63-64 (1960).

[113] Kerr, *Unions and Union Leaders of Their Own Choosing* 14 (1957).

[114] Id. at 13-15. Kerr suggests that, to make up for the decline of these four sources of union democracy, efforts be made to enhance six other possible sources: membership interest, "professional" leaders with a professional ethic, a new faith for the union movement, local autonomy, union decertification, and discharge of leaders through rebellion. See id. at 15-19.

[115] Id. at 15.

[116] Id. at 18.

opposition groups until the passage of the LMRDA. And the most recent legislation is really only a preliminary start in this direction, not approaching the provisions of Australian law on the subject. American legislators tend to see union democracy chiefly as a way of protecting individual members from the abuses of autocratic leadership; and this emphasis could not but divert their attention from the social processes which alone can make union democracy meaningful.

Although legislation can provide a framework for democratic functioning, it cannot alter the determining structural conditions of political participation which vary tremendously from union to union—the mechanisms of the union's relations with employers or the peculiarities of the occupations it represents, for example. It cannot assure that union members will actually take advantage of the formal framework it has established; it cannot make members more interested in union affairs, nor can it create opposition groups which will utilize the democratic machinery. Opposition groups cannot be artificially erected. Their existence depends on sources of disagreement within unions which can provide a basis for different policies, as well as a climate in which members of similar economic interests and similar views on union affairs can get together. Legislation, then, once it accepts the rights of opposition groups, can only assure the mechanics by which such bodies can express themselves within the union.

The effectiveness of opposition groups in improving democratic procedure and due process is evident even in the two efforts referred to earlier in which success was achieved by *institutional* means: the Australian legislation dealing with union government and elections, which has good enforcement clauses, and the Public Review Board of the United Auto Workers. In Australia there was a well-organized and coherent opposition to the dominant Communist leadership in the form of "Industrial Groups," established originally by Catholics within the Australian Labor party. A brief description of the way they functioned and their effect is relevant:

[T]he ALP Industrial Groups . . . provided imaginative leaders, some of them former Communists, and established their own publicity media to break the monopoly of the Communists on the trade union press in many industries. They constantly harassed and exposed Communist officials in trade unions, keeping them off balance . . . . The "Groupers" made use of the arbitration court "clean ballot" legislation to get an honest count and roused the trade union membership to a pitch which resulted in some of the largest total ballots recorded in the history of these unions.[117]

Similarly, a recent study of the operation of the Public Review Board, which points out that thirty-nine individuals have appealed to the Board against the union leadership, nevertheless concludes that "review works best where there is conflict within a democratic local framework."[118]

Under such conditions, the awareness of the rights guaranteed by the Board

[117]Weiner, "The Reduction of Communist Power in the Australian Trade Unions: A Case Study," 69 *Pol. Sci. Q.* 408 (1954).

[118]Harrington, "What Union Members Think of Public Review," in *Democracy and Public Review: An Analysis of the UAW Public Review Board* 51, 63 (Center for the Study of Democratic Institutions Report 1960).

reaches a larger section of the rank and file; the individual who has a grievance always has a union political to whom he can turn for advice and help in prosecuting his appeal; and any financial question that might inhibit access to the review mechanism can be solved on a group basis. In such a situation, review acts to strengthen democratic tendencies that already exist and to establish a rule of law for any struggle that will take place within the local.[119]

A. Does Opposition Weaken Unions?

Many who would like to see an extension of democracy and due process within the labor movement nevertheless oppose efforts to legitimatize factionalism or formalized opposition party rights within unions. They contend that the union, as an organization in constant conflict with a powerful business opponent, cannot afford the luxury of internal dissension. The problem was noted over three decades ago:

In the first place the trade union seeks to combine within itself two extremely divergent types of social structure, that of an army and that of a democratic town meeting . . . . It must develop something of the solidarity, discipline, and capacity for swift striking that an army has . . . . The impossible is demanded of the union and its leadership . . . .[120]

The argument that internal factionalism necessarily weakens trade unionism actually is not as cogent as it seems. In fact, the period with the most internal opposition in the life of most labor organizations has usually been when they were at their *weakest,* in the phase of early organization before employers accept them as a legitimate part of the industrial relations system. The United Auto Workers experienced a series of bitter factional fights at the same time that it was trying to organize the "big three" of the industry. Along with the achievement of greater strength vis-à-vis the external enemy, the auto companies, went tighter control of the organization by the union administration. A similar story may be told concerning most other labor unions. Parenthetically, it may be noted that in the Soviet Union, which at one time also justified a one-party monopoly of power on the basis of a need for unity against powerful capitalist encirclement, there was much more freedom and opposition rights while the capitalist threat was a real one, in the form of foreign and White Guard armies on Russian soil. The Communist Party did not formally establish its monopoly of political expression until *after* it had expelled its military opponents.

It may even be argued that regularized opposition strengthens, rather than weakens, the loyalty of members to unions. Thus it has been observed that in the International Typographical Union, which for over half a century has had an institutionalized two-party system in which turnover in office can and does occur, "the two-party system serves to deflect discontent among members and

[119] Ibid.

[120] Muste, "Factional Fights in Trade Unions," in *American Labor Dynamics* 332-34 (Hardman, ed., 1928). For recent statements along the same lines see Leiserson, *American Trade Union Democracy* 69-70 (1959); Taft, *The Structure and Government of Labor Unions* 239 (1954); Goldberg, "A Trade-Union Point of View," in *Labor in a Free Society* 109-11 (Harrington & Jacobs, eds., 1960).

opposition leaders away from the union itself and toward the party in power."[121] Dissident members will say that the particular set of officers is no good, but that the union is wonderful. Similar reactions to internal conflict are reported in a study of four union locals in the United Rubber Workers and the United Auto Workers. The local with the most factionalism was also characterized by a high degree of loyalty on the part of its members.[122]

More recently, the steel strike of 1959 occurred in a union in which there was considerable factionalism and membership discontent with its officials. Interviews conducted with steel workers during this strike indicated that many remained hostile to the McDonald leadership but were aggressively loyal to the union and so supported the strike. It may, in fact, be argued that where incumbent officers follow the more common pattern of completely identifying the organization with themselves, they potentially undermine loyalty to the union, because any discontent with the leadership is interpreted as, and often of necessity becomes, an attack on the organization.

A second argument with which many labor leaders justify repression of opposition may also be challenged: the notion that unions are still on the defensive within a business-dominated society. While this paper is not the place to present the evidence for the thesis that unions are now an institutionalized part of the American polity, much evidence to this effect does exist.[123] It may appear that the defeat suffered by the International Union of Electrical Workers in its strike against the General Electric Company in October 1960 negates this thesis. However, it should be noted that the IUE is the only national union to suffer such a defeat in recent years, and it was vanquished after its national leadership decided to strike against a contract offer that had been accepted as a fair one by almost all the other one hundred unions which represent the majority of GE employees, including the old left-wing United Electrical Workers Union. A large minority within the IUE, including the leaders of its largest GE unit, that in Schenectady, also opposed the strike as unnecessary before it started. Moreover, the IUE's position was weakened by the fact that it contained a *disloyal* core of oppositionists, UE supporters who seized every opportunity to attack IUE policy. When the Schenectady local finally voted to join the strike, petitions were circulated urging the workers to leave IUE and rejoin the old UE. And as Paul Jacobs has noted, unionism in general has been relatively weak at GE since many of the company's plants "are located in rural areas where workers from farms are recruited, and there is a very high proportion of women employed."[124]

In any case, with few exceptions, the major American corporations accept the legitimacy of the trade union in their industry. They will still fight it with regard to normal issues of collective bargaining, but they no longer engage in activities designed to eliminate unions. As powerful an industry as steel failed in its major objectives in the 1959 strike. Though conservative legislators are able to pass antiunion measures, on the whole there is general agreement, that,

[121] Lipset, Trow & Coleman, *Union Democracy* 269 (1956).
[122] Tannenbaum & Kahn, *Participation in Union Locals* 183-84 (1958).
[123] See Kerr, op. cit. supra note 113, at 4-5. Arthur Goldberg sharply challenges this thesis. See Goldberg, supra note 120, at 106-08.
[124] Jacobs, "The Showdown at GE," *The Reporter* (Oct. 27, 1960), p. 36.

while it may have made new organization more difficult, none of this legislation has affected the position of established unions.

As far as can be judged, the majority of the general public believe unions play a positive role in the society. In 1958, the voters in the five industrial states that balloted on "right-to-work" legislation turned it down by large majorities, and elected legislators and other state officials were generally committed to opposing such measures. And the survey data on public opinion trends between 1945 and 1960 indicates that despite all the exposés, the widespread support for labor has not declined.[125] On the other hand, a very large majority of those interviewed thought that unions should be regulated "pretty closely," and union members were actually more likely to favor government regulation than were nonunion manual or white-collar workers. In this respect, it should be noted that a breakdown of the answers suggests that the union members were more concerned with corruption and mishandling of union funds than with matters pertaining to democratic union government.[126]

Even if union leaders were to accept the idea that internal conflict does not necessarily weaken their organizations, and that the existence of the labor movement is not in jeopardy, the fact remains that anything which encourages internal opposition does weaken their *personal* security, and union officers, no more than others, can be expected to endanger the source of their own authority and status. The political assets that every union administration possesses by virtue of controlling the official machinery—such as the near monopoly of internal communications and political skills discussed earlier—make it unlikely that regularized opposition can develop. There is even reason to believe that most changes in the position of the trade union movement have operated to reduce rather than to increase the potential for such opposition groups.

B. The Potential for Internal Opposition

The stabilization of the position of trade unions, particularly in their relations with management, and the decline of radical political doctrines, has reduced the number of situations that serve to increase membership interest in the organization and permit men outside of the established leadership to gain a hearing. In stable and secure unions in which major crises are rare, there are few opportunities for aspirants to power to find any way of challenging the union leadership. The decline of the left-wing political ideology, which characterized many American union leaders of the early organizing period of both the AFL and the CIO, was caused in large part by the institutionalization of labor organizations, and to some degree by the weakness of the Socialist Party as a force in the larger society.

In general, the more politically involved a trade union movement is, the greater the likelihood of internal factionalism. The commitment, for example, to support a socialist party or general socialist objectives necessarily involves

[125] The data for 1960 are given in American Institute of Public Opinion, Press Release (May 13, 1960). For the 1945-58 trends, see Opinion Research Corporation, *Labor's 1959 Bid for Power* (1959).

[126] See Opinion Research Corporation, op. cit. supra note 125.

some commitment to accept discussion of differences in politics as legitimate.[127] Many British trade union conventions have spent considerable time discussing both economic and more general political issues stemming from differences within the Labor Party. Conversely, the stress on business unionism in the American labor movement has served to reduce the possibility of internal union disputes emerging out of differences in value orientation.

Various changes in the social situation of American workers also operate to weaken the forces making for membership participation in trade unions. In the past workers were often tied to their unions by the fact that they lived in occupational communities, and so were involved in a variety of off-the-job social relations with other workers.[128] The growth of metropolitan areas, improved transportation, shorter work weeks, and higher incomes, have lessened workers' mutual dependency. More and more workers live in suburbs and occupationally heterogeneous neighborhoods, and the removal of their former social ties to their occupations has brought a similar decline in their ties to the union.[129] These changes have consequences for union democracy, for when membership participation in unions declines it is more difficult for a potential opposition to gain strength.

Increased bureaucratization and centralization of authority in industry have also played a role in reducing the possibilities for enduring opposition within unions, since they engender a similar bureaucratization and centralization in labor organizations. The effective decision-making is taken away from the membership, and as the procedures become more complicated, members are increasingly reluctant to become involved in union politics, and to listen to or support opposition.

Another emerging pattern that serves to reduce this potential is the tendency many unions, even craft unions, have to become "general unions," that is, to include a large variety of different crafts and industries. The industrial unions of the old CIO led the way, but they have been followed by many unions which seemingly remained loyal to the craft ideology.[130] The Carpenters Union for example, has taken as its jurisdiction not only work made of wood, which

[127]The Communists, on the other hand, have contributed to a breakdown in democratic procedures and due process. The fact that Communists are agents of a foreign power and often use unscrupulous tactics in gaining or retaining power within unions has been used by their opponents as a justification for comparable methods. A totalitarian opposition by definition can never be a legitimate opposition and hence by its very existence undermines democratic "rules of the game."

[128]For a discussion of the role of the occupational community see Lipset, Trow & Coleman, op. cit. supra note 121, at 83-140.

[129]A pilot study of the "possible effects of suburban residence on the participation and attitudes of union members" based on intensive interviews with forty-six male members of two locals of the UAW reports that "The effect of suburban residence, with its heterogeneous or dominantly middle class environment, is to diminish both trade union participation and values of all but the work-group oriented." Spinrad & Goldstein, *The Influence of City and Suburban Residence on Union Membership* (Institute of Management and Labor Relations, Rutgers University, dittoed 1960).

[130]For a detailed statistical breakdown of this tendency toward the growth of general unions see Chamberlain, "The Structure of Bargaining Units in the United States," 10 *Ind. & Lab. Rel. Rev.* 3 (1956). Some of the consequences of these changes are elaborated in Kahn, "Contemporary Structural Changes in Organized Labor," in 1957 *Indus. Relations Research Ass'n Proceedings of Tenth Annual Meeting* 171-79.

includes diverse industries, but all commodities that once were made of wood or that would have been made of wood if different materials had not been developed. The proclivities of the Teamsters, the largest union in the country, to organize any firm which uses trucks, are well known. And, it may be argued, the more heterogeneous the constituency of a union, the fewer possibilities there are for maintaining internal democracy.

The growth of the general union increases the possibility that conflicts will develop within the union among groups composed of members with similar skills or occupations.[131] They will quarrel over whether each group's *special* economic interests are being adequately promoted by the Union as a whole. Unions which include members with a wide range of skills, such as the UAW and the IAM, have already experienced this kind of conflict. But such conflicts of *interests* cannot be resolved simply by a democratic vote, as these unions have found. The interest group which is in a numerical minority within the union must feel that it can expect fair treatment, or it may become disloyal. Such conflicts are more likely to be resolved by intraunion "arbitration," which takes the form of a decision from above, than by a majority vote.

Union opposition groups can endure only if, like political parties in the nation state, they can appeal to the body politic in terms of general political and social *value* differences, as well as to economic interests. Such differences are the meat of disagreement within relatively homogeneous unions such as the International Typographical Union or the American Newspaper Guild. Thus any trend, like that toward general unionism, which reduces the potency of disagreements flowing from varying values, and increases the possibility that the interests of different occupational or skill groups will become the basis for factional difference, serves ultimately to weaken the democratic potential of American labor organizations.

While most of the ongoing changes in the internal as well as the external situation of trade unions would seem to operate against the enlargement of opposition rights, there is one important trend that may have different consequences. As a result of the increase in the educational attainments of the American population and the decline in the proportion of unskilled and semi-skilled jobs in the economy, union members are becoming better educated and achieving higher status. Both education and status are associated with a heightened concern for democratic rights and due process, as well as adherence to conventional morality with regard to matters such as corrupt practices.[132] Insofar as American unionists are incorporated socially into the "middle class," either as well-paid blue-collar workers, or as part of the growing white-collar group, they will resent behavior which, in the eyes of their friends and neighbors, demeans trade union membership. The way in which these values operate may

[131] Clegg also suggests that the "danger of authoritarianism" is greatest in the general unions. Clegg, supra note 110, at 134. The two big general unions, the Transport and General Workers Union and the National Union of General and Municipal Workers, are the unions which are best known to him as those likely to "discipline factions or leaders of factions." The situations which he describes as examples of such behavior were occasioned by specific occupational groups such as the busmen or the dockers acting on their own. See id. at 126-27.

[132] See Lipset, *Political Man* 109-11, 115-20 (1960).

be illustrated by the active opposition of some milk drivers' locals to James Hoffa in the Teamsters Union. An official of one such local accounted for this as follows:

Our members deliver milk bottles to middle-class homes. Most of them come into day-to-day contact with the women on their routes. Whenever the papers describe how Beck or Hoffa are in cahoots with racketeers, or how various Teamster officials are taking money, our men come into the local and want to know what the hell is going on. Some woman on the route asked them what they were doing in a crooked union, or why they put up with Beck or Hoffa. The over-the-road men or those delivering to warehouses within the city couldn't care less about the exposés. As far as they are concerned, Jimmy delivers the goods for which he is paid, and most other workers they meet think they are lucky to be in as aggressive a union as the Teamsters. It's middle-class morality that gets the milk drivers down.[133]

Whether "middle class" morality will help create organized pressure within labor against violations of that morality is a moot question, given all the other forces operating to strengthen administration authority. As unions have become a legitimate, major American institution, however, the general community status and social position of union leaders have been increasingly improved. They live in middle-class suburbs, their wives and children mingle with people of diverse backgrounds, and anything which makes the union movement look bad hurts their social position.[134] These pressures on both members and leaders serve to reinforce the need for union officials to adhere to due process and membership civil liberties, regulated by legislation, as closely as is compatible with their own political security.

[133]Confidential interview.

[134]For discussion of the social pressures on trade union officials see Imberman, "Labor Leaders and Society," *Harv. Bus. Rev.* (Jan. 1950), pp. 52-60; Phelps, "Community Recognition of Union Leaders," 7 *Ind. & Lab. Rel. Rev.* 419-33 (1954); Gouldner, "Attitudes of 'Progressive' Trade Union Leaders," in *Sociological Analysis* (Wilson & Kolb, eds., 1949), 574-79.

Paul E. Sultan

DISSENT IN THE TRADE UNIONS

What are the sources of discontent among rank-and-file union members? What happens to union dissenters? Paul Sultan interviewed a number of them and recorded some of their frustrations.

. . . A prime cause of controversy was the issue of union security. Almost all respondents expressed opposition to union security agreements, a uniformity of opinion that is surprising even considering the fact that twenty-eight of the survey group were suggested by right-to-work committees. Thirteen respondents protested against union security agreements at their local meetings, and became even more antagonized when union officials attempted to silence them. Another twenty-one respondents aired their views on public platforms. Seven had testified before national and state government committees in hearings that were set up to expose abuses in internal union affairs. Four had appeared on television shows; many had written letters to newspapers declaring their support for right-to-work legislation, and six were involved in elaborate letter-writing campaigns, sending hundreds of mimeographed open letters to public officials describing the unfair treatment they believed they were getting from their union. One movie projectionist, reacting to the murder of a fellow dissident in Chicago the evening before he himself was to testify before a government committee, distributed a letter that named the union officials he thought would be responsible in the event of his own murder.

Let us look first at the spirit of this category of protest, and then indicate some of the underlying forces that caused such general concern with union security clauses. Some of the respondents simply could not accept the arguments utilized by the union movement to defeat right-to-work legislation. A rubber worker explained: "They ask their members to go around and tell the preachers and ministers that if right-to-work laws pass, wages would go down and unemployment follow; grass would grow on the streets, and church revenues would fall off." As to his own local: "I have a lot of friends there, but I might just as well be friendless. If I have got to sacrifice a principle to have friends, I would have to do without the friends." A motion was made to expel him from the union. "But I was fully protected. Even their own constitution sets forth freedom of speech and dissemination of ideas and opinions. But they think it is something awful for a person to speak up." He wrote a letter to the local newspaper supporting right-to-work laws, and received a threatening phone call. "They told me to button up my lip or I might not fare so good." From then on he carried a hatchet and knife in his car: "I heard about some of these goons and I didn't figure at my age I could take on two or three of them."

An auto worker became embroiled in controversy for circulating a right-to-work pamphlet at work:

Twenty minutes later I was in the office and got a written reprimand for passing out unauthorized literature. At a union meeting, I asked them if they couldn't stand any opposition. That was the end of the meeting. Seventeen members asked that their money be put into a separate fund instead of used for political education, and only seven of seventeen are still working. At least ten union members have threatened to run over me. I put in a union dues revocation order and both the business agent and the company personnel man gave me a bad time. I really got hot. I looked them in the eye and I said: "Fellows, I have had enough. Yesterday you called me a liar, and today you tell me that I am fouling you up. When General Motors is too big to listen to an individual employee they are too big. Whenever a union is too big to listen to an individual they are too big. And you two guys standing here are too big." They told me that I was asking for trouble, and I said trouble doesn't worry me since there is enough social security to take care of my family in case I am no longer with them. The same people that tore up Newcastle and Princeton were still around. I told these guys to either give me my rights or go ahead and crack my head, it matters not which. I am not afraid. After that I faced a lot of ostracism. The labor relations man told me that when you go and do a thing like that, it is like having an affair with someone's wife.

He felt that his job was in jeopardy:

If I'm the only one in nineteen hundred men to dissent on an issue, don't you think the company would go along to eliminate the sore spot? The only reason I have not been eliminated is because I have recourse to the courts. But I have to be beyond making mistakes in my job.

A woman respondent revealed a long history of protest against union policies. On one occasion, she described a controversy within the local over a seniority change that would reduce the protection afforded elderly women. Fifteen women stood up to protest the action at a meeting of their local, but they could not speak because the officers began a filibuster. When the respondent saw the women sit down one by one, she rose to her feet and delivered a fiery oration:

I told them that when the Declaration of Independence was signed, I'm sure that they discussed it first, and even though I was for the union motion, I explained why everybody ought to be heard. I got a lot of applause, but I was so angry that I didn't hear any of it myself. But the next morning these carrier pigeons, the union stewards, went all over the plant telling what an ass I made of myself.

She described another occasion when her local's elections were protested because nominations were closed before the faction opposing the leadership had nominated its candidates. An international representative arrived to supervise a second election:

Nobody would ask a question or say anything because the power of the international had dropped in on them. So I finally asked: "How do we know that this election is going to be any more honest than the last one?" The man just bounded off the stage . . . . I think he was coming after me, but in all the confusion a motion was made to adjourn.

On a later occasion she supported an underdog candidate for union office:

This fellow was supposedly a preacher. Seven years of college, he said, and he wasn't preaching because he had lost his voice. So I campaigned and went home early, losing my overtime, to make posters and put them on cars. So after the election they counted the ballots and after tabulating three hundred votes, they said they were tired and sent all the candidates home. Why, I wouldn't even trust my own grandmother with a ballot box. I cried, and I mean tears, for three days, to think that I had electioneered for a candidate that was more stupid than I was because even I know not to leave a ballot box.

Later, at a state convention of the AFL-CIO, she fashioned a picket sign to greet the arrival of Walter Reuther: "We Workers Love Reuther: We Want to be Sovietized." But she complained that not one in twenty-five understood the sign. She gave a series of speeches to the crowd that collected, and described the consequences in a letter:

It took three squad cars and two plainclothes policemen to control the situation. They came at the request of our top labor leader, but I was more glad to see them than they were. I am firmly convinced that I did get to many of the delegates with my ideas . . . my methods may not be practical, but in your opinion, was it psychologically correct?

It is likely that the stormy reception by the union movement of such views reflected the fact that they received so much publicity. One respondent had lost a close contest for the presidency of his local. He then led a protest against an increase in union dues but was told that the resolution would be introduced at every union meeting until it passed. He further antagonized union officers by appearing on television shows and at other public meetings in support of right-to-work laws. He was then quickly expelled from his union. His case received national publicity when he brought suit against his union. Although the newspapers inaccurately reported that he had lost his job, he suffered social rather than economic penalties:

The worst thing was the loss of prestige and hurt feelings. For many years I was always the person to whom people came for information and help. In fact they still do. I got a call at two-thirty in the morning from a chairman who had shut down the plant in the missile division and wanted help. I've always kept myself well informed on all the contracts, the constitution, and the by-laws. I think that's the worst thing; it hurts to be asked questions and not to have the right to tell them. In my own group, people talk to me just the same as they ever did; in fact you might say they're practically unanimous with me. But the business agent still comes into the plant and talks against me, tells them what a stinker I am.

In contrast, a railroad telegrapher appeared on television for the right-to-work movement without suffering any consequences:

I was told there might be some unpleasantness, that I might be knocked on my can. But nothing happened. But I did have a visit to my office by three men in shirt sleeves from another union, so I invited them to calm down and try to convert me. I say, "Maybe I'm wrong." But they would only throw some uncomplimentary remarks my way. I guess I've got a walrus hide.

Ironically, a few workers complained that there was little union reaction to their protests, contending that the fact that they were ignored was proof of the union's entrenched position.

But not all protests could be ignored. Following, for example, are excerpts taken from open letters given widespread distribution to public officials and newspaper editors, written by union critics. The provocative nature of these charges is immediately apparent. A veteran union member, defeated for office, wrote the first of these letters to his international president. The following are excerpts from five pages of his slashing criticism:

How can a crooked, corrupt union leader, who has broken every article in the Constitution and by-laws to benefit yourself, possibly write such dirty lies? . . . How decent men can even bear to have you around them is beyond me—that is, if they are union men at heart . . . . You don't like anyone to call you a hoodlum or a racketeer, but it is exactly what you are, so why deny it or try to punish me for reminding you? You are a coward at heart. I don't believe there is an honest bone in your body. Again I say you are a terrible disgrace to organized labor . . . . As I know you, you are nothing to my eyes but a strike-breaker and scab . . . . You had me expelled for daring to inform the members of these hoodlums and racketeer buddies of yours. How can you as a union man sit among good union leaders and act so innocent? Does your conscience ever bother you when you are asked to act on other unions who are before you for corruption and racketeering? Do you ever have trouble sleeping at night? . . . To me you are the country's greatest betrayer of union men, and I hope soon to let the world read of your life's history, and with all the publicity you get, maybe they could use you in the movies. You would be terrific playing a gangster, racketeer, hoodlum, a Judas, a betrayer of union men, or just any underworld type or character, as you've had so many years of real-life experience . . . . Hoping to have the great pleasure of hearing from you soon, I want you to know I shall never cease writing about you until I find someone brave enough in the AFL-CIO Executive Council or Ethical Practices Committee to challenge you, or till one of your goons "bump me off." So with best wishes for your early trial and conviction, I am, Respectfully,

P.S. 2000 copies of this "letter" to be distributed to union officers, Congressmen, Senators, Newspapers, etc.

The respondent was then faced with a two-hundred-thousand-dollar libel suit from the international president. He countered with an equally large libel suit of his own against the president.

This same respondent, after failing to gain an opportunity to testify before a congressional committee about his experiences, mimeographed an open letter to the President of the United States, declaring:

Surely this can't happen in America. What has really happened? Is this a dream? Were all the wars we fought for democracy all in vain? Have the gangsters, hoodlums and racketeers really got control? . . . What would the millions of

Americans who gave of their lives to protect our constitution and our American way of life say to this? What would these dead say if we could radio to them that many of our congressmen and senators have betrayed their trust and had "mortgaged" themselves to the AFL-CIO in return for their political support. Hoodlums, racketeers who with the funds of the dues paying members can pay for favors from a duly elected Senator or Congressman, who ever thought this could happen in America? Those senators and congressmen who have been sent to Washington AFL-CIO style. Many have turned traitor on those American voters or citizens who had entrusted to them the making of laws to protect our constitution and our country. Traitors in war times were usually shot at sunrise.

Another equally excited respondent wrote the following mimeographed letter, heavily laden with sarcasm, to fellow union members:

A few lines to clarify a few points, because you will never get an honest answer to any question asked of anybody who has anything to do with the running of the local. If you knew the truth you would get a club and clean house. The clique that runs our union have stood in your doors for 25 years with a big rock in their hand daring you to step out, if you did they would hit you, or bump whichever you call it. Well I stepped out and took the rock away from them . . . . These boys are right in [there] pitching for you every minute. They pitched away $102,000.00 last year, nobody received any benefits what so ever. The last quarter these boys put you in the hole over $500. This is for attorneys to try to beat a federal law. Yes sir, you have some fine men doing your negotiating . . . . Of course you will all be dead before you get anything. You boys sure have a progressive bunch, that is they would have been progressive 250 years ago. Fellows you do not *have to pay any fines or assessments of any kind . . . . Believe me fellows, I have just started, their death threats won't stop me, these are just a few things that happen in your local every year.*

The women in the office get a $150 a week, do you? Now men are mostly fools as you are aware, therefore, they let themselves be governed by fools. Men pulling and shoving in different directions, shouting one another down, so far the knaves and fools seem to have it. Let's hope it gets better.

In a letter to public officials, this same respondent explained:

As you know, my local is run by gangsters and they don't mind killing you . . . a whole lot of people are wondering what the NLRB exists for, it seems to all of us who have had dealings with them that they act as a buffer between the working man and the union to keep us from doing anything to the union.

Sir, until a part of Section 8A of the Taft-Hartley Act is changed, "For reasons other than the failure of the employee to tender the periodic dues and initiation fees uniformly required," until this is changed then the union goons, gangsters and political scum who play Tootsie with them will grow fatter. Where in the hell in the Constitution or Bill of Rights does it say I must pay goons, gangsters and commies to be allowed to work? When are some of your boys going to get enough guts to stand up to [various union] goon squads and give us some protection? . . . I think the rank and file have more votes than the goons. I still want to know why the NLRB seems to protect the unions.

A less strident challenge to unionism was offered by a female respondent.

She had been invited to become a correspondent for the union paper following a letter she had submitted to a local newspaper defending female employment. In rejecting the union invitation, she explained:

We face an intolerable situation—compulsory membership in an organization of which I am thoroughly ashamed, namely, the Teamsters' union. A disgrace to our nation in the eyes of the whole world, they have defied our government and all the laws of decency—yet we remain a part of them.

She pointed out that she had been a charter member and first secretary-treasurer of their local back in 1934

. . . at a time when the union was of the people, by the people, for the people. That is no longer true. The servant has become the master. Most union members, I find, are afraid to even think for themselves, lest their thoughts be disapproved by the union. I realize this is "heresy" of the first order, for in union circles the union can do no wrong and criticism is considered sufficient cause for expulsion. Be that as it may, no union or any other organization will ever "own" me to the point of depriving me of my freedom of thought or speech. I presume that in your estimation I am a "screwball," but at least you cannot say I am a hypocrite.

She felt considerable anxiety about repercussions from writing so frankly, but nothing came of it. The contrast between the tone of protest of the first two respondents and that of the last may in part be explained by the fact that the former two found themselves without employment in their trades and were unable to prove that the union had been responsible for their plight.

What reasons were given for such uniform opposition to union security agreements? The most articulate critics on this issue were those who were (or had been) members of the railroad brotherhoods. The twenty-one railroaders contended that they were not consulted when their unions decided to press for union security agreements. They resented learning of this contract agreement after management had agreed to it. Typical expressions include:

I personally had taken a poll of numerous terminals on my property with a petition in regards, "Are you in favor of Public Law 914 union shop?" The totals were about ninety-four against with only six for it.

Not being informed about it was my biggest objection at the time. I was local chairman for this Switchmen's Union at the time it went in, and I resigned right after the agreement went in for the simple reason that none of us were given a vote on it. In fact, they hadn't asked us or we had heard nothing about it. That of course was one of my biggest objections. The fact that they made an agreement with the company and hadn't notified the members. So I objected to the darn thing and told them that I wouldn't belong to it, that I resigned my job as local chairman and joined the Brotherhood of Railroad Trainmen. At its inception I'd say about eighty percent of the men were against it. I think it was the method, the way they done it.

Another respondent described urging his convention delegate to resist endorsing the union shop at the convention. At the train station the delegate exploded:

Let me tell you something. It isn't what you men want. It's what you get. Damn you. You're going to get union shop rammed right down your throat.

Several of the respondents had the impression that the 1951 amendment to the Railway Labor Act *required* that employers sign the agreement, a conviction not altogether consistent with the opinion that members should have been consulted on the issue before negotiations began for union shop terms. As one explained:

The employer has absolutely no choice. It's the law. Congress gave them that privilege. They could say "No," but they would certainly have trouble on their hands, such as other railroads. Of course, according to the law, all the union had to do was just write them [the employer] a letter and say that they desire to put the union shop agreement in and that's the way the law reads. It says that they must. The president of this railroad put out a letter saying that, according to the law, that they were forced to sign a union shop agreement with any organization that presented it, that they had no beef one way or the other, that it was immaterial to them which way it went. It seems strange to the average guy that if he objects to it, why he is doing it. Most of them don't know that the law says that you've got to do it, that you've got to sign an agreement if they come in and request it.

A second contention was that, while unions sold the principle of union security on the basis of spreading the cost of union organization to the "freeloader" or nonmember, once the agreement was signed union initiation fees and dues increased:

For fifty years they never had an initiation fee. As soon as the union shop agreement went in they put a five-dollar initiation fee on. Some locals put it at fifteen dollars. I went to the secretary-treasurer and said, "What's this crap putting in that five-dollar initiation fee? You guys ought to be tickled to death you're getting a member, let alone just absolutely putting a gun on him and telling him he has to pay you five dollars." He said, "Well, it's the union shop. He's got to join, don't he?"

We had the general chairman from Toledo talk on the union shop. What good would it do? It would decrease the dues because everybody had to belong. But we had very few men that didn't belong to the union. Since that time, the dues went up from $5.25 to–I believe they're paying $7.50 now.

A third complaint was that concessions were made by the union to get the union shop agreement–concessions that the membership thought more important than the union security agreement. One imagined the conversations at the bargaining table:

"Now John, we're speaking of you asking us to sign a union shop agreement. We've run this railroad for fifty years or seventy-five years without a union shop agreement. However, in the event that we sign this union shop agreement, we're going to ask you to strike out some rule that has been before this committee time and time again." So when you go into the yard office, you see on the bulletin board, "Beginning at 12:01 A.M., rule so and so does not apply after that date." That rule has probably been in effect for twenty-five years but we no longer have it. After we search our minds for a few moments we find out that just recently the rule committees have been in negotiations with management. So our thoughts are that something has been given for something that they take.

A Teamster found his local had renegotiated a contract in the fourth year of its five-year term. The intent of this strategy was to beat the effective date of the state's new right-to-work law. To secure this concession from the employer, he alleged that many benefits of the previous contract had been surrendered, including the amount of the minimum weekly wage guarantee. Although the new contract was voted down twice, a third meeting was held in another location without notice. The respondent tried to mobilize the opposition:

When we learned about it we tried to get as many of our men there as possible. They had a lot of strangers there. Five or six of them were great big guys, some "muscle" imported to see that the vote went the right way. So we lost the vote.

Subsequently, the respondent found that his dues had been doubled. His steward told him that a mistake had been made and to hold back in his dues payment until the matter was clarified. Without warning he was discharged by the employer for nonpayment of dues. In subsequent appeals to the NLRB, his position was upheld and his union membership reinstated. As he described the situation:

We are dealing with a rough element here, but so many people know about my case that I feel safe. Even my steward filed an affidavit to support me, and, when he did this, he was told he was no longer a union steward. This fellow knows that if he leaves his present employer he will never get another job. When you cross the union, you're done.

A fourth criticism was that union officers were indifferent to the members' needs once the agreement was signed, both in dealing with individual grievances and in negotiating contract agreements:

There's no point in jumping from one union to another, as one is as bad as the other, and it's bad enough to pay one of them without paying the other. We pay $6.15. It includes nothing. They used to have a burial fund, but now, if you died right there on the property, they wouldn't throw a lump of coal on you.

The union argued that if you get rid of the "no-bills" [nonmembers] your dues will be cheaper and that ain't come to pass. They go up instead of down. And, if you are forced to do something against your will, you may take a man's money, but he is not supporting you in the majority of things. You ain't doin nothin but tying a chain around your own neck. You are just paying for the right to work, that's the way I'd say it.

It gives the union complete control. They can raise the dues. They can go after increases, working conditions, decreases, throw your working conditions away. And you have no recourse. You can't drop out. You can't say: "If that's the kind of union you've got, I don't want to belong to it. I'm going to drop out." If you do this you're out of a job.

A movie projectionist expressed similar sentiment:

The union officers sit around over there with their feet on a desk because we haven't got voluntary unionism. They sit with their feet on the desk, smoking cigars and tell you to go to hell. Because we got to pay them anyway, see? Now go over in Arizona and check and see if they ain't got fighters in that union, because they got to produce something, my friend, or you *say, "Go to hell." Isn't that right? That's the way I finally figured it out. It always takes a year or two to sign a contract and then they come up with a nickel or dime an hour, that's all they ever get.*

A machinist explained:

Before the union shop we had the best representation we ever had. In other words, we saw a business agent sometimes two times a week, at least once a week. And they used to take the chairmen out into the lunch area at least once a week and inform them on things that were going on in different parts of the plant. New rules and regulations, new grievances that had been settled, and how things were being handled in different parts of the plant. Since we've had compulsory unionism, they've done away with the training programs. You never see a business agent except during election time, which is about every two years. They might get in once or twice a year, but it just isn't the same. It used to be that people would get a lift just seeing their business agent pass through once or twice a week. They knew that they were getting something for their money. And now the attitude is: "Well, if you do this, we'll do this for you. If you don't do this, we won't do anything for you."

Typically, the respondents believed that the freedom to resign from a union was the only effective control device over union policy:

Actually, there is no reason for any kind of government regulating unions. A union member can regulate it by saying: "If you don't do something and show me where my money goes and quit spending it in Florida and vacations and buying big yachts, I will take my money out." If they lost a thousand members they would certainly be trimming themselves up. That is the only way to control them. As long as the union member can be free to get out of there, he has all the leverage he needs without government interference.

This same respondent described the effect of right-to-work legislation on her relations with the union:

Immediately after the right-to-work law was passed they loosened their grip. They became a little bit more benevolent towards the union members. In fact, after they got over being shocked and angry at me, they did their best to welcome me with toothpaste smiles to the union meeting.

Closely related to the issue of union security were difficulties created by interunion rivalry, rivalries that were particularly severe in the railroad industry. According to the testimony of the twenty-one railroaders in the survey group, most railroaders were dissatisfied with their union representation. Discontent was said to have its origin in "top-down" control by the international office, the negotiation of "thin" contracts, the union surrender of work rules, the inability of railroad brotherhoods to secure contract terms that would provide economic concessions that were standard in most other labor agreements; and in general terms, the declining status and dignity of railroading attributed to ineffective representation. One railroader explained:

There's quite a few men who have read the constitutions of the respective brotherhoods. They have time to read these things when you're riding in the caboose. And railroaders have always been sort of independent anyway. And another thing, twenty years ago we were rated 4th as far as pay was concerned. Now we are 129th in wages.

The respondents also charged that the brotherhoods were more interested in insurance than advancing membership interests. Typical comments included:

My thought of the organizations in the railroad field is insurance. They're insurance peddlers, basically.

You see, the brotherhoods already had an insurance company established. . . . The insurance business in the railroads has become so enormous that they forgot about time claims and grievance matters. They were merely to be bargained away to keep from rippling the placid waters of this nice little lake they were in.

As far as they are concerned, it's strictly a business operation. Now in Canada they've got eighteen-thousand members. With the money they've gotten from Canadian members they've got nine-million dollars invested in Canadian bonds. Now how do you account for that? They get it from the insurance.

On January 5, 1951, a mass meeting of disgruntled railroad unionists was held in San Jose, California. The group decided to create a new union. One respondent explained: "In this union, the men would have the right to choose their own leadership and have a referendum vote on all their wages and working conditions at all levels, and the recall for every officer at all levels." The new union, called the United Railroad Operating Crafts (UROC), was designed to represent all operating personnel in all lines.

Interest in UROC spread rapidly, and while various respondents gave different estimates of its size at peak strength, ranging up to 22,500 members, an officer testified that an audited account in the summer of 1952 showed that the organization had 11,700 paid members. The Railway Labor Act amendment of 1951 permitting the negotiation of a union security agreement offered some flexibility to railroad employees as to what union they joined—a measure designed to avoid the necessity for constant reaffiliation with different unions, with the constant shift in job assignments. To overcome that difficulty, an employee could fulfill his membership requirements so long as he was a member of any union "national in scope." Thousands of employees resigned from their brotherhoods to join UROC, certain that the membership requirement of their agreement was still being met. However, the more cautious, suspecting that UROC might not be considered "national in scope," decided to "double-head" or maintain membership in both UROC and their old brotherhood until the issue had been resolved.

Ironically, the grass roots protest movement was immediately confronted with its own internal grass roots dissension. A Cleveland UROC local published a booklet that proposed a new constitution for UROC. It cataloged the failures of the existing organization: First, it condemned the fact that the UROC newspaper, *FACTS,* was not an open forum for all member opinions: "In sad fact, our own paper does not carry the facts except as the facts are laudatory or neutral in tone and matter." Second, the organization was run by dictatorial policies. In a cartoon captioned "You've got the referendum but I've got the Organization," the UROC president was depicted as showering down on UROC members, from the union structure, a stream titled "Lies and Distortions." On the union building were the labels: "What Have the Brotherhood Heads Got that I Ain't Got?" "I can make secret deals." "I control the Union Press; I appoint the editor." "I decide what we'll do." "I appoint the office staff." "I spend union funds as I please." In a second cartoon the brotherhoods, together with railroad employers, were pictured as jointly feeding a cannon, titled the "Union Shop," aimed at UROC members. Behind a stone wall, titled the "UROC Treasury," was located the UROC president, admonishing the UROC members to march on the cannon. The president urges: "Attack the union shop. Onward men! I am behind you. (But *I like* the union shop.)" The booklet went on to explain that the experience with the union shop problem "proves that one man rule does not produce workable solutions; it only muddies the waters." In another section it declared: "If we wanted to take orders from the top we would have stayed in the Brotherhoods." UROC policies were considered to be based on "sheerest opportunism," and when in March 1953 the president asserted in convention that the organization might support the union shop, the booklet explained: "The effort of the whole year in this area was wiped out in three minutes by one man without any discussion by the UROC membership."

The booklet acknowledged that the UROC organization "faced the same problem of every other social organization: how to delegate authority as we must, without losing our power." It urged the formation of a national council, made up of representatives elected from each local. The council would meet regularly, appoint newspaper staff, implement convention resolutions, and generally assume responsibility for all policy. National officers would report to the council, and it would in turn report to the membership for ratification of its decisions.

A more moderate criticism of the president was offered by a senior official in the movement:

Unfortunately, his thirty years of brotherhood activity seemed to shine through under his procedure as head of UROC, and even though his fundamental beliefs were very democratic, he ruled UROC with somewhat of an iron hand.

Difficulties began to pyramid for the new organization. There seemed an "unaccountable" delay in pressing for contracts. One UROC member described the problems involved in representing UROC members in grievances when UROC did not have a contract with the railroad:

If you have a contract, you could give away enough time slips and grievances to keep a drunk on the job. I've been sitting in on these "swappy for changy" deals between the local chairman and the superintendent. If you were an operating officer of a carrier and could clean up ten-thousand dollars of time claims by putting some stew bum back to work just because he is popular with the members, you have a nice deal. What a club you have.

If you have a contract then you can give away on the legitimate time-claim grievance matters. But without a contract, you have nothing to give. You merely plead and beg, and you are talking to a sphinx when you talk to a railroad official on a "forgive and forget." We had no contract and no bargaining power whatsoever. We had the legal right to represent and appeal but we had no horses to swap. So it merely ended up with a good pleading. But our client was still hung. It's fantastic.

Another respondent described the hostility building up against UROC:

The brotherhoods worked on the men mercilessly. In the east they went to work on us with court suits and in personal antagonism against all the men, and against the UROC organization, belittling it in every way that they could. They got men fired for any provocation, any way that they could.

Another described how union pressure had caused their president to lose his job:

The brotherhood saw to it that the company fired him for overstaying three or four days of his leave of absence, while he was president of UROC. So that after serving as an engineer for some forty-two or forty-three years, he was fired for overstaying a leave of absence for three or four days.

As the court decisions began moving against UROC, many of the men scrambled to gain readmission to the traditional brotherhoods, while those who had double-headed quietly surrendered their membership in the rump organization. There was considerable disagreement in the testimony offered by the respondents as to whether UROC had advised its own members to abandon membership in the other brotherhood until its own status was clarified. But one explained:

The very top of UROC nationally advised the men: "Sure, we're national in scope. Don't you join [the other brotherhoods]. Let them take you out of service. We'll get an attorney and defend you." Well, the first thing you know we had ten different cases going in ten different courts. You can imagine how quickly your money is drained away from you under those circumstances.

One respondent prepared his own mimeographed study on the technical issue of determining whether a union was "national in scope" and enumerated the contradictory rulings of various courts. That report also contained an exchange of correspondence, in which a UROC member asked for readmittance to his brotherhood in order to avoid discharge:

You will probably be surprised to receive this letter, but I have to try to rectify my mistake; and I'll have to admit that I made a mistake . . . . I would like for you to arrange for Lodge ___ to reinstate my membership, and I can assure you that I will never pick up another UROC receipt. If I am reinstated I can assure you and the membership of the B of RT that I will be a faithful member from here out. Waiting for an early reply and thanking you in advance . . . .

He received a reply:

I am not too much concerned about what you have to say . . . but I do know that you were willing to accept the conditions the B of RT got employees in the Baltimore & Ohio Railroad, such as the automatic couplers, air brakes, safety appliances, 16-hour law, 8-hour day, time and one-half for overtime and many other conditions too numerous to mention; yet you would desert these organizations and "go over the hill" for a rump organization that had no policies or conditions to sell the men. As I understand, you were very much interested in the UROC activity and had yourself elevated to the presidency of a local, but when you come down to face facts, you then become weak and yellow. You then turned against the organization that you so proudly supported . . . now you get on bended knees asking for forgiveness. I am compelled to tell you that you are now in the same boat as the others who have appealed [for] reinstatement. I have no regret in telling you that I do not have any sympathy for you or others who have gone the UROC route.

The booklet also contained a copy of a letter written by the general chairman of one brotherhood:

This bunch has at last got themselves in a bad position and are looking for an out, but, as far as I am concerned, they have had their chance, and if I have my way I will put them where they will bother us no more.

He complained of the passive and compromising role of the Firemen's brotherhood:

The Firemen, as usual, are taking no action whatsoever in their cases, but are waiting, as usual for us to do the work and pay the bill, after which they will say, "Me, too." I also understand they have taken several of these UROC members after we have held hearings for noncompliance. In other cases I have proved they predated receipts to help these rats.

One respondent who held a key position within the organization speculated on the numbers who lost their jobs through this confusion:

To my knowledge, and I don't have the full knowledge, we know of 425 men that lost their jobs nationally under the union shop Public Law 914, for belonging to UROC instead of the standard labor organizations. I think the number would run nearer to 600, but I know of 425. That's a lot of men, and many had from thirty-five to forty years' seniority. The public don't know anything about these things, and the brotherhoods are most careful that this information don't get to them. We were only a voice crying in the wilderness, you might say.

The consternation created by this turn of events was obvious. One discharged employee complained:

Why, it turned out that we belonged to nothing but the human race as far as they were concerned. We lost all our seniority. The moment we were notified that we were discharged, our name came off the roster so that at that moment we were through.

Further down the list of prime causes for disputes , . . . twenty-four respondents complained of the union's inadequate attention to their grievances. Several of these grievances related to loss of seniority rights.

In one case, a female respondent reported that she had been discharged following the negotiation of a contract term that called for equal pay for equal work. The employer contended that men could more easily handle the work assignments. Whether the company could make such discharges stick depended on whether it was bound by a single or dual seniority list. While the single list had recently been made a part of a bargaining agreement, the company reasoned that the layoffs were not covered by that provision. The displaced women protested.

The complainant alleged that, when the issue was put to a standing vote at a meeting of her local, the male members who had displaced the women were allowed to vote. In addition, several who were not members stood up and were counted in the vote. When she asked one nonmember why he was standing, he said he thought it was time to pledge allegiance to the flag. At a subsequent meeting she was denied the opportunity to vote because she was unemployed. "I asked why I couldn't vote, and they said that they had found it in a big book uptown, that they had read it in a big law book some place that I was not eligible to vote." She and her husband protested to the president of the international, the Ethical Practices Committee of the AFL-CIO, and the NLRB. But no relief was secured. They organized a protest faction. Meanwhile, they received phone calls that threatened them and their child. Unable to get a job, the respondent filed a $150,000 damage suit against the president of the local, charging him with collusion. After the suit was filed, the president of the local was made personnel manager of the company.

In a further case, a movie projectionist who moved from one California city to another was refused admission to the local even though he had been a member of the union for twenty-five years. He, and other men who had been similarly refused, took jobs with a commercial film-processing company. This job is considered less desirable because the work is paced faster than projecting films in movie theaters. The business agent for the local approached the respondent (and several others) to see if he would be willing to give up his job temporarily so that an apprenticed son of a regular member could get some experience. The respondent realized that under the provisions of the Taft-Hartley Act, the union did not have authority to compel him to step aside. But he felt the law might be repealed. If he insisted on his legal rights now, the union might be in a position to retaliate later. He gave up his job for a brief interval, but when unable to secure another was able (with his employer's help) to get his old job back. This annoyed the union officials. However, he and other "visiting brothers" demanded full membership in the local. The day before they were to be admitted, the local admitted the apprenticed sons of regular members to give them seniority.

Later, the respondent broke a union rule and was advised by his union to plead guilty. When he did so he was astonished to find himself suspended from the union, and from his job, for six months. When his suspension was up, the union refused to refer him to jobs, telling him that he would have to acquire additional experience:

The business agent says that I can't go to work in any studio, that I would have to break in to their way of doing things, and then he could get me a job. I say, "After forty years in the business, I've got to learn the business again?" Well, I went to one studio and worked around there without pay. And after three months I say that I'm broken in, and that I'm ready for a job. He said he would call me for work. But I didn't get any calls.

Without employment, the respondent found the forty-three-dollar quarterly assessment for union dues and insurance excessive. He resented paying for insurance he did not want, and refused to tender the insurance portion of the assessment. The union declared that the total amount—and no less—would be required. Subsequently he was expelled from the union for nonpayment of dues and gave up all hope of ever returning to his trade.

The protests alluded to in the table covered a wide range of other issues. For example:

A president of one of the local lodges of the Brotherhood of Railway and Steamship Clerks protested the terms of hospitalization insurance negotiated by the brotherhood because "this comes out of our pay." He explained: "Almost the whole local was up in arms to fight this thing, but when I got an attorney to represent us, my brother and I ended up alone fighting both the union and the company." While the case was before the courts, the contract was adjusted to allow for company contributions. "Not many employees were willing to jeopardize their employment rights in a fight with the union. In our battle, they must have had forty attorneys, half from the union and half from the company, all against one man for us." When he testified before a state right-to-work committee, the general chairman said he would be expelled from the union for such action, but he regarded this as a mild threat. "If I got expelled, I would just save me my dues."

In a second case involving insurance, a respondent had established his popularity with fellow workers with his skill in representing their grievances against both the employer and their union. He was a serious student of union constitutions and membership rights. He described one occasion when the insurance representative of the grand lodge of the Brotherhood of Railroad Trainmen attended the meeting of the local to support a resolution that an assessment of twenty-five cents be made to keep up the insurance of members fighting in Korea:

I studied the constitution and knew this was illegal, for the insurance department is separated from the lodge, and must be self-sustaining. I raised this question from the union floor, and the answer I got from him, which I will never forget, was "Brother, you got a good question." That was my answer, and that was the end of it.

Although he was expelled from his union for supporting the right-to-work movement, he felt he had the support of the membership:

Even the person who signed the charges said that, if he had known what he was doing, he never would have done it. None of the men have bothered me, but a few of the local officers have said: "Wait and see. Eventually he won't be working on the railroad." I think this is wishful thinking. They take pot shots at me in their paper and refer to me as a disgruntled and unhappy employee because I didn't hold an official position in the union. The officers don't like criticism. I asked a question at another meeting and they immediately called me a jackass and said I should go to Korea and do all the yapping I wanted to.

One respondent offered an endless stream of testimony on how he had been victimized because of a personality conflict with one of the chief projectionists in his industry. His difficulties began when he gave truthful testimony involving the misbehavior of a fellow member. The accused called upon his well-placed friend to avenge the damage done by this testimony. He described a long series of discriminatory acts. These generally involved layoffs, and in one instance he alleged that a chief projectionist discharged eight men in order to effect his discharge. He described a series of protests to the international, to the NLRB, and finally, to public officials. He became involved in a letter-writing campaign, giving widespread publicity to the corruption within his union and to the abuses he was exposing. His appeal to the international was rejected; but when he threatened to talk to the press, it was agreed that the "slate would be wiped clean," and he would be assigned to a new job. But he became involved in additional disputes. He was beaten-up at work, and while in the hospital received a telephone threat against his life. His wife also received threatening phone calls. Following the assault, his employer refused to reinstate him. "I began to smell something's rotten in Denmark . . . . I didn't get my two weeks' notice, I lost my insurance, my health and welfare, my seniority, and I was put on the blacklist." His efforts to organize resistance to the union intensified, and his attacks on the union became almost hysterical. His health broke down. The NLRB ruled that the union should cease discriminating against him, but he received only intermittent employment through the union. His further appeals to the NLRB were rejected, but he continued his letter-writing campaign. His charges now widened to include not only the local but the international, and several employers.

Political rivalry within a union was an additional cause of controversy. One Teamster, following an unsuccessful bid to be reelected president of his local, continued to criticize the winning candidate. He made frequent comparisons of the benefits he had obtained for the membership with those secured by the new administration and openly opposed the president's proposal to change the union bylaws:

I rose to my feet to protest, pointing out that the membership had worked for twenty-five years to build up those by-laws. I told them we needed three meetings to make a change. I'm a good talker and I got the membership pretty excited about this. The next day the regional head came by with two muscle men and took me to his office. "You made quite a row at the meeting last night." So I replied: "I'm against what I'm against. If you don't want any answers, you shouldn't ask any questions. If you want to take away the by-laws, why don't you just steal them?" So they shifted the meetings around to other towns to get what they wanted.

He subsequently found that he was not being dispatched to jobs. The international held a hearing on the charges he filed against the local's officers; the board ruled in his favor and ordered the local to stop discriminating against him. But eight months later, he had not yet been dispatched to a job.

The variety of penalties that the critics absorbed can likewise be classified. Eight respondents contended that, once they had been identified as critics, the union ignored their grievances on the job; 9 said they had been threatened with expulsion; and 11 more had been expelled. Eleven described the organized ostracism by fellow workers, and 14 the angry abuse they were subject to at local meetings. Five contended that union pressures had discouraged employers from offering them advances or promotions; 10 said they or their families had received insulting or threatening telephone calls; 9 of these alleged that threats had been made on their lives, and 2 of these described actual attempts on their lives. Four had been assaulted, of whom 2 had required hospitalization and surgery. Six respondents said that their dispute with the union had temporarily cost them their jobs, while 25 contended that they had been permanently denied employment in their trade because of union pressures.

The legal capacity of a union to invoke economic penalties against its members is extremely limited. Under union security agreements, a request for discharge can be made only if the employee refuses to tender his regularly required initiation fees and dues. In the absence of a union security agreement, a union is barred from discriminating against any employee for nonmembership in the union. By what devices, therefore, were unions alleged to exert pressure on employees who had taken critical positions?

Several respondents, particularly those in the railroad industry, indicated how the freedom of the union to expel them from membership (while not necessarily infringing on their employment rights) could cancel their insurance investments with the union. This could be a serious penalty, especially for older workers. In one case a local of the Brotherhood of Railroad Trainmen passed a resolution, to be sent to Congress, opposing the union shop:

The motion passed, but the secretary held the letter until the next meeting when an official from the national office came and threatened to expel any member who would sign that letter. Some of these men have had insurance in the brotherhood for a long time. When they are expelled, they lose that insurance.

Another railroader testified:

In the case of these older fellows like my father-in-law, who had been forty years on the railroad, he would remain in the organization even though he didn't believe in what was going on because of the fact that, back forty years ago, he had taken out insurance policies with his organization, and he stood a chance of losing all that. Now if a man pays into one of those policies for forty years, he is getting up to the point when he is going to retire, and he surely isn't going to take a chance of losing that.

Another explained:

Once you are expelled from a local lodge, then you are expelled from your insurance and everything. Yeah, you get a small part of it. But for myself, I dropped my insurance a long time ago. I realized that by just having that threat over me, they had too much control, too much monetary control. I don't believe in a labor union becoming an insurance company because they become too interested in premiums and not enough in grievance matters. And you would be amazed at how interested they do become in insurance.

Other respondents said that if workers criticized the union, they would receive no union protection should any controversy develop with the employer. A machinist testified:

I think they were afraid. A lot of union members are afraid of their jobs. They don't just feel confident to take care of themselves. They need somebody to help them, and they're afraid to oppose because they're going to lose that help. You might say they are more afraid of the company than the union. So they're afraid that if they oppose the union, they wouldn't get the protection, that the union would hold back on them, not protect them, let things go.

A further union control device was the discretion it could exercise in the matter of seniority. A projectionist described how his union crushed any opposition:

Well, if you give them any arguments, you ain't going to stay on the job very long, I can tell you. You can go get a job, another job. And then immediately, in two or three weeks, they send somebody else, and that's it. And then we got old-timers where the son came in. We got old-timers down there that'll tell you: "God damn you, you better not bump my son, cause I'll quit my job and come down and bump you off that job, and then I'll go back and take my job." Cause they'll put a low-number man on his job so he can go back and take it away from him. Oh it's nice, unionism is nice, my friend.

In railroading, one respondent explained how "shared" seniority rights in a yard facility could be juggled to penalize rebel members:

We have certain seniority rights within a defined limit of railroading. When a train comes into a terminal, maybe men on one division have a certain amount of seniority in this terminal, yard facilities, switching facilities. And they will share two different seniority divisions in a terminal. Now the brotherhood can penalize a rebellious group in one seniority district and give more rights to the adjoining division, causing the loss of jobs for this group.

A Teamster described the manner in which the brother of the business agent "poked a hole in the seniority board," and how his protests aggravated his relations with the officers in the local. An electrician described his problems in accepting promising job opportunities outside of the geographic area represented by his local: "There is a geographical limitation to your work, and you cannot get out of it. It is strictly up to the business agent. He's a regular dictator." A projectionist pointed to the illegal application of union seniority:

I stayed and stayed on my job, but they finally got me off. They have union seniority—it's right in the contract—even though it's against the law. You can't have no union seniority. The union can have nothing to do with taking you off the job—nothing at all. They're not supposed to, but they do it. So they changed their seniority; the old boys are still number one and everybody else was just exactly like they was. They can't call it union seniority so they call it county seniority. Now you have to go before the executive board to ask for a job.

A further contention was that employers were responsive to union interests, and would cooperate with a union to establish a pretext for the critic's discharge. Or if the person were a known critic, the employer would not want to antagonize the union by offering any promotions to him. A further variation on this theme was that an employer would not knowingly hire a union critic, for fear that this might be interpreted by the union as an unfriendly gesture. An electrician explained:

I had the opportunity for the foreman's job, but then the company officials refused to let me have it. I asked how they picked the foremen, and the company told me that an official of the union always gets the job. You see, it is company policy to try to get along with the union. The foremen and the general foremen really work for two masters. The company figures it this way: "If we get along with the union heads, we can get along with the men."

A Teamster described a series of unsuccessful efforts to secure employment:

After discussing the prospects of a job with the manager, he asked if I would talk with the board of directors. This I agreed to do, and I really hit it off with them. The company had twelve trucks and seventeen men. I knew I could handle the job and the men. But then I never heard anything from them, and they finally told me: "We seem to be going down different roads . . . ." I knew then that the union had killed that job for me. I went after another job and the story was the same: "Stay away."

I worked thirty days for one employer, and the union spotted me at work. I was supposed to go to work at 1:30, but I got this call saying, "Don't come in." So I said, "What's the deal on me?" And the foreman replied, "I think you've been laid off. . . ." I had an appointment to see the manager but he never turned up for it. But I saw his car at the union office so I knew what that meant.

A member of an Iron Workers local had battled with his local, and found himself unemployed for over thirteen months:

Each time I went to the union they said they had no job for me. And I knew they wasn't about to give me no job. I went to several contractors for work and several of them said, "Look, I don't want to get involved." When they called up the union, the union was telling them I was a troublemaker. The union sure put me behind the eight ball. Why, even if you get a job through the union and the union doesn't like you, usually the foreman is a union member. He can put you on the spot easy so you get fired.

An additional form of economic coercion was found in union refusals to dispatch critics to any except unsatisfactory jobs. Here the respondents alleged that they might be dispatched to work that was known to be of very short duration. After a few day's work, they would be laid off, and their names dropped to the bottom of the hiring hall list. Another device was to dispatch the critic to a job in the distant part of town, one known to be unpopular. Many of the respondents alleged that the technical requirement that the union not discriminate against nonmembers or expelled members could easily be overcome by juggling the books.

In much of this testimony relating the devices available to the union for getting even with critics, it was stressed that foremen were often union members, and therefore served as the disciplinary arm of the union. Another projectionist explained that the chief projectionist, as a member of the union, was obligated to hire members dispatched through the union. In the film industry members are forbidden to solicit jobs on their own, under penalty of fine or expulsion. As a consequence, the member is completely dependent on the union for employment. As one respondent complained:

I cannot solicit work on my own. Nor can I get work through the union. I filed charges in court against the union, as well as with the NLRB. To compensate for my trouble I received deadly threats, blacklisting, discrimination, threats, and today I'm being unemployed, living from hand to mouth.

4

Professional Associations

Corinne Lathrop Gilb

PROFESSIONAL ASSOCIATIONS AS GOVERNMENTS

The government of professional associations, Corinne Gilb notes, reflects a number of tendencies also evident in public government: national integration, planning for the citizen, a tendency toward more bureaucratic and more oligarchic administration—and at the same time, paradoxically, a more intense spirit of democracy.

* * *

Twentieth-century professional associations are fundamentally guilds in form as well as in function. Their internal governments have taken over some of the patterns of business corporations, and because they cover wide geographic areas in an age of far-reaching communication and rapid transportation, they have imitated some aspects of the American federal system of government.[1]

Officers of professional associations are more like business corporation officers than like public administrative officials. Except for the executive secretary, they are normally elected for brief terms, either by the board of directors from among its members, as in a business corporation, or by the delegate assembly, or occasionally through mailed ballot to the members.

The boards of directors (or boards of governors or executive councils) that make detailed policy are directly comparable to the boards of business corporations, though they might also be compared to the British cabinet or even in some cases, according to Oliver Garceau,[2] to the central executive committee of Soviet Russia. An association may have two or three executive-administrative bodies: a council or board, an executive committee, and a board of trustees. The particularly powerful executive boards of national associations virtually run the organization, because the assembly of members or their representatives meets so briefly and infrequently (at most twice a year) and because delegates to the assembly are far-flung. The meetings of many boards, both state and national, are by express rule or custom not open to nonboard members of the association.

[1] Sources for this section are the general books on the national professional organizations cited for Chapter 2. Also John M. Hancock, "Report on the Organization of the American Chemical Society," *Chemical and Engineering News,* 25 (February 17, 1947), p. 442; American Library Association, *ALA Bulletin,* 55 (December 1961); constitutions and bylaws of the AMA, ABA, AIA, ADA, NSPE, NASW, and ALA (the ALA constitution is in the above-cited bulletin, p. 989 et seq.). Also state and local constitutions and bylaws for teachers, accountants, physicians, dentists, chemists, engineers, social workers, librarians, nurses, and lawyers. The author has attended national conventions of the ABA, ACA, ALA, and the National Society of Professional Engineers (NSPE), as well as numerous academic associations, and state and local meetings in California of judges, lawyers, physicians, dentists, social workers, teachers, and nurses.

[2] Oliver Garceau, *The Political Life of the American Medical Association* (Cambridge, Mass.: Harvard University Press, 1941), pp. 16, 17.

Clearly Montesquieu's doctrine of separation of powers, which had so much influence on American public government, has not significantly affected the government of American professional associations. The boards of directors operate in part like a legislative upper house, but they also function as the executive and possibly the judicial branches of the association. In these respects the governmental structure of professional associations is similar not only to corporate government but also to American colonial government, which bore many resemblances to the government of joint-stock trading companies.

The structure of professional associations is like the structure of American public government in that, for example, the professional associations have written constitutions, though only limited judicial review. They have representative government, universal suffrage for all members, secret ballot, parliamentary procedures. Local units elect representatives to a delegated legislature at the state level, and the state in some fashion sends delegates to a national legislature. Their legislatures, which are often larger than American public legislatures but meet for briefer durations, resemble public legislatures in some of their forms and procedures. There are similar problems in determining the basis and manner of apportionment of representation; many of the private legislatures have speakers and standing and interim committees like those of public legislatures; state delegates to the national private legislatures caucus as state delegations do in the federal House of Representatives; and "program" comes down from above to private legislatures, as it does from the executive branch to public legislatures.

In the large national associations, such as the National Education Association [NEA], the American Bar Association [ABA], and the American Medical Association [AMA], the delegate assembly usually elects the president, for he is the public representative in national affairs for the whole, presumably nationally united, profession. The president of the association not only has presiding and administrative duties but also is spokesman for the profession before public legislatures and the public at large. Though much power is formally vested in the president, the office is regarded as honorary and presidents are expected to stay within established patterns. Association presidents, like mayors in cities operating under a council and professional-manager plan, are primarily for ceremonial purposes.

Change and Paradox

The internal development of many American professional associations in the twentieth century parallels similar developments in American public government in three major ways.

1. *Decentralization and centralization. There have been gradually more regulatory and service activities at all geographic levels, more independent activity on the part of units at all levels, and at the same time more national integration.* In short, more government at the national level has not necessarily meant less local government, but rather more government at all levels.

Like many other phenomena in twentieth-century America, professional associations have been undergoing processes of both magnification and miniaturization; that is, the whole has got bigger while the parts have become more clearly articulated, differentiated, and integrated into the whole. The number of associations at the local and state levels has increased, and many of them are vigorous and opinionated vis-à-vis the national association. On the other hand, methods of integrating the associations at various levels have become more effective, and broad forces are at work that tend to increase the importance of national unity and of the national associations.

Seen from the national perspective, the associations tend to fall into three categories: those that are unitary, whose membership is directly in the national association and whose local chapters are subsidiary units of the national group; those in which local, state, and national associations are tied together in various degrees and modes of federation; and those in which the various geographic units go their separate ways. Whichever way they begin, associations tend to gravitate to the federative mode of organization.

Very often unitary organizations do not have strong governing powers over their own members. They rely on persuasion and influence to accomplish their goals and are not, in any complete sense, private governments. Professions whose local, state, and national associations are partially independent of one another tend to have more disciplinary power over their members than do those whose local chapters are subsidiary units of a national association.

The long-range tendency, both in organizations that begin as unitary and in those that begin in a disjointed fashion, is toward the pattern the general medical associations now follow, an integrated organization with each level having its own major function. This form of organization appears to be the most effective for control over membership. Physicians in all but a few states join the American Medical Association and their state medical association by being admitted first to a county medical society. Until AMA dues were made separate in 1950, joining a local component automatically meant membership in the AMA.[3] The governing structure of these organizations is pyramidal: The local units elect delegates to the state association's house of delegates, which elects delegates to the national house. The local units are chartered by the state associations, and the constitutions at each level must not conflict with the constitution of the level above. The state and local associations work with and through their national association in matters of professional education, public education, and federal legislation. At best, national integration is still only partial, though it is increasing, and one of the strongest deterrents to complete integration is the continuing decentralization in American public government.

Decision-making in professional associations is divided geographically somewhat as it is in American public government, but for many associations decisions made at the national level apply only to the internal affairs and public program of the national association or to the profession's federal legislative program. State associations, through their own representative bodies, make most of their own decisions. Most of the rules and policies that directly affect members are enacted at the state level.

Normally state and local units determine the procedure for selecting their

[3] David R. Hyde and Payson Wolff, "The American Medical Association: Power, Purpose, and Politics in Organized Medicine," *Yale Law Journal* 63 (May 1954), p. 938.

delegates. Persons selected customarily have been major leaders within the state and local associations; the national assembly is an assemblage of state and local leaders. Men come to the presidency of national associations typically through a long chain of organizational service, local, state, and national.

Two classic problems like those arising under the United States Constitution —the problem of who shall interpret jurisdictional issues, and then enforce a decision, between associations at different geographic levels, and the problem of whether the national body has direct jurisdiction over individuals or must work only indirectly through state and local units—have not been resolved in professional associations in the same manner as they have in American public government. There is no clear-cut federalism, with its brilliant conception of dual jurisdiction, in professional associations. The concept of judicial review has been only imperfectly developed.

The American Medical Association has the most well-articulated and integrated judicial system, but—as in American public government—the issue of states' rights constantly looms. One problem has been an absence of effective sanctions against recalcitrant units. Expulsion is always possible, but as Garceau has said, "A voluntary association cannot afford to contribute too lavishly to its own dismemberment."[4] Excommunication is sometimes used when the heretic was going anyway!

Like the American federal government, the national professional associations have resorted to the carrot (more than the stick), the national conference, the deploying of contact men, and propaganda as techniques for bringing about more uniformity and conformity among their component units.

Whatever the pulls in the opposite direction, there has been a gradual tendency, as in American public government, toward more national uniformity and centralization of decision-making. The national associations have promoted uniformity from the beginning; their efforts have been more successful partially because of improved communication, undoubtedly also because of changed mobility patterns among their members. For some salaried professionals who are in short supply (e.g., nurses, teachers, engineers), movement about the country is easy and common. Uniformity in state practices both eases mobility and results from it. Some fee-basis professionals—architects and engineers, lawyers, accountants—of high rank within their profession regularly offer their services on a national or even an international basis while maintaining an office or offices in fixed locations. They, too, find uniformity an advantage. Centralization of decision-making has also come about because of increased activities by the American federal government in areas affecting the professions. In these respects professional associations are like trade unions, in which centralization and departure from local autonomy have been inevitable by-products of the nationalization or regionalization of business.

Centralization has important internal political implications for professional associations, for, as in American public government, the broader the geographic jurisdiction of the governing body, the higher the educational and occupational prestige level of the governors and the greater their lifelong commitment to organizational politics. Centralization means that more and more decisions will be made by urbanites occupying positions of authority within the professions;

[4]Garceau, op. cit., pp. 116-17.

by specialists within the profession rather than generalists; and by people remote from the day-to-day problems of the average practitioner. And this leads to the second point about internal development.

2. *Democracy, bureaucracy, and oligarchy. The problems are becoming more technical, complex, and interconnected, requiring more expertise on the part of policy-makers; more bureaucratization of staff means that many important decisions are made by a few administrators at the top; yet there is also more internal democracy—more universal suffrage, higher participation, more communication between leaders and members.*

Most professional associations include higher percentages of the profession as members than formerly. In 1912 the AMA represented only 50.6 percent of all physicians in the United States; the percentage rose to 65.1 in 1929, declined again to 60.8 in the depression year of 1935, and increased again to 66.8 by 1940. In 1957 it was estimated that 90 percent of all private practitioners in the country belonged to the AMA. The ABA's membership rose from a total of only 3.2 percent of the lawyers in the United States in 1910, to 9.2 percent in 1920, to an estimated 46.2 percent in 1960.

The same trends have been apparent in state associations. In 1907 only 14.7 percent of the teachers in the United States were members of state teacher associations; by 1916, 34.1 percent; and by January 1923 membership had jumped to 61.5 percent. Associations in southern states showed the least increase in membership.[5]

For most professional associations, although some have more rigorous admittance standards than others, the rise in the percentage of the total profession represented has been due in part to a deliberate change in policy from more to less exclusiveness. During the ABA's first quarter century, five years had to elapse after a lawyer's admission to the bar before he could be a member of the ABA. This was then changed to three years; and in 1928 any lawyer in good standing was eligible for membership, though a member could still be excluded by negative votes from four members of the association's board of governors. Not until 1912 did the ABA aggressively attempt to increase its membership; the NEA did not seek a broader membership base until 1917.[6]

Voluntary nonmembers often include the very young and the very old; the very poor, men working on salary (e.g., in the armed services, for various branches of government, for industry, teaching in professional schools), where the profession consists primarily of fee-basis practitioners; people working in rural areas; and people who are in a marked minority by reason of race, religion, or sex.

But there were many involuntary nonmembers. In the early years the medical societies excluded men who subscribed to unorthodox methods of practice. Medical societies, bar associations, and even some teacher associations did not accept women; eventually all let down the bars. And race has long been

[5] American Bar Association House of Delegates, Midyear *Proceedings* (1961), p. 184 .... Granrud, p. 11.

[6] Edson R. Sunderland, *History of the American Bar Association and Its Work* (Boston, 1953), p. 96. See also Martin, *Building a Teaching Profession, 1857-1957* (Middletown, N.Y.: The Whitlock Press, 1957). Membership may still be denied in ABA on the basis of four negative votes on the board of governors (*ABA Journal,* 48 [February 1962], p. 101).

a basis for exclusion, though in recent years the professional associations have begun to desegregate.

The American Medical Association has refused to accredit its Negro counterpart as a constituent society, but the national teachers' and nurses' associations have taken steps to integrate Negroes more thoroughly into the association. In 1947 a joint committee of the National Education Association and the (Negro) American Teachers Association recommended that Negroes be fully integrated into the NEA; in 1948 the NEA welcomed Negro delegates from three states that also sent white delegates. The American Nurses Association [ANA] at its convention in 1946 voted unanimously to recommend to state associations that they integrate as soon as possible. Tennessee, the first to comply, was followed shortly by sixteen other states. The ANA made special provisions for direct membership of Negro nurses still barred from their state associations. By 1962 all the nurses' state associations were integrated.

At the state level racial exclusion is still practiced, even in states outside the South. As late as 1953 a bill was introduced in the California state legislature, but did not pass, to attempt to require the State Bar board of governors to adopt a rule prohibiting the recognition of any bar association that denied membership on the basis of race, creed, color, or national ancestry. The majority of the county medical societies in the South still exclude Negro doctors.[7]

In the Cold War years after World War II most associations also excluded persons who advocated the overthrow of the government by force. In 1941 the American Federation of Teachers reported it had uprooted the communists in its ranks. In 1949 the NEA passed a resolution, with only 5 out of 3,000 voting no and with almost no debate, barring communists from membership.[8]

Medical associations have also excluded or attempted to exclude applicants who participated in closed-panel prepayment plans, but the courts have declared that it is unlawful to deny membership on this basis.[9] But except for political subversives, the tendency has been more and more to admit categories of persons formerly excluded. Indeed, the trend of public law appears to be the same for professional associations as for trade unions: to prohibit arbitrary exclusion or possibly any exclusion at all and—in the case of the state bars—even to uphold compulsory membership. If membership were the only criterion, it could be said that now, far more than ever before, the professional associations speak for the great preponderance of their profession.

As a result of membership changes, persons of middling rank in the profession have more opportunity to hold leadership posts. At one time the National Education Association had as presidents such men as the presidents of Harvard,

[7]Hyde and Wolff, op. cit., p. 941; Garceau, op. cit., p. 105; Sherwood Dean Fox, "Voluntary Associations and Social Structure" (unpublished dissertation, Harvard University, December 1952), pp. 155-73. See AB 1475, introduced in the California legislature in 1953.

[8]*The Washington Teamster* (October 24, 1941), p. 6, col. 5; Fox, op. cit., p. 203.

[9]Complete Service Bureau *v.* San Diego Medical Society, 272 P2d 497 (1954); Group Health Cooperative *v.* King County Medical Society, 237 P2d 737 (1951); AMA *v.* U.S., 317 U.S. 519 (1943); U.S. *v.* Oregon State Medical Society, 343 U.S. 326 (1952). However, see Medical Society of Mobile County *v.* Walker (Alabama, 1949) 16 S2d 321, 324. Of interest is Lane Lancaster, "The Legal Status of 'Private' Organizations Exercising Governmental Powers," *Southwestern Social Science Quarterly,* 15 (1935), 325-36.

Columbia, and Stanford. During its first sixty years, administrators and professors overwhelmingly dominated the NEA, partially because offices tended to go to positions rather than to individuals—positions of authority and held by men. As a result of the revolt in 1910, a woman became president, but she was a superintendent, not a teacher. The first classroom-teacher president was chosen in 1928, but not until after administrator-versus-teacher pressures had been building up for a long time. Since then presidents more frequently have been classroom teachers. The same is true in state associations. In 1918, 72 percent of the California Teachers Association's Council were administrators; by 1927, 68 percent; by 1942, 50 percent; and by 1962, only 22 percent.[10]

The new democratic spirit in education associations reflects not only a closing of the formerly wide gap in education and quality between the leaders and the run-of-the-mill members of the profession, and an increase in the percentage of the classroom teachers who belong, but also a change in philosophy. In the late nineteenth century councils of notables or elders governed national and state education associations. The NEA organized in 1880 a fifty-one-member council consisting of prominent educators and some college presidents. It was to be an elite group, with somewhat ambiguous constitutional authority, that would pass on its wisdom to those less wise. The oracular nature of the council was gradually diminished by additions to its size—until a limit of 200 was established in 1940—so that by the mid-1920s it no longer had its former distinctive quality, and in 1947 it was discarded altogether. The new empiricism in education and learning was partially responsible for its downfall; social science research methods replaced the dogma of the notables.[11]

Although boards of directors, particularly of national professional associations in which the membership is scattered and remote, exercise a high degree of discretion and power, historically the trend has been to try to make boards more democratic through shorter terms, greater limitation of the number of terms, and increases in the size of the board. Other tests of democracy yield mixed evidence. Although most associations appear to be dominated by "ruling cliques," there is enough turnover in office to permit the would-be office holder access. Another test of democracy is whether there is factionalism within the organization and whether real contests for office occur. The authors of *The Worker Views His Union* maintain that leaders and active members of trade unions regard factionalism as necessary for local democracy. Factions, they say, keep close watch on one another, permit the development of rival centers of power, keep members informed on issues, add interest to meetings and elections, help develop leadership ability independent of the administration, give members an opportunity to choose between competing programs and candidates, increase

[10] See Edgar B. Wesley, *NEA: The First Hundred Years* (New York: Harper & Row, Publishers, Inc., 1957), p. 326, on the election of the NEA's first woman president . . . . R. C. Gillingham, "The California Teachers Association" (unpublished diss., University of Southern California, 1949), pp. 82, 101, 238. In 1947, 67 percent of the CTA's State Council were administrators; 33 percent were teachers. In 1958 the CTA elected its first woman president, but her husband was a county superintendent (*CTA Journal,* 54 [May 1958], 7).

[11] Wesley, op. cit., Ch. 23; see also Roy W. Cloud, "The History of CTA," *Sierra Educational News,* 29 (October 1943), 9.

the importance of membership meetings as decision-making bodies, make officers discreet in their actions, and hold them accountable.[12]

Some professional associations practice factionalism privately and deplore it officially. Others encourage contests for office. Election of the first woman president in the National Education Association followed a year-long campaign of letter writing and vote soliciting by a militant women's group, who nominated their candidate from the floor in opposition to the nominating committee's choice—and won. More recently it has not been unknown for an election contest in the NEA to be waged for a year.[13]

The American Medical Association passed a resolution in 1902 that soliciting votes for office was not in keeping with the dignity of the medical profession and would be considered a disqualification for office. State associations may also forbid electioneering. However, it is not unusual for several candidates to run for president-elect and for elections to be preceded by considerable behind-the-scenes maneuvering. This does not necessarily mean that candidates represent different viewpoints. It is customary for men who rise to office in the AMA to have for years worked their way up gradually from county society office. Basic differences between opposing candidates are unlikely; elections for delegates to the AMA House are rarely contested. In Alabama the president has appointed the delegates. Only four out of twenty-four state societies, in the early 1950s, reported competition for AMA delegates' posts. The Kansas medical association is unusual in that it requires two nominees for each position.[14]

The AMA, strongly desirous of maintaining a united front to the public, deplores open disagreement. *The Journal of the American Medical Association* rarely prints opposing views; nor are most state journals controversial, the *New England Journal of Medicine* being a notable exception.[15]

Organized opposition to incumbent policy has developed in medical associations in California and New York, but overthrow of established leadership is rare.[16] Medical associations usually manage to maintain a united front, which may not mean that dissent is quelled, but rather that the majority of physicians agree with or are willing to go along with the stands their associations take. Surveys and polls of physicians indicate that this latter interpretation is correct. Even when dissident groups within the national AMA form over public policy issues, they do not attempt to capture the association's governmental machinery.[17]

Free debate is more commonplace and more accepted in bar association circles, probably because lawyers are accustomed to opposing one another

[12] Siedman et al., *The Worker Views His Union,* op. cit., p. 209.

[13] Wesley, op. cit., pp. 324-7.

[14] Hyde and Wolff, op. cit., p. 945. See Garceau, op. cit., p. 80, on solicitation of votes. On p. 82 he states that there are often four names for president, but other offices may go uncontested.

[15] Hyde and Wolff, op. cit., p. 946.

[16] *Encyclopedia of Associations,* Vol. 1, p. 945; David Truman, *The Governmental Process* (New York: Alfred A. Knopf, Inc., 1951), p. 208.

[17] Committee of Physicians, Garceau, pp. 147-51. On going along with the AMA, see Hyde and Wolff, op. cit., p. 947, and Garceau, op. cit., pp. 133-7. See also Oliver Garceau, "Organized Medicine Enforces Its 'Party Line,'" *The Public Opinion Quarterly,* 4 (September 1940), 408-28 . . . .

in their daily work and have well-established traditions permitting underlying fellowship and unity despite strong advocacy of opposing views. Controversy is their style of life.

With the possible exception of the medical associations, the absence of dissent appears to result from membership apathy as much as or more than from any effort to quell dissidence. Until 1936 only about 2000 to 3000 attorneys attended the annual ABA convention, less than 2 percent of American lawyers. An American Medical Association survey indicated that 60 out of the 64 societies with more than 300 members reported attendance of under 50 percent; 48 of 581 with fewer than 100 members reported less than 50 percent; whereas 111 of the smaller societies reported 90- to 100-percent attendance. The New York Medical Society considered 25-percent attendance at business meetings "good."[18]

Voting participation, particularly for nurses' associations, is often low, even when voting is by mail. In fact, some associations report that mail ballots result in cut-and-dried elections or give an edge to men who have been well publicized.[19] Since members are given the opportunity to vote and are permitted or even urged to put themselves forward for office, their indifference to these opportunities might imply a form of consent. If they disagree with the policies of the leaders, often they apparently do not disagree strongly enough to make their dissent known and felt. In any case, democracy in many associations—as measured by membership, participation, voting, and office holding—has increased over the past several decades.

On the other hand, there is evidence of oligarchy and bureaucracy: long tenure in the more powerful positions; the path to high office at the national level normally through long service in offices at levels below; and positions of power tending to be held by persons of high (but not the highest) prestige and authority within the profession. Further, permanent staff members play an increasingly important role in making or guiding decisions.

Recent studies of the major associations for teachers and the leading fee-basis professions show that despite the democratization that has occurred, the leaders are still people who occupy positions of relatively high prestige and authority within the profession (administrators and professors), men rather than women except where women outnumber the men in overwhelming numbers, Caucasians rather than non-Caucasians, urban rather than rural, middle-aged rather than young men, persons who have some control over their own time (which means men from large law firms with big clients, surgeons, education administrators, and supervisors). They make an avocational career out of association politics, serving in offices at every level and throughout their lives. Often they have ample opportunity to communicate with one another outside the professional association because they belong to the same large law firm or practice in the same hospitals, because they frequent the same clubs or socialize (within a profession, not between professions) in the same places. Especially at the higher levels they have worn and do wear several hats—within the professional association at various geographic levels, by teaching as well as practicing

[18] Hyde and Wolff, op. cit., p. 944 . . . .

[19] *California State Nurses Association Bulletin . . . CSNA Bulletin,* 52 (January 1956), 8 . . . .

or perhaps administering a professional school, by serving on public boards and advisory committees, and by holding office in other specialist professional associations or on the boards of special foundations. The higher the level of office, the more the professional schools from which the office holders have originated are the schools of high prestige.

In two careful statistical studies of leaders in education organizations—one for the United States as a whole and one for the Inland Empire region of the Northwest—two Stanford masters' candidates have shown that for the United States as a whole, "the vast majority of educators in elementary schools have little or no voice in their professional associations."[20] Whereas most of the members have been women working in rural communities and teaching at the elementary level, and not in administrative capacities, teacher organizations have been controlled mainly by men from cities with populations over 25,000, teaching at the high-school level, and in administrative capacities. The broader the geographic jurisdiction of the association, the more this tendency is revealed. Only in large urban associations have women classroom teachers had reasonably proportionate representation in leadership positions.

Garceau's studies of leadership posts in the AMA and selected state medical societies indicated a comparable pattern. He found that they were dominated by urban specialists who had well-established practices and could leave their patients to assistants or partners while they did medical-society work, or who had independent incomes or practices where the unit return was exceptionally high. He also noted a higher preponderance of professors than their proportion in the profession would warrant. The longer the tenure, the higher the proportion of professors and urban specialists; the more powerful and important the post, the higher the percentage of these men.[21] A more recent study has found that in 1949 there were 72,500 general practitioners, 55,000 specialists, and 23,000 in mixed categories; yet 90 percent of the AMA officers were usually specialists. [A]ll but one of the members of the 1954 board of trustees were specialists, and all presidents, vice presidents, and speakers since 1947. About half of all doctors in private practice in 1957 were family physicians, but only 35 members of the 192-member House of Delegates of the AMA were family doctors.[22] A study of the Massachusetts and Colorado houses showed the same balance in favor of urban areas and the same difference between long- and short-term men.[23]

There have been no such thorough studies of other professions, but a rough tabulation of members of the board of governors, officers, and committee chairmen of the California State Bar for the 1950s indicates a high proportion from two or three law firms in Los Angeles and five or six in San Francisco—large law firms with a high proportion of corporate clients. Although nurse administrators and professors constitute only a small percentage of all nurses, they hold most of the officer posts in nurses' associations. Dentists, too, tend to select specialists

[20] Wayne T. Toivanen, "The Occupational Composition of the Officers of Teachers Organizations in the Inland-Empire-States Region" (unpubl. thesis, Stanford Univ., 1942), pp. 112, 113, 169, 181-5; John Mongan, "The Professional Composition of the Controlling Bodies of Teachers Organizations" (unpubl. thesis, Stanford Univ., 1941), pp. 10, 68, 86, 93-94 . . . .

[21] Garceau, op. cit., pp. 54-5.

[22] Hyde and Wolff, op. cit., p. 947.

[23] Garceau, op. cit., pp. 52, 56-7.

as state and local leaders, although in 1961 the ADA [American Dental Association] house had only 47 specialists, including 22 orthodontists, out of 416 members.

Since the number of specialists has been rising in proportion to general practitioners among physicians, dentists, and lawyers, it can be expected that their professional associations will have more rather than fewer specialists as leaders. As the association gets larger and its affairs become more complex, it requires more leaders who can spare the time. The president of the California State Bar reported in 1961 that it took the members of the board of governors about 6,000 man hours a year to serve; there were forty actual meeting days plus all the time required for preparation.

As the association grows older, larger, and wealthier—as most of the large ones have—it hires more and more staff people. For a long time professional associations resisted hiring professional public relations men and legislative advocates on the grounds that it was "unprofessional" or "undignified." Then, beginning tentatively in the 1930s and capitulating rapidly in the 1940s and 1950s, they did hire such men, as well as special legal counsel and research directors. In the 1950s some of them were also adding actuaries for their many insurance problems and special directors for radio and TV.

Staff members often wield considerable, though sometimes inconspicuous, power, and staffs are increasingly professionalized and bureaucratized. Many staff members do not belong to the profession they serve and, in fact, are in a specialist profession of their own or the National Association of Association Executives. As staffs grow in size and permanency they are given pensions and other benefits, resulting in a low turnover in the higher offices. If they move, it is apt to be from the professional association in one state to the association in another state. Ruler of the staff roost is a salaried executive secretary, whose job is not an easy one. During 1953 the executive secretary of the California Teachers Association attended 141 conferences, conventions, and committee meetings; made 72 speeches, necessitating more than 125,000 miles of travel and over 100 nights away from home; and directed the operations of headquarters. Under the executive secretary may be a deputy and several assistants, each in charge of a major aspect of the association's activities.

The power of executive secretaries varies, and this is undoubtedly due not simply to individual personalities but to differences in the nature of people drawn to a particular profession. The executive secretaries of bar associations tend to have less power than their counterparts in medical and teacher associations. In most associations, however, the executive secretary not only is chief administrator over a corps of subordinates but also serves as public relations man and legislative advocate for the association. He is the pivot wheel in the professional association and probably its most powerful individual, though nominally he takes his directions from other people. He is the expert among amateurs, for he usually holds his post a number of years, whereas association officers and board members come and go.

For years the American Medical Association was said to be the lengthened shadow of the editor of its journal, who was called the "czar of the medical world . . . the most dynamic, the most vocal, the most capable in terms of myth-making and business management."[24] The executive secretary of a state teacher

[24] Ibid., p. 86 . . . .

association not only greatly influences everything that goes on within the association but also may be one of the greatest single influences upon public education in the state.

As problems become more technical and complex the amateur and transitory officers of associations more than ever must put their faith in staff men to map out programs and make the daily decisions. Staff men are to the professional associations what the civil service is to public government.

Although an egalitarian democracy is lacking within professional associations, there is no reason to presume that professional associations are less democratic than American public government, where voter turnout in local elections may also be low, where turnover in Congress is markedly below turnover in the houses of some professional associations, where a bureaucratized civil service has replaced the spoils system, where more and more decisions are made at the top by those in command of the necessary technical information, where not only is there more government at all levels but also the national government plays an increasingly important role, and where the median education and social rank of top national decision-makers are markedly above the median for voters at large. As in professional associations, in public governments there has been some increased democratization: suffrage has gradually been extended to those without property, to Negroes, and to women; political parties have been transformed from private to public associations; and open primaries augment the convention system of selecting candidates.

With the advent of an interdependent division of labor, with the maturation of an economic organism whose frame of reference is increasingly national rather than local, there is greater articulation of the parts at the same time that they are more integrated into the whole—in the professional associations and in public government. Since it is a highly complex, rational system, the comprehension and consent of the participants are necessary if it is to function well. What is true of the economic system is also true of the political system, which interacts with it. And so we have the seeming paradoxes of centralization and decentralization, bureaucratic oligarchy and democracy.

3. *Individualism and community. There is strong ideological stress on individual freedom, and yet at the same time more and more is done for the welfare of the citizen-member, more socialization of risk among members has developed, and more emphasis has been put on the member's duty to the association—the corporation "family" of the community.*

Since the paradoxes in the development of professional associations also appear in American public government and in other private organizations, it is reasonable to conclude that none of the traits is accidental, but rather that each is an integral part of the total development of the American socioeconomic-political system. The seemingly contradictory traits are different facets of a whole, necessary to one another.

The Vertical Integration of Government

The degree to which a profession is interested in some kind of formal regulation of itself outside of the institutions of work is a product of its power in the private socioeconomic sphere: The more vulnerable its position, the more it wants outside regulation. Professions vary greatly in the amount of regulation they seek.

What do the associations use public government for?

It should be remembered that for most professionals public government is not simply an abstract sovereign or a detached public agency to which they relate as an ordinary citizen might relate. When public government is their employer, as it often is, relations are comparable to those of a private employer and employee. When public government is their client, as it is sometimes for architects, engineers, and accountants, the relationship is comparable to that with a private client. Public government subsidizes directly or indirectly the work of many professions. Lawyers and accountants are intermediaries between private citizens and public government. Where the profession neither serves the general public directly nor has a direct relationship to public government in its everyday work, but is instead employed by private organizations—such as independent or quasi-independent colleges and universities, large engineering corporations, and large research institutes, even if the financing comes from government—then that profession does not often turn to public government for aid in solving its problems. The most essential relationship of these professions is with the private employer, and to define itself, its work, and its rights vis-à-vis that employer, the profession relies on a national association, stressing the "mystery" of the profession's skills and knowledge, or it takes the course of unionization. The organized professions or segments of professions that serve the public or have an everyday work relationship with public government tend to depend heavily on government—primarily state government—to provide them with recognition, tools, and sanctions so that they can exercise control over the circumstances of their work. When they turn to public government, for most of them "control" and "work" are the key words. Although bar associations have broad legislative programs and some medical societies have tried to repeal the federal income tax, seldom (for some, never) are professional associations officially concerned with governmental actions on issues not related to their work or to work circumstances.

When professions seek governmental help, they do so with the following aims in mind: (1) to control preparation, entry, and practice; (2) to maximize favorable public opinion and so obtain guarantees of freedom on the job; (3) to rationalize work; (4) to maximize economic returns; and (5) to facilitate their work.

1. They want help in gaining control over preparation for and entry into their vocation, as well as control over those who are in the profession, when they do not have sufficient control over the job market to gain these ends by private means. Usually this is the case when they work for many dispersed employers or for individuals on a fee basis.

If a profession gains control over the qualifications, preparation, and examination of all those who enter the profession, it has taken the first major step toward more comprehensive control over its own work. Unless it can gain a private monopoly on the job market, which is difficult indeed when preparation for the profession is no longer solely by apprenticeship, the only way to control entry into its ranks is to borrow the coercive power of an organization that embraces the whole community—namely, the state. The professions do not want to, and in fact do not, stand in relation to the state as governed to those who govern. Rather, they go to the state for a seal of approval, for public recognition of their identity and merit.

Where they feel that their status is sufficiently high in the public eye, in relation to employers and in relation to competitive professions, they ask the state to delegate to them a good deal of self-governing power. To the degree that they feel insecure in their private position vis-à-vis the public, employers, or competitors, they are content to be delegated less power and have more regulation done by and in the name of state agencies, providing they are strong enough to get favorable regulatory laws in the first place. They prefer to have the state as a go-between where they are particularly vulnerable to attack, but they seldom give up the idea of self-government. Consequently there is a close tie between the state board or agency and those who are supposedly regulated. The associations seek from public government tools to help them organize more effectively; for example, statutory authorization of payroll deductions for teacher associations or recognition of the right of publicly employed professionals to form unions for collective bargaining. It is a question of balancing factors, counter-balancing the forces impinging upon them, using the state as a buffer, borrowing its power and dignity, to create as large a sphere of self-government as possible.

Statutory delegation to professional associations of the power to set and enforce rules of behavior, with the backing of the public law, constitutes the apogee of professional status. With their tenure rights and their rights to testify in cases of dismissal, teachers demonstrate that a measure of autonomy and self-government is possible even for vocations employed entirely by public government. Teachers and lawyers provide interesting examples of the fusion of private and public authority. Groups having such self-governing rights and freedoms protected by law have parallels in the medieval situation. The Anglo-American jury system is based on the principle that a man should be judged by his peers. In the stratified feudal social system this meant judgment by his equals, who were also familiar with the circumstances of the case. The state bars' disciplinary system, one that teacher associations seek to establish, harks back to ancient ways, and other professions would willingly follow suit.

2. All of the professions want some measure of status—that is, prestige in the eyes of the public—and some measure of freedom on the job, and they believe that the two go together. They think maximizing favorable public opinion entails both controlling the nonconformists within the profession, who might jeopardize the reputation of the whole, and creating as large a sphere of autonomy and freedom for professional practice as society will allow. They strive for a balance between freedom and conformity, using the latter to gain the former. Consequently they seek governmental statutes and regulations that will guarantee their freedom or help neutralize public pressure that threatens to encroach on their freedom. Publicly enforced definitions of their freedom are, of course, more reliable than mere private claims. Public statutory declarations of conformity to community norms are more convincing and conspicuous than private declarations.

Teachers want a share in decision-making in the school systems, and they want freedom in the classroom. Since administrators, parents, and the general public cannot be relied upon to grant this kind of freedom, teachers welcome state laws that define their rights. The teachers' union, which represents those teachers who feel the most constrained, places heavy stress on civil liberties of all kinds and seeks laws prohibiting discrimination on the basis of race, age, and sex.

Each of the professions wants its authority to be accepted and respected in its own sphere. To succeed, it has to reassure the public that it will not violate the fundamental standards of the community. The form this reassurance takes is writing into law provisions that persons who have been convicted of crimes involving moral turpitude relating to practice of the profession will not be admitted to practice or retain the right to practice. In other areas of special tension between the profession and the public, individual clients, or patients, a statutory law may clarify the situation. As long as public pressure for book censorship exists, librarians want state laws that will keep the local censors at bay but will also spell out censorship rules so that the librarian is not in too vulnerable a position.

A profession may also want from public government commemorative postage stamps and ceremonial weeks. Sometimes even a special public agency, bureau, or department, possibly with a cabinet post directly pertaining to the profession, is sought not only because it provides access and service but also because it symbolizes the profession's "arrival," legitimacy, and importance. It then wants as much control as possible over the agency's decisions; in this way it can control its own fate in the name of the community at large.

3. The professions employed by government want to rationalize the work process—make work uniform and predictable—and mitigate the more conspicuous instances of personal influence or chance that affect professional advancement. They are in the process of defining rights and obligations in terms of vocational status. Their efforts in this direction are only partial and sometimes not articulate, but discernible nonetheless. Uniformity aids in controlling the profession; on the other hand, control is used to achieve more uniformity. Even though the group stresses individualism vis-à-vis outsiders, conformity is sought within the group. In this way the professional has a buffer between himself and those who might otherwise exercise arbitrary jurisdiction over him.

Teachers, particularly, resort to state law—to regulate class loads and hours of work, to achieve a more uniform standard. The teachers' union has a strong leveling bent; it seeks to equalize salaries so that there is less differential between old and young. All teachers are interested in protecting themselves against arbitrary lay whim, and they rely on state tenure laws. As a result of their lobbying, New Jersey passed the first statewide tenure law in 1909; by 1957 thirty-three states had tenure laws, some not yet statewide in application. Many state colleges and universities provide tenure for teachers. Civil service reform has similar aims, but does not stress peer-group determination of rights and obligations. The independent fee-basis professions lean in this direction when they feel they have more freedom to gain than to lose by this approach. They also want control over the circumstances surrounding their work. Unlike the trade unions of skilled craft workers, the professional associations turn to statutes and administrative rules, rather than private contract, either because the employer is government or because employers are too dispersed for the purpose of bargaining.

Since most professionals other than teachers are privately employed, the issue of tenure has been irrelevant or has not been a state matter. However, since the number of professionals employed by government is constantly increasing, the issue may become significant in the future; other professions may look to the teachers as a precedent.

4. The professions want to maximize their economic returns. If public government is employer, client, or subsidizer, the profession may seek larger appropriations to finance the projects in which members of the profession are employed. This is not always true. The incomes of lawyers and tax accountants are deeply affected by the extent of governmental activity, since much of the profession's work is to aid clients in their relationships to public government, and yet both groups often espouse a laissez faire ideology. A few professions want both floors and, to some extent, ceilings on professional incomes in order to permit control and to safeguard against public discontent. They may turn to public government if the need seems urgent and if their private bargaining power or control over pricing of services is manifestly inadequate. Similarly, professions have sometimes turned to public government to establish minimum salaries or fees and have also sought governmental aid in matters of retirement and, for teachers, sick leave.

Public law profoundly influences the economics of demand for professional work and the salaries paid. Since teaching jobs depend on school financing, this has been a central concern of the National Education Association and state teacher associations.

5. Finally, the professions seek to use the tools and resources of public government to carry out their professional work. Despite what cynics may believe, the motivations of the professions are not entirely narrowly self-interested ones. All of the professions evince genuine interest in the end purpose of their work; and when public government plays a role affecting that end purpose, they take an interest in that government action.

Many professions are forced to be concerned with public government because it is through public government that other groups seek to alter the nature or terms of professional work. If a profession does seek regulation, in order to place a protective buffer zone of peer-group standards between the individual professional and the layman, then it generally finds that the internal sanctions of the professional association are not enough and that some kind of reinforcement from public government is necessary. In order to achieve that reinforcement, the association has to integrate its internal structure more closely and keep its members more cohesive—in short, it has to regulate in order to get regulation. And so the reciprocal relationship between private government and public government becomes ever more reciprocal. The more regulation there is at either level, the more there is at the other level, and the structure of government in both cases is affected accordingly.

Since professional associations need the aid of public government, many of them have at some point fallen necessarily into the classification "pressure group"; but they have not been ephemeral pressure groups, and the phrase is not an accurate description of their present relationship to public government. They have evolved slowly, some of them for more than a century, as part of the maturing of the industrial revolution. Although they have been throughout this time in the process of realizing an idea (in the Hegelian sense), of developing their basic nature, which was present or latent all along, they have changed over the years. They have grown large, stable, organizationally skillful. Their ties with other segments of the community have become deeply rooted. Professional associations are now regarded as part of the institutional framework of the socio-economic-political system. To sustain and advance their position in relation to the ordering of work and authority in the whole socioeconomic system, they have relied increasingly on public government. A secure position, once achieved, has in turn contributed immeasurably to their access to public government. Whereas once the older associations were the sounding boards of public officials, and later pressure groups clamoring in the lobbies, they have become so institutionalized as law-proposing mechanisms in their own fields that for most work issues they are no longer pressure groups but constitute instead preliminary arenas of public lawmaking.

*   *   *   *   *   *   *   *   *   *

The Continuum of Government

What, then, is the relationship of professional associations to the structure of public government?

1. *Private governments.* To some extent some professional associations are autonomous private governments. Yet it is surprising how little purely internal control the professional associations exert over their members, as distinguished from control via, or in collaboration with, public government; even the lawyers who govern themselves via state bars do so in the name of the state.

Members of the associations, of course, vote to install or accept internal services from the association or to embark on a particular program. But participation in such programs usually remains optional for individual members. Government implies something more than the pronouncement of group opinion, the teaching of informal consensus, or the giving of mutual aid. It implies enforcement, sanctions. Other than the structural, housekeeping rules for the operation of the organization itself, almost the only rules professional associations have enacted that are designed to guide the behavior of the members in their everyday work are those contained in the codes of ethics or rules of professional behavior. The small number of these that are formulated and enforced in a purely internal manner, without resort to public government, are the rules concerning advertising, solicitation, or public criticism of the profession; that is, rules designed to minimize internal competition and maximize professional cohesion. On most other matters the associations rely on state law to set the guidelines for professional behavior.

2. *Preliminary arenas of public lawmaking.* One of the commonly used models of American public government presumes that the process of legislation takes place primarily in the public legislature. Private organizations are viewed as pressure groups attempting to influence legislative decisions from the outside.

For most laws affecting the detailed work of professionals, this is not a fair picture of the facts. It is more accurate to say that the legislative process begins, among other places, with the formulation of legislative proposals within private organizations; that the process within organizations by which group consensus is reached is part of the broader process; that negotiations between groups on issues that have not yet reached the public arena are a further extension of the process, which culminates in public battles and the final legislative vote. This latter picture is more accurate in the light of the fact that private organizations, such as professional associations, are responsible for the initiation and much of the content of a high percentage of the legislation directly related to their work. It must be emphasized, however, that they serve as preliminary arenas for the formulation of public laws only in relation to *some* kinds of public issues, those having the closest and most narrow connection with the ordering of professional work.

3. *Agencies for the enforcement of private and public law.* Professional associations perform a governmental function in two administrative ways: in policing activities in their arena of work and in policing their own members. In both instances their collaboration with public government is such that it is difficult to tell where one begins and the other leaves off.

The AMA, for instance, as a private association tests and passes judgment on new drugs, medicines, dietary and other special-purpose foods, and therapeutic and diagnostic devices; but the AMA was also instrumental in getting public pure food and drug laws passed, at both federal and state levels, and it assists public administrative agencies in the work of enforcing the public laws.[25]

Only some of the associations attempt to enforce upon their membership either the organization's own internally articulated codes or the public law. Bar and medical associations are the most active in this respect. Nurses', architects', and engineers' associations often have no operative formal disciplinary machinery at all.

When a profession is weakly organized, there is usually little internal or public control over the profession. Where organization is strong, there may be more internal control, but the association also relies heavily upon the sanctions of public government. A profession deems itself to be in the strongest position when its organization exercises control over its members, but does so by virtue of public delegation of authority with the sanctions of public government. If the phrase "private government" is taken to mean organizational autonomy in controlling its membership, then none of the associations is truly a private government.

The associations often make no clear distinction between internal rules and sanctions and those that are integrated with the public law. In some cases their application of private rule and public law is so mixed that it is difficult to segregate enforcement that refers only to internal rules; though for violations of the public law the penalties are often more severe, and the process of appeal and final enforcement of penalties takes place in public rather than in private agencies of government. Government, for the stronger professional associations, is a continuum, a matter of continual interaction and close integration between private and public governments. This does not mean that they are being closely regulated by an alien state, since they do in fact write much of the public law pertaining to their profession, as well as participate to a considerable extent in the task of enforcement. They borrow the sanctions and the legitimization of public government in order to accomplish their own ends. At the same time, the public government—in granting its seal of approval and lending its resources —does exact a price.

[25] Hyde and Wolff, op. cit., p. 960 . . . .

David R. Hyde and Payson Wolff

THE AMERICAN MEDICAL ASSOCIATION: POWER, PURPOSE, AND POLITICS IN ORGANIZED MEDICINE

How does the American Medical Association govern itself? The editors of the Yale Law Journal, *David R. Hyde and Payson Wolff, report on the results of a questionnaire sent to a number of state societies and then consider the issues raised by the conflict between self-interest and professional responsibility.*

In its hundred-odd years of existence the American Medical Association has attained a position of undeniable authority and influence over medical affairs. The power of organized medicine affects not only the physician but also everyone who requires the assistance of the healing arts. AMA successes in raising the quality of medical education, practice, and care are beyond question. However, in these endeavors it has acquired such power over both public and practitioner that it can channel the development of American medicine. Dangers inherent in such power are compounded by the layman's ignorance of medical matters and the AMA's monopoly position as spokesman for the profession. Out of this situation arise questions of grave significance. The AMA is motivated both by obligations to the public and loyalties to its own members. The demands on it from these two points of view underlie all its activities and suggest the possibility of conflict. To what extent does professional self-restraint, combined with present laws and institutions, assure that this conflict will be resolved in favor of the public interest?

Membership

The American Medical Association consists of 53 state and territorial (constituent) societies and 1987 county (component) societies.[1] Each county society sets its own qualifications for membership and its members automatically belong to the state association.[2] Aside from racial barriers in most southern counties,[3] all "reputable and ethical" licensed M.D.'s are eligible for membership.[4] And in most areas virtually every practicing physician belongs to his local society.[5] Until recently, all members of county and state medical societies were also automatically members of the national association. But in 1950 payment of dues, previously assessed only by the county and state groups, became a prerequisite to AMA membership. Now some physicians belong only to their county and state societies, and are not members of the American Medical Association.[6]

"The AMA: Power, Purpose and Politics in Organized Medicine" by David R. Hyde and Payson Wolff. Reprinted by permission of the authors, The Yale Law Journal Company, and Fred B. Rothman & Company from *The Yale Law Journal,* Vol. 63 (May 1954), pp. 938-47.

Note: Due to space limitations, footnotes appear at the end of this selection rather than at the bottom of each respective page.

On the other hand, since belonging to a county society is a prerequisite to admission at all levels, membership in the AMA depends upon acceptance by the local organization.

Reasons for membership. Many factors contribute to the high percentage of physician membership in organized medicine—a proportion unique among voluntary professional associations.[7] With membership in the society, the doctor receives ready access to the social and professional contacts indispensable to the growth of his practice—contacts which may lead to patient referrals and consultations.[8] Additionally, there is the all-important factor of association with men engaged in his own science, with opportunities for exchange of knowledge and acquisition of professional status. The medical societies disseminate the latest scientific information through professional journals which are available to members either at no cost or at reduced rates, and through lectures, exhibits, and medical libraries which the societies support. In addition to these professional services, the local and state societies aid members by providing group malpractice insurance,[9] and by offering legal advice.[10] Many of the larger societies maintain bill collection agencies.[11] There may also be direct economic benefits incident to membership. Since the societies often contract to furnish medical care to indigents[12] and veterans,[13] participating physicians have a supplementary source of income from these programs. Membership can also be a conduit to such professional advancements as hospital staff appointments,[14] teaching positions,[15] and specialty ratings.[16]

Beyond the advantages which accrue to the member physicians, there are services which the society renders to the profession as a whole. The AMA has improved curricula and facilities in American medical schools. It gives financial support to research projects and publicizes medical discoveries through its journals and meetings. Moreover, many doctors look to the American Medical Association to protect their interests against encroachment. Thus, the AMA spearheaded the drive against compulsory health insurance and other governmental inroads into private medical practice. And the Association has worked to rid the profession of quacks, as well as licensed physicians thought guilty of malpractice, and to limit the activities of nonmedical practitioners. Since the entire profession profits by these efforts of the AMA, physicians may feel obligated to join and give their material and moral support.[17]

Reasons for nonmembership. However, a substantial number of American doctors do not belong to the American Medical Association or its component units.[18] Many of these are retired physicians who let their membership lapse, or young practitioners who have not yet fulfilled the residence requirements for their local society.[19] Doctors who do not conform to the code of medical ethics are not eligible for membership.[20] And many southern societies exclude Negro physicians.[21] Salaried doctors, such as those on the staffs of universities and research institutes, and civil servants often do not join medical societies;[22] here professional advancement is available through channels other than medical society membership. In remote areas, services which the society can render may be so negligible that doctors have little incentive to join.[23] Some physicians may find the dues prohibitive; for example, in parts of California the total of county, state, and national dues runs as high as $190 annually.[24] Undoubtedly some doctors do not join because of apathy,[25] while a small minority of physicians do not choose to belong because they disapprove of the policies of the AMA.[26]

Formal Structure

The formal structure of the American Medical Association provides for the largest measure of direct democratic control in the county medical societies, and increasingly indirect representation at the state and national levels. Members vote directly for county officials and representatives to the state "legislature," usually known as the House of Delegates.[27] These delegates select their own state officers and elect the state representatives to the national House of Delegates.[28] This body elects the President and other AMA officers and the nine-man Board of Trustees.[29]

In theory, the policy-making function of the American Medical Association is vested in the House of Delegates. However, since the House meets semi-annually, many administrative and policy decisions are necessarily left to the Board of Trustees.[30] Although it is responsible to the House of Delegates, the Board functions with little supervision when the House is not in session. The members of the Board perform the typical role of corporate directors: they approve all AMA expenditures, and generally the Chiefs of the Association's operating bureaus are responsible to them.[31] The Trustees also appoint the Secretary-General Manager[32] and the editor of the *Journal.*[33] The President has little formal power in formulating AMA policy, although he enjoys tremendous prestige as chief spokesman for the organization.[34]

The AMA functions through standing committees or councils elected by the House of Delegates or appointed by the Board of Trustees.[35] Each council directs the activities of the Association in a particular field with the assistance of a full-time staff. The 900 employees of the national organization are supervised by the Secretary-General Manager of the Association, who has chief responsibility for the day-to-day decisions of the organization between meetings of the Board of Trustees.

Real Power Structure

While democratic procedures exist at the county level,[36] many members do not have sufficient interest in activities to attend meetings.[37] Doctors are extremely busy with their practice and have little time to devote to the problems of organized medicine. In New York, for example, 25 percent attendance at a business meeting is considered good.[38] Thus, the few doctors who are interested in medical politics can easily wield power and influence out of proportion to their numerical strength.

The nominating process for elections within the American Medical Association allows the officers in power to have the dominant influence in deciding who shall succeed them in office. At the county level, the President appoints a nominating committee which puts up a slate of officers and delegates for the state House of Delegates.[39] The state President functions in the same way in the selection of national delegates.[40] These elections are rarely contested.[41] In at least one state, Alabama, the delegates are appointed by the President.[42] The election of the official slate is made easier by the fact that the state and national organizations forbid electioneering and soliciting votes for office.[43] Even where the official slate offers alternative nominees, basic differences between the candidates are unlikely.[44]

The nominating process, in combination with the apathy of the average doctor,[45] assures domination by a single faction within the AMA.[46] In New York—one of the few states where an organized opposition has developed—these challengers have had little success.[47] State societies report that reelection of delegates is common,[48] the same names appearing on the ballot year after year. Frequently officers progress steadily from county, to state, to national prominence as they acquire seniority.[49]

One of the major obstacles to the formation of any opposition is the lack of an effective forum for dissident opinion. The *Journal of the American Medical Association,* which is the publication most widely read by members, rarely prints opinions in disagreement with positions taken by the House of Delegates or Board of Trustees.[50] In response to criticism of this policy the American Medical Association asserts that members can present their views initially in their county societies; that if these views win approval, delegates will present them to the state society, and finally the members' opinions will be presented to the national House of Delegates for consideration.[51] In practice, however, because of the indirect system of elections,[52] such a procedure eliminates any dissident viewpoints above the county level unless they win majority support. And while a member can oppose official policy in his local society, the structure of organized medicine makes it almost impossible for him to effectuate his opinions within this framework.[53]

One study of the American Medical Association has concluded that the physicians who rise to power within the medical societies are predominantly urban practitioners and specialists.[54] Although there is only a slightly larger number of specialists in the United States than general practitioners,[55] usually over 90 percent of the officers of the AMA are specialists.[56] Specialists, whose incomes are above those of the average practitioner,[57] are probably better able to devote time to medical politics. Statistics also reveal that cities contribute a larger proportion of officers than rural areas.[58] And in the AMA House of Delegates those who have served long terms are primarily from urban localities, while the shorter term delegates tend to be from the rural areas.[59]

Although these officers are not "average" American doctors, it would not be accurate to say that their policies are unrepresentative. The support of the membership is clearly shown in the immediate response of most members to a voluntary assessment voted by the House of Delegates.[60] Most members also seem willing to distribute literature and advocate AMA policies. But perhaps the most indicative fact is that groups organized to oppose AMA policies regarding the economic and political aspects of medical practice have never gained widespread support among the doctors. No group of any significance that has been formed to modify or review AMA policy has offered itself as an alternative to the AMA. Doctors are free to join such organizations while retaining their AMA membership but few have enrolled.[61] Even though the actively controlling group within the American Medical Association is a self-perpetuating minority its viewpoint is readily accepted by the passive majority. This acquiescence assists that governing minority in excluding dissident opinion from organized medicine.

Notes

[1]AMA, Guide to Services 4 (1952). Each component society serves a separate geographical area, and there can be no more than one county society in such an area. E.g., Va. Med. Soc. Bylaws Art. 3, Sec. 2 (1953). However in some rural areas a local society may cover several counties. E.g., Colo. State Med. Soc. Bylaws c. 11, Sec. 1 (1951-52).

[2]E.g., id. c. 11 Sec. 5. Some county societies in Kansas admit "associate members" although the state society will not recognize them as members. *Reply to Questionnaire,* Kansas Medical Society, Question No. 10. (Hereinafter cited as *Questionnaire* No. ___. A comprehensive questionnaire was sent to . . . 48 state medical societies and to the Medical Society of the District of Columbia. The following twenty-four fairly representative societies responded in varying degrees of detail to the 83 questions: Alabama, Arkansas, California, Colorado, Connecticut, Florida, Illinois, Iowa, Kansas, Louisiana, Maine, Massachusetts, Missouri, Montana, New Hampshire, New-Mexico, Pennsylvania, South Dakota, Texas, Utah, Vermont, Virginia, Washington, and West Virginia. The original answers from each society and a compilation of all the answers given to each question are on file in the Yale Law Library.)

[3]See note 22.

[4]Many county societies impose additional requirements upon applicants for membership: e.g., they must be graduates of an AMA approved medical school, United States citizens, present medical practitioners within the county, and practitioners of nonsectarian medicine. *Questionnaire* No. 9.

[5]*Questionnaire* No. 5. Half of the societies report over 90 percent membership among eligible, active physicians in their states. Only two states–Pennsylvania and Washington–report two-thirds membership or less.

[6]The AMA claims a membership of over 140,000. *Its Your AMA* [1] (1953). Although in one society–New Hampshire–less than 60 percent of the state society members pay dues to the AMA, more typically 95 percent to 99 percent are AMA members. *Questionnaire* No. 8. And in Illinois, the Society's constitution and bylaws require all members to pay AMA dues. Illinois *Questionnaire* No. 8.

[7]"How the Doctors Solved the Coordination Problem," 21 *A.B.A.J.* 221, 223 (1935).

[8]See Group Health Cooperative of Puget Sound *v.* King County Medical Society, 39 Wash. 2d 586, 626, 237 P.2d 737, 759 (1951); Garceau, *The Political Life of the American Medical Association* 103 (1941) (hereinafter cited as Garceau).

[9]A 1950 survey showed 35 percent of the county societies maintaining group malpractice insurance for their members. AMA, *Activities of County Medical Societies* 6, 7 (1951). Three state societies reporting now offer this insurance to their members, and two others formerly did so. *Questionnaire* No. 55.

[10]See, e.g., *You and the Medical Society of New York* 14 (1952) (legal defense provided for members involved in malpractice suits).

[11]Seven percent of the county societies responding to an AMA questionnaire had collection bureaus for their members. AMA, *Activities of County Medical Societies* 6, 7 (1951).

[12]In Iowa the county societies conduct indigent patient clinics and in four other societies membership is a prerequisite to physician participation. *Questionnaire* No. 54(c); Iowa State Medical Society, *Handbook for the House of Delegates* 20-44 (1950) (county societies reporting upon relief contracts held with local Boards of Supervisors). See, generally, Stern, *Medical Services by Government* 23-26 (1946).

[13]Iowa State Medical Society, *Handbook for the House of Delegates* 55 (1950) (reporting contract with Veterans Administration to furnish medical care in veterans hospitals); *You and the Medical Society of the State of New York* 53 (1952) (reporting fee schedule negotiations with the Veterans Administration for physicians serving veterans).

[14]See Group Health Cooperative of Puget Sound *v.* King County Medical Society, 39 Wash. 2d 586, 620, 623-5, 237 P.2d 737, 755-6, 757-8 (1951).

[15]E.g., in Illinois, Kansas, and Pennsylvania. *Questionnaire* No. 54(a). *Hearings Before Senate Committee on Education and Labor on S, 1606,* 79th Cong., 2d Sess. 2642 (1946) (nonmembers of the Chicago Medical Society ineligible for staff membership of teaching or research institutions). But see text note 23.

[16]"We [nonsociety members] cannot be accredited by various specialty boards because membership in the local medical society is a condition of eligibility. This is an increasingly serious handicap, since many hospitals are making certification by a specialty board an

absolute condition for practicing within those hospitals." Testimony of Lawrence Jacques, M.D., in *Hearings,* note 16, at 2642. See also Group Health Cooperative of Puget Sound *v.* King County Medical Society, 39 Wash. 2d 286, 626, 237 P.2d 737, 759 (1951).

[17]The AMA and the state societies solicit support by emphasizing their contributions to the profession. See, e.g., *It's Your AMA* [1] (1953): "We can take great pride in our AMA. It is the largest, most influential and most active medical association in the world. Even if you are not a member, it is your AMA to a certain extent. The Association began helping you the day you entered medical school and continues to aid your practice and guard your freedom. Though, for one reason or another, you do not share the responsibilities of membership, you benefit daily from the Association's work." See also *You and the Medical Society of the State of New York* 4 (1952) ("The freedom with which you practice and your very livelihood would be seriously jeopardized if the physicians of New York were not organized into a statewide association.").

[18]Of the 215,000 licensed physicians in the United States, *World Almanac* 779 (1954), about 140,000 are AMA members. Note 7. Some non-AMA members belong to local and state societies. Note 5.

[19]*Questionnaire* No. 5. Connecticut, for example, has a one-year residence requirement, and reports a corresponding lag in admitting physicians newly arrived in the state.

[20]E.g., Tex. Med. Ass'n Const. Art. 1, Sec. 3 (1952).

[21]The majority of county medical societies in the southern states deny membership to Negro physicians. Of those southern societies responding to the *Questionnaire,* four report no Negro members. *Alabama, Louisiana, Texas, Virginia Questionnaire* No. 11 Cf. 140 *Journal of the American Medical Association* 1278 (1949) (hereinafter cited as *JAMA*).

The unsegregated National Medical Association is the organization to which most Negro physicians belong. In 1870 the AMA House of Delegates refused to accredit the NMA as a constituent society. Cobb, *The First Negro Medical Society,* 2 (1939). In rejecting the NMA's then tiny membership the AMA established a policy, since written into the bylaws of many state societies, of one component society only in a given geographical area. E.g., Va. Med. Soc. Bylaws Art. 3, Sec. 2 (1953). Members of the colored Medico-Chirurgical Society of the District of Columbia, for example, cannot become AMA members through their present organization since, as the component society for that territory, the District of Columbia Medical Society fills the field.

There have been some signs of progress in the eradication of racial barriers on the local level. Recently, previously exclusionary local societies in the District of Columbia, Florida, and Missouri have admitted Negro members. Cannon, *Why I Am a Member of the Physicians Forum,* Physicians Forum Bull. (Sept. 1951), p. 10. See also *Arkansas, Florida, Missouri Questionnaire* No. 11 (reporting some Negro members). In 1950, New York sent the first colored member, Dr. Peter Murray, to the AMA House of Delegates. 140 *JAMA* 1278 (1949). Dr. Murray has since been elected to office in the New York County Medical Society. *N.Y. Times* (May 27, 1952), p. 29, col. 4 (Vice-President); id. (May 26, 1953), p. 31, col. 8 (President-Elect). And members of the NMA have attended AMA's county, state, and national scientific sessions, and NMA "observers" have been invited to AMA conventions. See, e.g., 140 *JAMA* 1278 (1949).

But the AMA as a national organization has failed to take steps toward a fundamental change in membership policy. Its spokesmen assert their inability to act, pointing out that each county society has absolute control over its own membership qualifications. Cannon, see text at 9; *Chicago Tribune* (May 19, 1939, Editorial). However, a group of New York physicians obtained state society approval of a resolution providing that "no constituent association shall exclude from membership any physician for other than professional or ethical reasons." The resolutions failed in the AMA House of Delegates. "Medicine: White or Black," 68 *School & Society* 70 (1948). Similarly the Medical Society of North Carolina made an unsuccessful attempt to challenge the one component society geographical rule when it proposed admittance of the colored Old North State Medical Society as a constituent organization. 147 *JAMA* 1241 (1951); 150 *JAMA* 1684 (1952).

The AMA has, however, deemed it politic to court colored nonmember doctors for support in its opposition to compulsory health insurance. At the 1950 NMA convention, an AMA representative cited Dr. Murray's election to the House of Delegates as an indication of equality in medicine. Cannon, see text at 9. The NMA, seeking the full benefit of AMA membership for all colored physicians, treated AMA overtures with caution. It avoided the endorsement of either the AMA's or the Truman Administration's position on health insurance, perhaps hoping that its strength of 4000 members might be a bargaining lever to gain full affiliation. *Time* (Aug. 22, 1949), p. 32. But with the compulsory health insurance issue at least temporarily mooted, the southern colored physician will have to look for a change of heart from within the AMA before he can expect full equality with his white colleague.

[22] *Questionnaire* No. 5; Garceau 105.

[23] Cf. *West Virginia Questionnaire No. 5.*

[24] *California Questionnaire* Nos. 12, 13. Several societies mention inability to pay dues as a cause of nonmembership. *Questionnaire* No. 5. Other societies mitigate the dues requirement in cases of financial hardships. See, e.g., Colo. State Med. Soc. Bylaws c. 1, Sec. 5a (1951-52); W. Va. State Med. Ass'n Bylaws c. 1, Sec. 5 (1952).

The range of county society dues within a state may be wide. E.g., Texas: $1 to $100; California: $5 to $125. *Questionnaire* No. 13. And state society dues vary from $15 to $55 a year; the average is about $25. *Questionnaire* No. 12.

The AMA assesses its members $25 for annual dues. AMA, *Guide to Services* 10 (1952). However it grants exemptions for the following reasons: financial hardship, retirement from practice or reaching the age of 70, internship or residency within five years of graduation. Id. at 17.

[25] *Questionnaire* No. 5.

[26] See, e.g., "Dr. J. H. Means resigns from AMA to protest levy to fight Federal Insurance," *N.Y. Times* (June 22, 1951), p. 14, col. 4.

[27] Each county society is entitled to at least one delegate although representation in state Houses is generally proportional to membership in the local society. Apportionment ratios vary among the societies from one delegate for every ten members to one for every hundred; the average representation is one delegate for every twenty-five members. *Questionnaire* No. 19. Densely populated areas tend to be under-represented. E.g., in New York, Schuyler County has one delegate for its eleven members. While New York County (Manhattan) has only 24 delegates representing its 6954 members. Kings County (Brooklyn) also has 24 delegates for 3467 members. *You and the Medical Society of the State of New York* 32 (1952).

[28] An AMA delegate's term is two years. State societies are represented by one delegate for every thousand members or fraction thereof. A representative from the Army, Navy, Air Force, Veterans Administration, and U.S. Public Health Service, and twenty representatives from the specialized medical fields within the AMA also serve in the House. AMA Bylaws c. 9, Sec. 1(B) (1952).

[29] The President, President-Elect, Vice-President, and other AMA officers are elected annually. The President and President-Elect serve on the Board of Trustees. The other Trustees are chosen for staggered five-year terms and may serve not more than two successive terms. *It's Your AMA* 3 (1953).

[30] Ibid. The Trustees meet six or eight times a year.

[31] AMA Bylaws c. 13, Sec. 4(A) (1952). The powers of the AMA Board of Trustees are duplicated on the state level. E.g., the Texas Board of Trustees serves "as a board of directors, within the meaning of the corporate laws of the state." Tex. Med. Ass's. Const. Art. 4 (1952).

[32] AMA Bylaws, c. 13, Sec. 4(D) (1952). After he is appointed General Manager by the Trustees, he is elected secretary by the House of Delegates. Unlike the officers and Trustees, he is a salaried employee. *It's Your AMA* 3 (1953).

[33] AMA Bylaws c. 13, Sec. 4(C) (1952). Until recently the editor of the *Journal* was the dominant figure in the Association. Mayer, "The Rise and Fall of Dr. Fishbein," *Harper's* (Nov. 1949), p. 199.

[34] The President's official duties consist largely of addressing the House of Delegates and nominating members for various committees, subject to confirmation by the House or Trustees. AMA Bylaws c. 12, Sec. 1 (1952). Prior to his term of office, the president serves as president-elect for one year, during which time he presides over the General Sessions and Council of the Scientific Assembly. AMA Const. Art. 7, Sec. 3; AMA Bylaws c. 12, Sec. 2 (1952). However, the "President's Page" in the *Journal* and his frequent appearances before Congressional Committees increase the president's importance as "chief spokesman for the Association on policy matters." *It's Your AMA* 3 (1953).

[35] For a general description of the AMA's operational structure, see *It's Your AMA* 1-6 (1953); *AMA, Guide to Services* 8-9 (1952).

[36]See, however, AMA, "Putting PR to Work," 13 (1st Public Relations Institute, 1952): "You would be surprised how many county societies do not even have a semblance of democracy in their sessions." (Statement of county society official.)

[37]The results of an AMA survey showed that urban county societies had the lowest average attendance at meetings. Sixty of 64 societies with more than 300 members report attendance of under 50 percent, while only 48 of 581 societies having less than 100 members were in this category. And 111 of the smaller societies report 90-100 percent attendance. AMA, "Activities of County Medical Societies," 3 (1951). Although the AMA regards these results as indicative of generally good attendance at local meetings, a former AMA President has remarked that "if 10 percent of the membership [in many areas] attend a meeting it is about average and it is usually the same 10 percent at each meeting." Bauer, "The Importance of the County Medical Society in the State and National Programs" (address before the Medical Society of the State of New York, January 27, 1947) (copy on file in Yale Law Library).

County societies list as their best attended meetings those featuring speeches on general medical subjects by "well-known" and "respected" members of the medical profession. Meetings on socioeconomic problems are ranked as poorly attended, "despite the increased interest in . . . [these] problems by members of the medical profession during the past few years." AMA, "Activities of County Medical Societies," 4 (1951).

[38]Richardson, "Freedom of Speech and Organized Medicine," 4 (undated typewritten manuscript on file with Physicians Forum, 510 Madison Ave., New York City).

[39]E.g., *Pennsylvania Questionnaire* No. 18. In Virginia the county president alone chooses some of the delegates to the State House. *Virginia Questionnaire* No. 18.

[40]E.g., Kans. Med. Soc. Bylaws c. 6, Sec. 1 (1952) (Nominating Committee for the selection of state society officers composed of five former Society Presidents); Colo. State Med. Soc. Bylaws c. 6, Sec. 1 (1951-52) (nominations from the floor permitted); *Connecticut Questionnaire* No. 20 (same).

All state society delegates to the AMA House must meet the AMA constitutional requirements of two years' prior membership in the AMA and its Scientific Assembly. AMA Bylaws c. 9, Sec. 1(A) (1952).

[41]*Questionnaire* No. 21 (only four of 24 state societies report competition for position of AMA delegate). Kansas requires Nominating Committees to present two nominees for each delegate position. Kans. Med. Soc. Bylaws c. 6, Sec. 1 (1952).

[42]*Alabama Questionnaire* No. 20.

[43]E.g., Kans. Med. Soc. Bylaws c. 6, Sec. 4 (1952); AMA House of Delegates Standing Rule, adopted June 13, 1902: "Resolved that it is the sense of the House of Delegates of the AMA that the solicitation of votes for office is not in keeping with the dignity of the medical profession, nor in harmony with the spirit of this Association, and that such solicitation shall be considered a disqualification for election to any office in the gift of the Association." Although the Judicial Council has stated that this rule, as phrased, was unenforceable, Fishbein, *A History of the American Medical Association,* 419-20 (1947) (hereinafter cited as Fishbein), it was found to be an "effective moral influence," ibid., and it has never been repealed. Id. at 224.

[44]Richardson, op. cit., note 39, at 3-4.

[45]The inertia of the majority of AMA members has been attributed to the consuming nature of medicine, the drive toward material success, and an aversion against "politics." Garceau 61-3. Consequently the membership is said to turn to the AMA, thus saving itself from the "awkward predicament of having to think." Id. at 101.

[46]Richardson, op. cit., note 39, at 4.

[47]The Physicians Forum was organized in 1941 by members of the Medical Society of the County of New York to defeat a proposed amendment to the state society constitution. This amendment provided that members "shall not initiate or participate in any activities outside the structure of the Medical Society of the State of New York, which are contrary to [its] policies . . . ." Chapters have been formed in other cities and the group has promoted health insurance and other measures counter to "official AMA doctrine." 12 *N. Y. Medicine* (Nov. 20, 1952), p. 13 (letter from Ernst P. Boas, M.D., chairman of Physicians Forum). Although the Forum was successful in defeating the amendment and in electing "several liberal minded physicians" to county officerships, its influence was of short duration. Richardson, op. cit., note 39, at 16.

[48]Several societies report that all delegates are reelected while others estimate that between one-third and one-half of the delegates are rechosen. One replied that "receptive delegates" are reelected and another characterized the tenure of delegates as extending "until they choose to retire." Only three indicated that few or no delegates were "repeaters." *Questionnaire* No. 23.

[49]An example of "devotion to medical society office" is the career of former AMA President Rock Sleyster who served as Secretary of his county society, Secretary, President, Treasurer, and Editor of the Wisconsin Society, Delegate and Vice-Speaker of the AMA House, and member and Chairman of the Board of Trustees. Garceau 59. For further illustrations see id. at 58-61.

The "active physician" in the New York Society proceeds from membership in a standing committee to its chairmanship. The second vice-president, who automatically becomes President within a few years, is chosen from such members. Richardson, op. cit., note 39, at 3.

[50]Davis, *America Organizes Medicine* 175-176 (1941); Medical Economics, July 1952, p. 12. Spokesmen have emphasized their desire that organized medicine present a united front. See, e.g., *JAMA* 936 (1938) ("Once the House of Delegates has spoken its actions should be supported by the united voice of American medicine."); 49 *N.Y. State J. of Med.* 2527 (1949); cf. 139 *JAMA* 788 (1949). Perhaps the *Journal's* practice is a result of this attitude. However, this policy has been widely criticized. See 1 *N.Y. Medicine* (Aug. 20, 1945), p. 11 (editorial advising that "some further consideration . . . be given to [the *Journal's*] policy with reference to publication of dissident opinions and views."); 244 *N. Eng. J. of Med.* 307 (1951) (reporting resolution of Mass. Medical Society urging "that the *Journal of the American Medical Association* welcome and provide space for the presentation of considered discussion from varying points of view . . . ."). Cf. *N.Y. Times* (Nov. 30, 1952), p. 54, col. 3 (Editor of *Atlantic Monthly* criticizing *Journal's* refusal to accept paid advertisement of article on compulsory health insurance.)

State society journals have been similarly criticized. Davis, op. cit.; Garceau 100; 27 *J. of Pediatrics* 196 (1945). However, there are some exceptions. The *New England Journal of Medicine* maintains that its columns are open to comment critical of the official AMA position and has published divergent viewpoints. 240 *N. Eng. J. of Med.* 397 (1949).

[51]149 *JAMA* 1227 (1952). But see 5 *N.Y. Medicine* (March 5, 1949), p. 41 (county society member describing his inability to have his views heard); note 37.

[52]See text at note 40 et seq.

[53]But cf. 149 *JAMA* 1227 (1952) (example of individual member's securing passage of previously unconsidered resolution concerning physical selection of airplane pilots without prior official support).

[54]Garceau 55-58.

[55]There were, in 1949, approximately 72,500 physicians exclusively in general practice, 55,000 exclusively practicing a specialty, and 23,000 general practitioners "giving attention" to a specialty. 3 President's Commission on the Health Needs of the Nation, *Building America's Health* 140 (1952-53) (hereinafter cited as Magnuson Rep.).

[56]All but one of the present members of the Board of Trustees and all AMA Presidents, Vice-Presidents, and Speakers since 1947 have been specialists. Compilation on file in Yale Law Library.

[57]4 Magnuson Rep. 247.

[58]Only seven of 31 recent and present high officers and Trustees of the AMA practice in communities of 25,000 population or less. Compilation on file in Yale Law Library.

[59]Garceau 50.

[60]Only one state society indicated that less than 50 percent of its membership paid the 1948 assessment. And 14 societies reported that from 60 percent to 96 percent of their members contributed. *Questionnaire* No. 15.

[61]Thus, the Committee of Physicians for the Improvement of Medical Care has functioned within the AMA with about 700 members. *Means, Doctors, People, and Government* 147-51 (1953); Davis, *America Organizes Medicine* 298 (1911). The Physicians Forum is open only to members of county societies or the National Medical Association, 12 *N.Y. Medicine* (Nov. 20, 1952), p. 12, and has never drawn much support. See note 48.

David Hapgood

HOW DOCTORS CONTROL THEIR OWN SUPPLY

Because it controls accreditation and licensing, the American Medical Association can restrict the supply of doctors. David Hapgood charges the medical profession with failing to live up to its responsibility to provide medical care adequate to meet the needs of the public, especially those of the underprivileged.

* * *

An American viewing the state of the industry on which his health may depend is bound to wonder: How did we get where we are? The answer lies in the politics of medical manpower. The action takes place almost entirely in state government. The guilds control manpower through state licensing, and their most effective block against outsiders is the diploma.

Licensing of doctors by the states began in the last years of the nineteenth century. The other guilds came later, and some newcomers are still struggling for the power of the license. Licensing may be permissive or mandatory. Under permissive licensing, you can practice the trade without a license but you cannot claim the title: You can cut people up, but you cannot call yourself a surgeon. Under mandatory licensing, you cannot practice the trade at all without the license. The trend over the years has been for the guilds to seek permissive licensing first and then, when they felt strong enough, to consolidate their power through mandatory licensing. The doctors, of course, got there first.

Even in the early days of licensing, there were indications that the motives for licensure went beyond its primary purpose: the protection of the consumer from quackery. Licensing laws were adopted by state legislatures with the support of people who at the same time strongly opposed other forms of health protection, such as the regulation of working conditions. The Supreme Court favored the guild. In 1889 the Court upheld licensing of physicians, but in 1905 it ruled that regulation of hours and working conditions in bakeries was an unconstitutional restriction of freedom of contract. This is inconsistent, Professor Lawrence Friedman points out, because it gives a person the right to work in an unsafe (unregulated) bakery but denies him the right to contract with an unsafe (unlicensed) physician.

The American Medical Association's power was vastly increased as a consequence of the Flexner Report of 1910. That report was aimed at eliminating the many schools considered to be diploma mills. But the legislation that followed Flexner gave the AMA control of medical education and, thereby, a stranglehold on the supply of doctors. Today you cannot become a physician unless you are graduated from a medical school accredited by the AMA, through its Council on Medical Education.

The power over the diploma that the AMA gained after Flexner has allowed the guild for half-a-century to practice what is widely known as birth control. The figures are dramatic. In 1910, the year the Flexner Report was published, the medical schools produced 4,400 graduates. In 1920, the number was down to 3,047. In 1940, the total had climbed back up, but only to 5,097 (117 *fewer* than were produced in 1900). Doubtless many would-be quacks were kept out, but there is no reason to believe that the U.S. needed a reduction in the number of doctors during a time of rapid population growth (immigration plus natural growth). The policy that was not followed was to improve doctors' training while keeping up the supply.

That this would happen was predicted a long time ago by Adam Smith, the apostle of laissez faire capitalism. In 1776, more than half-a-century before the birth of the AMA, Smith offered this definitive comment on guilds: "People of the same trade seldom meet together, even for merriment and diversion, but the conversation ends in a conspiracy against the public or in some contrivance to raise prices."

The AMA was able to practice the economics of scarcity because the states placed control of licensing in the hands of the guild itself. Licensing is controlled in each state by an appointed board generally known as the "Board of Medical (or Dental, etc.) Examiners." These boards—and here's the political essence—are controlled by the people they are supposed to regulate. The state's power of appointment is meaningless because it appoints board members from lists submitted by the guild. In 25 states, all board members are doctors; in the other states and the District of Columbia, doctors are in the majority (except Kansas, where doctors hold five of 11 seats). In no state does the public have effective control of the board. In no case does a state department of health control licensing.

This is nirvana for any interest group. No industrial lobbyist in Washington, even in his most fevered dreams, would dare imagine such bliss. The analogy would be for the law to require that all the members of the Federal Communications Commission, for example, be named by the communications industry. It is true that any industry tries to capture its regulatory commission, with more or less success; but no one has seriously suggested that they be handed that control by law. The fact that what is denied industry was given to the doctors tells us something about the American culture. Because they are professionals, not businessmen, we apparently consider them above the profit motive.

The medical board is only one, though the first and by far the most powerful, of the boards that control manpower in the health industry. Two-thirds of the industry's 3 million jobs are guild controlled; and, of the rest, 800,000 are aides and attendants, jobs that the guilds evidently feel are not worth conquering. Some 25 health and health-related occupations are licensed by state boards. Besides physicians, these include dentists, the various classes of nurses, pharmacists, optometrists, and so on. With one major type of exception, each of these boards is controlled by the guild it is intended to regulate: Dentists regulate dentists, pharmacists regulate pharmacists, etc.

The exception occurs when an occupation is controlled by a guild above it in the medical hierarchy. Dental hygienists are regulated not by their peers but by the dentists' guild; their boards include no hygienists. Similarly, the two registered nursing guilds (the American Nurses Association and the National

League for Nursing) hold power over their underlings, the licensed practical nurses. In New York, for example, both registered and practical nurses are controlled by a 15-member board that includes 11 R.N.'s and four L.P.N.'s. Just to keep the status distinctions clear, the L.P.N. minority is not allowed to vote on matters concerning only the R.N.'s—although the R.N. majority votes on questions concerning only the L.P.N.'s.

Through its control of the state board, a guild has extensive powers over the number that can enter the field. The board writes and grades the examination you must pass to be licensed; it issues the license and can revoke it; and it approves the school whose diploma you need in order to take the examination. The protective wall is complete; there is no way to slip through without the approval of a guild-dominated board.

A study by Benjamin Shimberg of Educational Testing Service cites a system rigged against those who did not attend the right school. Florida and New York impose "very difficult written examinations" for ophthalmic dispensers. If you attended one of the nation's three training programs, you can probably pass the test. "But the typical applicant, who has served an apprenticeship with a licensed ophthalmic dispenser, has virtually no chance of passing . . . . The licensing examination thus serves to guarantee ophthalmic dispensers a source of cheap apprentice labor with little or no likelihood that the apprentices will be able to obtain licenses and go into business competitive with the established dispenser," Shimberg writes. This situation is particularly ridiculous, since most eyeglass lenses come already ground from bulk manufacturers and need only be fitted into spectacle frames to be ready to wear.

Hierarchy

The guilds have created a hierarchy in which power flows down from the top. At the top of the pyramid sit the AMA and such specialty boards as the American College of Surgeons. They hold sway over the lesser craft guilds the way the merchant guild held sway over the lesser craft guilds in medieval towns. Although only one in ten people in the industry is a doctor (compared to one in two half-a-century ago), the AMA still holds more power than all the other medical guilds put together. The AMA controls or influences the lower guilds through a variety of mechanisms. Ten lower orders allow the AMA to set their standards, and often schools for other occupations are accredited by the AMA; medical technology and *its* lower order, certified laboratory assistants, are examples. Frequently there is an interlocking directorship in which members of AMA specialties sit on the boards that regulate the lower guilds.

The health industry's social system has been compared to the feudal structure in which the duke pecks the count who pecks the baron who pecks the serf who has no one to peck but his dog. The comparison is unfair to the Middle Ages, for those in the feudal pecking order also had obligations to their inferiors. The baron was obligated to protect the serf he pecked. There is little evidence that the AMA or the other guilds feel any similar obligation toward the attendants and nurse's aides who are the dogless serfs of the health industry.

In many respects, however, the systems are similar. The authoritarian structure of the health industry is reflected in an extreme range of incomes: It includes just about the worst and the best paid people in America. At the bottom, the aides and attendants earn less than $100 a week, often as little as $40. In Charleston, S.C., they struck in an effort to get above the minimum wage of $1.30 an hour. They are light years distant in every sense from the doctors. In between, the nurses earn $5,000-10,000. The rest of the industry falls between the aides' $3,000-5,000 and the doctors' $35,000 (self-employed physicians).

Since the industry provides no way to climb by merit or experience from one level to the next, there is no reason to do your job better than just well enough to avoid being fired. Each layer in this stratified system is sealed off from the next by the diploma. The aide is prevented from becoming a nurse by two diplomas: a high school degree and a diploma from nursing school. No number of years of experience, no amount of proven on-the-job learning, will shorten by as much as a day the time the aide must put in at school in order to be promoted. The only way she can climb is to leave the industry and go to school, where on the first day of the term she will be on the same level as the freshman who has never been inside a hospital. If she or her parents could not afford what those diplomas cost before she went to work, she can hardly finance the time and tuition on an aide's wages. It is a classic dead-end job. The same principle—promotion by diploma only—applies at every level in the health industry.

Ranking people by diploma has class and racial overtones. It costs around $60,000 to spend the years in school decreed by the AMA if you want to become a doctor; so most of them come from upper-income white families. At the bottom, the blacks, and in New York City the Puerto Ricans, get the serfs' jobs. The trend in the industry, as in the nation, is toward an increasing stratification along the color line. The bottom is getting blacker while the top gets whiter as the percentage of black doctors decreases.

Unperturbed by the crisis around them, the guilds keep on trying to lengthen educational requirements in order to make it still more difficult to get into fields already short of manpower. An unpublished study of guild practices and licensing by the Health Careers Program at Lincoln Hospital in New York finds no sign that the guilds are changing their attitudes: "The associations continue to close their ranks, using the excuse that they are protecting the public." Dr. Edwin F. Rosinski, formerly of HEW, comments, "These subgroups are so preoccupied with credentials and pretensions of professionalism that they're overtrained."

Nurses

The nurses are trying to improve their status by the diploma method. Their guilds want to eliminate hospital-based schools of nursing and put all nursing education on the college campus. At present most nurses come from a three-year hospital course. Others come from two- and four-year campus courses. Now the nursing guilds would like to see only two types: a "professional nurse" (four years of college) and a "technical nurse" (two years). The latter would replace the licensed practical nurse, who gets 9-18 months of training. This would erect still another diploma barrier, since the "technical nurse" would need a high school diploma, which the L.P.N. does not require. One more avenue of advancement for the uncredentialed would be cut off.

The motive for the current maneuvers of the nurses' guilds may have more to do with a need for status than with occupational birth control. Nurses, like cops and teachers, are usually white Middle Americans who occupy an ambiguous status position. To the doctors above them in the hierarchy, nurses are nonprofessional underlings who command little respect. To the aides and L.P.N.'s below them, nurses are the main dispensers of petty oppression. The nurse stands halfway up the ladder. Her hands reach upward to assume some of the duties traditionally performed by doctors and administrators. Meanwhile her heels are firmly planted on the hands of those below her. At present the registered nurses are trying to dislodge the L.P.N.'s from jobs they already hold in extended care facilities–jobs which the L.P.N.'s were able to get because of the shortage of registered nurses, a shortage which the nurses' guilds' policies can only worsen. Of course patient care in many nursing homes is substandard, but it is the quality of the performance, not the titles of the performers, that should be criticized.

The nurse's values and attitudes come down to her from above. If she insists that her fellow nurses have a college diploma, it is because the nurse is accepting the values of a society in which the college diploma is required for above-the-middle status. Seen from this perspective, the attitudes of the nurses' guilds are pathetic as well as nasty. Those who hold the college badge–a category that doubtless includes most readers of *The Washington Monthly*–might reflect that their own attitudes toward uncredentialed people like nurses are responsible for that Middle American behavior which the credentialed so righteously deplore.

Certainly the nurses have yet to hear a different tune from the superguild that dominates the industry. To those who hope that the AMA may soon respond to the crisis, an answer is provided by the guild's Council on Medical Education. The Council was describing the "essentials" of training for certified laboratory assistants. The assistants work for members of an AMA-controlled guild, the medical technologists. Technologists need three years of college plus one year of training; the assistants need one year of training without college. Among the "essentials" listed by the Council:

"Acceptable schools (for assistants) must be separate from AMA-approved schools of medical laboratory technology . . . there must be complete physical separation of the two types of students."

Though it sounds like Mississippi circa 1910, the Council's report was made in 1967. We can only speculate on what the Council feared might happen if the peasants studying to be assistants were to climb the wall separating them from their future bosses. Perhaps they would find that their schooling, though separate, was equal; that they were learning as much as the technologists who were going to be above them in status and income. And that might make them restless.

Nor is the AMA making any substantial effort to help the consumer, despite the efforts of the individual doctors. Although doctors' productivity has greatly increased, the patient has yet to feel the effects. As health economist Rashi Fein of Harvard rather gently puts it: "Past increases in productivity seem to have been translated into higher incomes rather than shared in lower prices." The trend to longer training for more doctors also translates into higher prices. The AMA has done nothing effective to prevent the gradual disappearance of the general practitioner, who is at once the least costly of doctors and the only one who sees the patient for what he is: a whole, rather than a collection of irrelevancies attached to a favorite organ. The number of G.P.'s has dropped from

109,000 in 1940 to under 70,000, and many of these are older men. Only two percent of those now coming out of medical school are headed toward general practice. They are following their noses: The rewards and prestige today are in research and specialization, not in delivering medical care to human beings.

* * *

Daniel Rich

PRIVATE GOVERNMENT AND SCIENTIFIC SOCIETIES

Scientific societies are exercising increasing influence over their members' professional activities and prospects. A number of them now have a licensing authority similar to that traditionally exercised by the legal and medical professions. As Daniel Rich points out, this broadening of power and responsibility raises a problem of legitimacy also encountered in other private governments: How extensive should the powers be, and who should decide how they are exercised?

Contemporary scientific societies, like the American Chemical Society and the American Meteorological Society, continue to perform functions and serve purposes which were characteristic of their late nineteenth- and early twentieth-century predecessors: They are mainly dedicated to fostering scientific communications by publishing journals and sponsoring meetings. To some extent, however, they also engage in activities which set them apart from their historical counterparts and which suggest a growing resemblance to modern professional associations in such fields as medicine and law. In this respect, they are becoming influential private governments which attempt to exercise uniform and decisive control over the professional lives of their members and the relationship of the profession to society. (See the Gilb paper in this reader.)

The operation of scientific societies as private governments poses serious problems of legitimacy. As they have grown, scientific societies have evolved a complex array of functions and clientele. As a result, much confusion and uncertainty have arisen concerning what these institutions should do and whom they should serve. The problem of determining legitimate functions and purposes has thus emerged as the principal dilemma of contemporary scientific societies.

The Functions of Private Government

The traditional functions of scientific societies have greatly expanded along with a growth in membership and the explosion of scientific research following World

"Private Government and Scientific Societies" is an original article based upon studies related to a dissertation to be published by The M.I.T. Press.

War II. In performing these functions, scientific societies operate as private governments insofar as they influence the distribution of rewards in various fields. For example, since publication is a criterion for achieving scientific status, decisions by scientific societies with regard to whose research will be published and whose papers will be presented at meetings may influence the status of their members. Moreover, since publications are often a standard for employment in jobs with higher economic rewards, scientific societies may also affect not only the status but also the income of their members.

So long as their operation as private governments resulted solely from the performance of their traditional functions, legitimacy was rarely a problem for scientific societies. On the contrary, that role was expected and accepted. A basic tenet of the social system of science is that all scientific institutions ought to embody meritocratic principles, that decisions ought to be made about the scientific worth of the work, and that rewards ought to be distributed accordingly. The question of legitimacy becomes a problem only when an individual or a group believes that meritocratic principles have been violated.

Particularly since World War II, scientific societies have engaged in activities which resemble those of professional associations and which have broadened the scope of their authority as private governments. They have become increasingly involved in the economic lives of their members. Most often such involvement has been initiated as a response to an apparent economic crisis in particular fields. The American Meteorological Society, for example, became more actively engaged in employment services immediately after World War II, when it appeared that there would be insufficient job opportunities for meteorologists because of reductions in military needs in the postwar period. The Society then launched a program of reorganization and professionalization with specific attention to employment services such as counseling and job placement. Recently, leaders of other societies have reported increasing pressure from some of their members to expand such economic services.

This pressure has largely resulted from currently rising unemployment rates in scientific and technical fields. For example, some members of the American Institute of Aeronautics and Astronautics have looked to their society to provide help in coping with unemployment resulting from cutbacks in the aerospace industry. A similar pattern is evident in the field of physics. While the American Institute of Physics has offered members employment services, such activities were generally regarded as of secondary importance. Currently however, many physicists have demanded that greater attention be given to economic services. Dissident members have in fact established a separate society, the American Physicists Association, to promote their economic interests, and leaders of the Institute recognize the existence of a competitor as creating further pressures for the expansion of economic services.

In addition to employment services, some scientific societies offer members group insurance and medical plans as well as pension and retirement plans. Some societies are now considering the establishment of a portable pension plan. One effect of such a plan would be to reduce long-term financial dependence of the individual member on a particular job and to intensify his attachment to a society.

A second area in which scientific societies have become involved is the establishment and application of standards of professional admission and practice.

The societies have become increasingly active in influencing professional education; they perform a wide range of services including student recruitment, counseling, and guidance as well as the establishment of curricular guides and plans. In addition, most local sections of societies sponsor student branches whose activities are designed to foster professional socialization.

Admission to most scientific societies has become more restrictive as these institutions have become more professionalized. In most cases, societies distinguish among grades of membership based on professional accomplishment. The lower grades continue to be open to virtually anyone demonstrating an interest in the field. Most often, however, only membership at a higher grade carries with it voting privileges or the right to hold office in the society.

A number of societies have established or have considered establishing codes of ethics or uniform standards of practice. Thus, the American Meteorological Society has created a code of ethics and a Board of Professional Ethics to investigate cases of alleged unethical practice. Moreover, a recent survey of scientists indicated broad support for increased activities of this type; over 52 percent of the respondents supported the idea of a scientific code of ethics comparable to those in the fields of medicine and law, and less than 6 percent indicated opposition to such an enterprise.

Some societies have become engaged in the licensing and certification of practitioners. In the past, most societies avoided such activities since it was thought to be an appropriate function only for institutions concerned with the application of scientific knowledge; consequently, it was viewed as appropriate for engineering but not for scientific societies. Over the last quarter century, however, virtually every field of science has developed applied branches, and the distinction between scientific and engineering fields has become blurred. Thus the American Chemical Society supports two national certification programs for clinical chemists and has worked with the Council of State Governments on a model bill to regulate clinical laboratories and their personnel. Similarly, the American Meteorological Society conducts a certification program for consulting meteorologists and a program for evaluating and distributing seals of approval to radio and television meteorologists.

Scientific societies also perform activities designed to control the relationship of their professions to society at large. Many of these activities are designed to protect and promote the public status of the profession. Societies such as the American Institute of Aeronautics and Astronautics and the American Institute of Physics employ public relations personnel to provide information services to the press, radio, and television and to promote public understanding and consciousness of the profession. Societies also conduct seminars for science writers and sponsor public forums and publications about their professions.

Leaders of some societies indicate that they want their institution to become the spokesman for the profession. It is often hoped that the public will come to associate the society with the science in a way similar to the public's association of the medical profession with the American Medical Association. The views of the leaders are often reinforced by the wishes of their members for the society to become more active in promoting the public status of the profession. Indeed, a recent survey of the American Chemical Society indicated that members desired greater activity in this regard.

As scientific societies have become more influential as private governments, the legitimacy of their operations has come under question. Some leaders and members suggest that the sole purpose of scientific societies ought to be the advancement of science through the performance of traditional functions. It is argued that other functions represent an unjustified distortion of the underlying purpose of scientific institutions. Such attitudes serve as a latent source of resistance to the growing influence of scientific societies as private governments. In addition, even advocates of professionalization are uncertain about the implications of that process; should professionalization proceed as it has for associations in such fields as medicine and law, or is there something unique about science as a profession? Assuming that scientific institutions should no longer be singularly dedicated to the achievement of purely intellectual goals, to what additional goals should they be committed?

Who Governs Scientific Societies?

Who governs is related to what government does. As the functions of scientific societies have been expanded, the structure of power within these institutions has been modified. The emerging structure can best be labeled as a limited managerial oligarchy.

Formal power in scientific societies is usually vested in an elected council and president. The council operates as a legislative body while the president serves as chief executive official. Although formal power is vested in these bodies, the actual influence which councils and presidents exercise varies from one society to another; it also varies from time to time within a particular society depending upon such factors as the interest and personalities of officeholders. Generally however, councils and presidents exercise only limited influence over the day-to-day affairs of their societies. First, occupants of such positions tend to have short tenure—limited to a few years at most. Not infrequently, by the time they become truly familiar with the activities of the society they are replaced by others. Moreover, there are usually few incentives for council members and presidents to devote a great deal of their time to governing their societies. In most cases they receive no material compensation and often must pay their own expenses. Invariably, they are employed in other jobs demanding a sizable time commitment. Not infrequently, council members and presidents are geographically isolated from each other and from the societies' headquarters. In fact they tend to meet together as a governing body only a few times a year for short periods. In addition, the rewards for holding office are largely honorary and council members and presidents gain whatever prestige an office carries regardless of the time they devote to their positions. Thus, the opportunities and the incentives for exercising influence are limited. Consequently, the tendency is for these formal governing bodies to devote their attention to a few of the more salient issues facing the institution at a given time. On such issues they may exercise decisive influence, but on most other matters they tend to defer to others.

In the early years of most societies, when their resources and functions were limited, power tended to gravitate to a single individual or a small group which accepted responsibility for administering the day-to-day activities. Often the founder or founders of a society tended to retain significant control in the early years. Since in some cases the publication of a journal was virtually the only activity of a society, the editor of that journal frequently was most influential. Generally it appears that power fell to anyone who was willing to do the time-consuming and often unrewarding work of the society.

As scientific societies have grown in size and complexity, the structure of power has changed. Such change is most evident in the growth of complex bureaucratic structures designed to manage enterprises which have tens of thousands of members and budgets rising into the millions. Reflecting on growing bureaucratization, one member of a large society pointed out that "running that institution is like running a big business and you need a professional bureaucracy to keep it running smoothly." The larger societies thus have staffs numbering in the hundreds and complex hierarchies of authority. Formally this staff is empowered only with the authority to implement decisions—in fact authority for the implementation of decisions carries with it authority in making decisions. Consequently, in many societies, the executive director, as head of the managerial staff, has emerged as the single most influential individual.

In most organizations the scientist is the expert, and the manager is the client; in scientific societies this relationship is inverted. Executive directors gain influence because they possess general managerial expertise. Moreover, because they tend to hold their jobs for long periods of time, they also develop expert knowledge about a particular society. As heads of the administrative bureaucracy, they also command significant resources to reinforce their own expertise.

Executive directors possess the power but not the legitimacy to make policy. Consequently, their influence tends to be applied covertly, through suggestion and persuasion rather than direct pressure. Not infrequently, they operate by co-opting the legitimacy of those who hold formal power. Thus, a number of executive directors define their relationship with the elected president of the society as critical to the effective exercise of their own influence. Presidents rely on executive directors to execute policy in their names, executive directors depend on presidents to legitimize their own influence. Not surprisingly, then, executive directors indicate that their position is made difficult when a presidential incumbent attempts to exercise his formal power in the day-to-day affairs of the society. On such occasions, it is difficult for the executive director to apply his influence without appearing to usurp the formal prerogatives of others.

The lack of legitimacy is thus one of the principal limitations on the influence of executive directors. In the day-to-day operations of the society, those who hold formal power defer to his authority. On particularly crucial issues, when those who hold formal power are determined to exercise it, his influence is limited; however, he may still retain significant influence if only because those in power will continue to be dependent on his expertise in the society's affairs.

The influence of the executive director is also limited since many decisions require scientific expertise which neither he nor his administrative bureaucracy commands. This limitation has become more acute as scientific fields have become more specialized. As a result, there has been a rapid growth of specialized committee structures within scientific societies. These committees are often delegated complete authority in making policy within defined areas. The rise in government by committee has resulted in a dispersion of authority which limits the influence of elected officials and managerial staff alike.

In the past, the locus of power in scientific societies has not struck most members as a matter of major concern. Indeed, if societies were unrepresentative or undemocratic it was as much by default as by design. Thus, for example, in many societies the percentage of members who vote in elections has been consistently low. Often certain structural characteristics, such as complicated nominating procedures and voting restrictions, have tended to limit participation. For the most part, members have shown no signs of being perturbed by such limitations. Generally they have demonstrated little incentive to take an active part in governing their societies. So long as the functions of these societies and their influence on professional life were limited, participation did not appear crucial.

While the influence of scientific societies as private governments is increasing, there remains little evidence of a rise in member participation. On some occasions, however, there have arisen "grass roots" movements built around a specific issue. The American Physical Society, for example, has experienced a great deal of conflict over the issue of involvement in public policy. Some of its members organized a movement to amend the Society's constitution and thus make it possible to take stands on issues such as the Vietnam War. When the amendment was defeated, the dissident members formed their own society. The movement seems to have had some long-term success inasmuch as the American Physical Society is again reevaluating its political role. Other societies have also experienced sudden upswings in participation on particular issues. Yet, on the whole, there is little member participation in the governing process. Most issues are resolved at the upper levels of policy-making, and most conflict is limited to confrontation among the leaders.

The structure of power in scientific societies continues to be best described as a limited managerial oligarchy. We can probably expect, however, that as scientific societies become more influential, the incentives for member participation will increase, and the present structure will change. It is also likely that, to the extent that scientific societies assume professional functions which pose problems of legitimacy, the level of conflict will increase.

The dilemmas of legitimacy facing contemporary scientific societies are symptomatic of the confusion and uncertainty which has characterized the scientific community as a whole since World War II. Science and its related technologies have become crucial forces in society. At the same time, scientific work has become more dependent on public support. This growing interdependence of science and society has been accompanied by much bewilderment concerning how science and society ought to be related. Old standards no longer apply, but new standards have not emerged. The dilemmas of legitimacy in scientific societies, as in other scientific institutions, cannot be resolved unless accepted standards for relating science to society are established. Unless such standards are established, either explicitly or implicitly, the operation of scientific societies as private governments will continue to rest upon an uncertain basis of legitimacy.

Thomas P. Ference, Fred H. Goldner, and R. Richard Ritti

PRIESTS AND CHURCH: THE PROFESSIONALIZATION OF AN ORGANIZATION

The reforms of Vatican II gave the bishops and laity a greater voice in the affairs of the Roman Catholic Church. At the same time, these reforms have also stimulated demands for a greater share in authority at the lower levels of the ecclesiastical hierarchy. In this groundbreaking study, three sociologists examine the recent steps toward professionalization of the priesthood.

Change: Enabling Mechanisms

The long-term secularization trends in industrial society have exerted continual external pressure for changes in the Catholic Church. Internal pressures have also been present for over a century (O'Dea, 1968). But it was not until Vatican Council II (1962-1965) that any of these changes were realized (Rynne, 1968). But since then there have been a number of changes brought on by the continual interplay between ideas and institutional arrangements which originated with Vatican II.

Change in the Church, as elsewhere, frequently comes about through "enabling mechanisms" which either permit pressures to surface or which create new situations and definitions. Vatican II was both the origin and the best example of a number of such mechanisms in the Church. It was the first time that most of the attending bishops were together as a body for legislative purposes. During their stay, they were removed from their administrative duties and the responsibilities of "handling" those below them. As O'Dea (1968: 123) has put it, they were there to "discuss."

Issues that had not been previously discussed in public were raised, as were those for which bishops, in their administrative role, had had neither the occasion nor time to consider. Unconfined by day-to-day administrative chores, they were able to call upon the ideal values that appealed to the core of their religion but that so often were submerged by what appeared to be organizational necessities. As one attending bishop reported (in a private conversation with one of the authors) about the final documents: "If the council documents were given to the 2000 bishops at the beginning you couldn't have gotten 100 signatures—including mine."

The Council increased the bishops' awareness of their common interests and illustrated their ability to promulgate change even over the opposition of the Curia. Accordingly, they attempted to institute a similar arrangement by providing for regularly scheduled synods composed of representative bishops from each country. However, the Curia preceded them by urging irregular synods to

From "Priests and Church: The Professionalization of an Organization" by Thomas P. Ference, Fred H. Goldner, and R. Richard Ritti. Reprinted from *American Behavioral Scientist,* Volume 14, number 4 (March-April 1971), pp. 507-24 by permission of the Publisher, Sage Publications, Inc. and the authors.

Authors' note: We thank Arlene Daniels for her comments.

be called only by the Pope and with his agenda. Previous to a recent synod, one of the bishops recounted (in a private conversation) how it had come to be created and how they now hoped to change it:

Debate in the Council was leading inexorably to a synod but not this kind –[rather] a synod of bishops in collegiality. Before it happened, the Pope announced the setting of a synod he could call. Everyone applauded, but we were had. They [the Curia] walked all over us. Now we have to fight it to change it to a statutory meeting. This is where we were headed. You have to give them credit. We were innocents abroad. They were the experts in infighting.

No longer did the bishops confront the administrative center of the Church only as individuals. In concert, they realized their common interests and, during that subsequent synod, they arranged to meet regularly and to originate agenda items. Even back in their administrative posts, they were now willing to decentralize the Church still further—at least to their level in the organization.[1]

But whether they had intended decentralization to proceed below them or not, they had now legitimated such pressures in the eyes of the priesthood. It became increasingly difficult to claim that decentralization should not apply to the bishop-priest relationship now that it was in effect at the bishop-Pope and bishop-Curia levels.

The crisis of the Church is most salient at the level of the priest and with the governance of this level. But the priests have become less reverent toward those above them. It has become clearer that bishops are only "other" priests; they have been divested of any sense of greater divine nature. Priests are apparently less willing to recognize that the consecration of bishops confers a higher status within the spiritual profession. Wide and intense publicity given to the internal workings of, and political maneuvering among bishops at Vatican II played a large role in this.[2] It is unusual for an organization, other than an explicitly political one, to have the deliberations of its leaders openly available to all members. If, as Thompson (1961: 70-71) has maintained, status rank is a function of ignorance, then such publicity will reduce the chances that members of the hierarchy will be held in awe by subordinates.

New Organizational Forms

The major organizational change at the diocesan level was the creation of priest senates or associations. Following Vatican Council II, Pope Paul VI issued a *Motu Proprio:* "Ecclesiae Sanctae," Article 15 of which provided for the creation in each diocese of a senate of priests which would be representative of that body of priests. In many dioceses the senators were elected by the priests, while in

[1] For an account of the historical relationship between popes and bishops, see Bassett (1969).

[2] See Rynne (1968) for an example of this. It is especially noteworthy that his book first appeared as a series of articles in a popular magazine–*The New Yorker.* It should also be noted that the author's name is a pseudonym. The *National Catholic Reporter,* a newspaper originated after Vatican II, has also played a large role in this country in continuing to disseminate information about changes and conflicts in the Church.

others they were appointed by the bishop. In still others, they were either not created or the bishops refused to recognize them.

Until now, the relations between the priests of a diocese and their bishop or his staff at the chancery were on an individual basis. Occasionally, when there was more than one priest in a parish, they might act jointly, but priests from different parishes seldom acted together. Common problems, such as relations with the laity (their clients) or with their bishops, were discussed informally, if at all, when priests were together socially. No mechanisms existed for joint action, and the formation of one was not perceived as a legitimate endeavor. Besides, there already was a mechanism to take care of any diocesanwide problem—the administrative staff of the bishop. Nothing in their history or value system made any attempt to organize priests an easy one.

Nor, despite their successes, has it been. As long as the priest performed the tasks required by his organizational role within this professional organization, he had quite a bit of time and personal autonomy. This was especially true before the advent of parish councils (described below). A logical form of counterbalancing the organization's power was in an individual direction, rather than joined with other priests. The interpersonal and interprofessional relations required by the former were far less cumbersome than those by the latter.

The creation of senates now legitimated concerted action on the part of priests. For example, associations (as opposed to officially recognized senates) were created in a number of instances when a bishop balked at starting or recognizing a senate. These senates and associations then went one step further when many of them combined to form the National Federation of Priest Councils (N.F.P.C.). This was an even more daring move, for nothing in the formal structure of the Church provided for any nationwide unit. The bishop of each diocese dealt directly with Rome. The dioceses were completely autonomous from each other. Diocesan priests do not transfer from one diocese to another. While there was some form of cooperation among bishops at the national level, it was with regard to the place of the Church in the political structure of America. Although it preceded the N.F.P.C., the nationwide unit of bishops (the National Conference of Catholic Bishops) has only become a more viable unit since Vatican II and with the advent of the synods.

By its very nature, the N.F.P.C. is parallel to, dependent on, and is in some form of opposition to the bishop's national organization; it can now deal with issues that transcend more than one diocese. However, as yet there have not been many such issues. It provides a body to represent priests as a class with bishops as a class, rather than as a body representing the priests of a diocese to their immediate superior.

Some standard of comparison or of potential is important for any new organization, without its own history. The combination of senates or associations into the N.F.P.C. provided a yardstick by which each of them was able to judge itself. What one senate did became at least a potential for any other that knew about it. The N.F.P.C. provided the means for the exchanging of information and experience.

The provision of a comparative framework goes to the heart of the issue of legitimation. It helped each area examine its own basis of legitimation on an issue that was not uniformly accepted by the American bishops. As we have said, there are still dioceses without senates or others where senates are controlled by the bishop. It was not just that one diocese had something another did not, but that activities forbidden in one part of the Church might be conceived and recognized as legitimate in another. Those who had not seen the relative structure of the Church or had only thought about it abstractly were forced to confront it. It taught that what was still considered illegitimate in one area was legitimate elsewhere. Having a senate present and unquestioned in one area made it more difficult to question elsewhere. A precedent had been established.

The creation of these organizations of priests reversed the usual order in the process of professionalization. Occupational groups usually form a professional association as one of the early steps in the attempt at professional recognition and in the attempt to gain exclusivity from official state sources (Wilensky, 1964). The association of priests, as priests, followed long after the existence and recognition of their profession. Instead of being formed to gain professional status, their association was formed as an organizational tool to deal with bishops. As part of the longest-lived profession, they did not have to compete with a welter of established ones in order to gain professional status. The national association was formed to reduce the power of specific others rather than to gain general power. At the least, it was to question the power of the bishops, if not overtly to reduce it.

Bureaucratization and Professionalization—Simultaneous Pressures

The first order of business for most senates and the N.F.P.C. was with the position of priests as "personnel" in their dioceses. Their first concern was over the assignment and promotion of priests. Heretofore, the frequent transfer of priests had been made by the bishop or, more likely for the younger ones, by a chancery official. In any case, the moves were made largely on the basis of personal knowledge and feelings about individual priests or despite the lack of any knowledge about younger ones. Recourse was provided only by the pleadings of the involved individual.

At first glance, the demands of this group of professionals to produce standardized personnel procedures with uniformly applied criteria appeared to be an attempt to bureaucratize their relationship—a strange request from professionals. A closer look reveals a more complicated picture. If most of the transfers in the past were made on a personal basis—unpredictable and unstandardized—promotions from curate to pastor were almost always predictable because they were largely based on seniority. The exceptions were made for those who stood out at either extreme of the bishop's favor. In neither case were distinctions of merit involved. While seniority met the conditions of being rational, impersonal, and standardized, it was not directed toward improving the organization or the profession.

The issue of differential merit has been a difficult one for most professions. Professionals are usually reluctant to admit to laymen that some members of the profession are without merit.[3] Within the profession, however, they are

[3]See Freidson (1970) for an account of the use of this and other autonomy maintenance mechanisms among physicians.

constantly evaluating others through invidious comparisons. Similarly, priests have readily made distinctions among themselves between those who were good or bad leaders and administrators, but they have been loath to evaluate a man as a good or bad priest. Up to now, however, seniority procedures assumed an identity between spiritual professionalism and leadership or administrative skills. Some priests have now questioned this identity. They have urged the use of merit distinctions among priests as a criterion for promotions to pastor while leaving unchallenged the notion that a man remains a priest for life. At the same time, another group has been urging the elimination of the pastor-curate distinction. Although these simultaneous pressures may be conceptually confusing, they should make it clear that organizations can contain many different and even opposing pressures at the same time. And in this case, the pressures for greater bureaucratization were from the desire for individual autonomy and to further the goals of the profession.

An even more significant and far-reaching attempt at greater professionalization was made by priests in their effort to gain greater control over the assignment of personnel. As we have seen, priests are more a part of an organization than are other professionals. None of them operates as an independent practitioner. The attempt at greater personnel control was much more typical of those in professional organizations than of those professionals who were part of larger, nonprofessional organizations.[4] But some senates went further than almost any professional organizations. They moved toward a system whereby elected representatives from their ranks were responsible for the task of drawing up the criteria for promotion and transfer, utilizing them, and making the moves (although the bishop still held final appointive power). This went beyond most professional organizations where, although it is a fellow professional that makes the decision, he does so by right of his hierarchical position and not on the basis of representative legitimation.

For the first time, the diocesan priests have become an association of professionals, although not an association of independent professionals. More importantly for comparison to other professional organizations, they are an association of professionals within the confines of a containing organization, albeit a professional one. They meet as colleagues, as equals, to help run their organization. This, despite the fact that many of them are the subordinates of others. The pastors and curates have equal voices binding on both. And, in a few places, as mentioned above, priests have even begun to talk of doing away with the distinction between pastor and curate. They are professionals in an organization increasingly run by the professionals in combination rather than by a vertical hierarchy. They wanted, then, both greater bureaucratization by altering the mechanisms for personnel decisions and greater professionalization by changing *who* was to be involved in the decision.

Organizational Change: Shifting Boundaries

Vatican II created changes in the Church's relations to the laity that have further complicated organizational relations within the Church. These changes will, in

[4]See Rogers (1969) for an account of this phenomenon in the schools.

fact, redefine what is internal and what is external.[5] The boundary has already started to shift with the creation of parish councils. Each parish is to have a group of laity who, together with the pastor and curates, will serve as a kind of executive committee to run the parish. While the activities of these councils, where they do exist, range from passivity to complete control over the finances of the parish, there is no doubt that they will encourage greater lay involvement in the Church. In fact, the laymen have created their own national organization to promote lay influence in the Church.[6] Although they may not be influential in any local diocese, the National Association of Laymen has been able to exert pressure through the national press. For example, its report attacking Church financial records was featured on page one of the *New York Times* (New York Times, 1970).

There is ambivalence among priests over the inclusion of the laity, with the younger ones generally favoring it. This ambivalence highlights the tenuous nature of the processes now at work in the Church. For example, the lay members of some parish councils are picked by the pastor, while in others they may be elected. The discussion of these alternative methods came up at a regional meeting of priest associations more generally devoted to greater freedom from bishops, including the notion that bishops should be elected. However, they could not agree that lay council members should be elected by other laity. Instead, their compromise resolution stated they should be democratically "selected."

There is ambivalence even among the proponents. The priests still see themselves as embodying a set of values in human relations not always embraced by their congregation. The spirit in which they wish to include the laity as colleagues among the People of God, they also expect to see embodied in the laity's actions toward the less fortunate and the "minority" groups. They fear that a sharing of power to do good will result in a parochial view.

An argument is thus raised that more power to parishioners—more decentralization—will hurt the chances of the diocesan-level church to carry on good works. Whenever the issue was brought up at the meetings of one senate,[7] the senators were reminded of one of the parishes that insisted on spending a million dollars to build a new building at a time when the Church did not want to expend capital because of the shortage of funds for "good works." They recited the opposition of this parish toward giving their monies to any other groups—especially if the blacks would get part of it. The actual story was not that clear-cut, but it was used a number of times before anyone questioned it. The problem of more power to the people when those people turn out not to think like those who urged it for them has always been with us.

Increased lay participation may appear to be similar to Protestantism on the parish level, but it is highly unlikely the two religious organizations could end up structurally similar. Most religions other than Catholicism are organizationally important at the local level. Few of them have dominating international or

[5] The laity's influence on the Church is but one example of the many pressures for change from outside the priesthood. We deal with these in more detail in a forthcoming work.

[6] There have been a number of lay organizations throughout recent Church history. However, these organizations, such as the Knights of Malta and the Knights of Columbus, are service or social organizations and have not played a political role in the Church.

[7] One of the authors has attended priest senate meetings. The authors have been jointly engaged in a study of the priesthood utilizing interviews, observations, and survey data.

diocesan-level organizations. No matter how much more organizationally involved Catholic laity become, they will be doing so in an already established international organization of great sophistication. The emergent result will be something new, as will the professional-lay relationship.

A series of norms has been established and expectations raised that will be hard to put aside. Change has been initiated as a way of life in an organization noted for its historical resistance to change. Conflicting forces have been set in motion to produce a continual process not before encountered.

Conclusions: The Organization of Change

The inherent contradictions generated within the Church have been brought to the surface. The Church is now going through a period when a series of overt pressures is moving it in different directions. Even among those aspects that characterize its clergy as professionals, there are conflicting movements. It is thus set upon a course of inevitable, though uncertain, change.

The clergy, for example, are involved in a series of conflicting pressures about their assignments. On the one hand, they are attempting to bureaucratize the procedures for transfer and promotion and to gain colleague control over these procedures. On the other hand, many of these same priests—especially the younger ones—urge that the laity through parish councils be given a voice in Church procedures. In addition, they emphasize that the most important criterion for promotion should be the interpersonal competence of the priest—the most immeasurable and unbureaucratic criterion. Decentralization to their level gives them more power and is, in fact, more professional than even doctors in hospitals. But decentralization to the level of the laity removes some of the power.

Democratizing the Church means more stress and conflict, because it raises the necessity of mobilizing forces and supporters for various positions. Democratizing it means politicizing it, which means more conflict and continual change.

Differences from one part of the Catholic Church to another have existed side by side for centuries. Whatever uniformity or coordination had to exist was taken care of at the center, whether it be at a diocesan level or in Rome. The differences existed side by side with unity because there was no need for them to confront each other. But unity and subsidiarity at the same time is not an easy thing to achieve. As the priests form associations which must come to some kinds of agreements among themselves, then these differences will come into the open.

The Church as profession and the Church as community have always been in a state of tension. Now the potential for conflict which had always been present will be realized. The forums and mechanisms are there. The inclusion of the laity within existing Church decision-making units will further confuse our attempts to understand the nature of this "profession as organization." Nevertheless, it is clear that questions of organizational decision-making processes will become an increasing part of professionalism. And, in this profession, the struggles over questions of hierarchical authority, to which we have referred above, may give way to struggles over issues of general Church policy and practice.[8]

There should be no surprise that there are pressures which conflict with each other, although there may now be a discernible trend toward decentralization and liberalism. What is interesting is that different groups are able to use the ideologies associated with the priestly role and with religion to justify each one of these conflicting pressures. Appeals for each of the changes or arguments against them are based on prevailing ideologies. For example, as the priests help support the rise of lay influence, they threaten the present organizational structure of the Church. But they are able to do so based in ideologies of Christian community. The history of the Church is long enough to permit the claim that any ideology is based on traditions from the past. At the same time, greater lay voice may permit the priest greater autonomy vis-à-vis his bishop. Yet the laity will remain suspect in light of the more advanced position of the clergy on social issues.[9]

All of these ideologies exist at the same time, to be dredged up whenever any one of them supports a position. It is thus interesting that conflicting ideologies can exist at the same time and not really be brought up unless a fight takes place. The creation of new forums and avenues of dissent within the Church now makes it more likely that such ideologies will be brought forth and that fights will be fought. Even when the fight does occur, there is not necessarily a specific and open confrontation among these ideas. They may be cited and ignored respectively.

Any structural social entity, whether a religion or a profession, carries within it a series of beliefs and ideas which answer to an assorted number of problems. They usually do not get called all at once, but sequentially. None of us is individually consistent, for our principles are organized around a set of problems and can never be absolute. They are not applied or translated to other areas where they are not considered appropriate—but it may be possible for someone to translate them so as to cause embarrassment. Organizational changes and shifts in professional-client arrangements provide occasions for the confrontation of such ideologies. The Church and the profession of priest are now in such a state.

If we again consider the Church as "profession as organization," it then serves as a model for other professions characterized by organized practices. Accounting and law firms, in their relationships of the professional to the organization, resemble the Church of the past; though the persons who made all the decisions were also professionals, they made these decisions by right of their hierarchical position. The Church is now trying to move to a collegial authority structure after centuries of hierarchy. If it happens, it will serve as a model for other professional organizations.

[8]An assertion that engineers are similarly engaged in such struggles over technical policies in industrial organizations is contained in Ritti and Goldner (1969).

[9]For an account of a similar relationship in Protestantism, see Hadden (1970).

References

BASSETT, W. (1969) "Subsidiarity, order and freedom in the Church." Presented at the Canon Law Society of America Symposium on Unity and Subsidiarity in the Church, Dayton, Ohio.

ETZIONI, A., ed. (1969) *The Semi-professions and Their Organization.* New York: The Free Press.

——— (1964) *Modern Organizations.* Englewood Cliffs, N.J.: Prentice-Hall, Inc.

FICHTER, J. H. (1966) *Religion as an Occupation.* Notre Dame, Ind.: Univ. of Notre Dame Press.

FREIDSON, E. (1970) *Professional Dominance.* New York: Atherton Press.

GOLDNER, F. H. and R. R. RITTI (1967) "Professionalization as career immobility." *Amer. J. of Sociology* (March): 489-502.

HADDEN, J. K. (1970) *The Gathering Storm in the Churches.* New York: Doubleday Anchor (Doubleday & Company, Inc.).

MORRIS, J. D. (1968) "Priests widen dispute with O'Boyle." *New York Times* (October 3).

New York Times (1970) "Catholic laymen score 23 dioceses." (November 16): 1, 41.

——— (1968) "Catholics in poll back birth curbs." (September 1): 46.

O'DEA, T. F. (1968) *The Catholic Crisis.* Boston: Beacon Press.

RITTI, R. R. and F. H. GOLDNER (1969) "Professional pluralism in an industrial organization." *Management Sci.* 16 (December): B233-46.

ROGERS, D. (1969) *110 Livingston Street.* New York: Vintage Books (Random House, Inc.).

RYNNE, X. (1968) *Vatican Council II.* New York: Farrar, Strauss & Giroux, Inc.

SCHURMANN, F. (1968) *Ideology and Organization in Communist China.* Berkeley: Univ. of California Press.

THOMPSON, V. A. (1961) *Modern Organization.* New York: Alfred A. Knopf, Inc.

VOLLMER, H. M. and D. L. MILLS (1966) *Professionalization.* Englewood Cliffs, N.J.: Prentice-Hall, Inc.

WILENSKY, H. (1964) "The professionalization of everyone?" *Amer. J. of Sociology* (September): 137-58.

5

Universities

Clark Kerr

GOVERNANCE AND FUNCTIONS

Since universities are "many things to many people," it would be wrong and unworkable, Clark Kerr maintains, to try to govern them in accordance with a single ideology or in terms of some calculus of power. Instead, he argues, they should be governed pragmatically and pluralistically, with recognition of their complexity and particular differences.

The governance of the American college and university is a residue of traditions and arrangements that are more the gift of history than of conscious thought. This system of governance is now in crisis as never before, and history alone will not dictate the future. The way out of this crisis, if there is a way out, will be extraordinarily difficult because of the peculiarities and complexities of the academic institution. The campus is inherently difficult to govern—even in theory.

One way of looking for solutions is from the perspective of the several functions of higher education which, in their many and changing combinations, affect both the general character of individual institutions and the degree of their internal variety. This functional approach suggests one general strategy for working out the manifold proposed adjustments now in controversy.

The Residue of History

Academic governance in the United States has at least four features that distinguish it from patterns elsewhere. The first is the heavy reliance on a board of trustees, regents, or managers composed of people drawn primarily from outside academic life and from outside governmental authority. There are boards or councils in Britain, Canada, and Australia, among other countries, as well as at some of the private universities of Japan, but they are nearly always much weaker than American boards in their exercised authority and are usually of a more mixed representation, including faculty and sometimes student representatives.

The second special feature is the comparatively strong role of the president, who is appointed without a specific term of office as a full-time executive with a relatively large administrative staff. He has considerably more authority and opportunity for initiative, narrow as these limits may be, than his counterpart vice-chancellor or rector.

A third characteristic is the monolithic nature of the campus. To begin with, there is a campus as compared with the scattered endeavors, for example, in Paris or Buenos Aires. And on the campus, the central administrative organization is

"Governance and Functions" by Clark Kerr. Reprinted by permission of *Daedalus,* Journal of the American Academy of Arts and Sciences (Boston, Mass.: Winter 1970), *The Embattled University.*

a single college of letters and sciences or arts and sciences. It includes most of the instruction and much of the research. Residence halls are simply residence halls, and not also academic units. Departments within the college are clearly subsidiary administrative units, as compared with the organization of a series of more or less autonomous faculties in many universities abroad—faculties of science and philosophy and law and medicine. Some of these monolithic colleges of letters and science in the United States are quite huge and have a single curricular policy and a single grading system.

The fourth identifying trait is the importance of external, but nongovernmental forces in the conduct of the affairs of the campus. In the United States, the alumni have an influence found almost nowhere else. Industry, agriculture, and professional associations have their points of contact, their advisory committees, their influence over funds. Private foundations advise about and finance endeavors according to their own systems of priorities.

This system of governance contrasts with others around the world. In Britain, the organized faculty has predominant influence, with the power of the University Grants Committee growing steadily. Universities are generally smaller in size and more divided internally into colleges and institutes (as in London, the largest, which still has under 25,000 students). In France, authority has resided until recently with the separate faculties and their deans and with the Ministry of Education; in Germany, it has rested with the individual full professor directing his area of scholarship and with the State government; in Russia, with the government formally and the Party informally and with the Academy that stands outside the universities with a degree of independence; in Japan, with the organized faculty; and in Latin America officially with the faculties, under their deans, and unofficially and intermittently also with students and heads of states. In Latin America, as elsewhere, Catholic universities give more power to the rector and more influence to the church than do others. As a general rule, faculties and governments are the dominating forces outside the United States.

The American system bears the marks of its origins in the Protestant sects of the early colonies. These Protestant sects emphasized the supremacy of the parishioners over the ministers; it was natural that they should also provide control by leaders of the community over the new colleges. If there was a model outside the colonies, it was probably Edinburgh which had a council largely composed of town councilmen and clergy. Similar arrangements existed at Leyden and Geneva. The earliest local councils were established in Italy when faculty members took refuge in the protection of the city fathers from the harsh rule of the students. Thus the rise of the city under control of its burghers was also a precedent for the board of the American college. It would have seemed natural, at a time when the church and the city were being placed under citizen control, to apply the same principle to the college. The populism of the nineteenth century in America added strength to this tradition—the college served the people and the board represented the people.

The president of the early college was like the minister of a Protestant church—in fact, most presidents were ministers drawn from the church. When the corporation became a more dominant institution, the president became more like the head of a corporation.

The single college of letters and science grew out of the unified classical college with its single curriculum and single faculty. Only at the University of

Virginia, apparently following the French system, were the professors originally organized into eight separate schools. As the campus grew and departments were established, particularly after the Civil War and after the rise of science as against the classical curriculum, the college of letters and science became the administrative unit for the departments and the central unit for the budget, faculty appointments, approval of courses, and curricular requirements.

The involvement of private groups from outside the campus grew out of the dedication to service by the campus, particularly since the Civil War, the positions of power in society held by industrial and agricultural groups, and also the reliance on the private philanthropy of alumni and, later, of foundations as well.

Changes have taken place. Board members are no longer primarily from the ministry, but from business—as Veblen pointed out and did not like fifty years ago, but then he had not liked the ministers either. The president is no longer a minister, but an executive. The college of letters and science is no longer so dominant, with the growth of professional schools, research institutes, and graduate divisions. The outside private forces have shifted in importance from the churches to agriculture, to industry, to the professions, to the contiguous population. Faculty members have organized into senates and increasingly attained dominant power in academic areas, particularly since World War I. Students have gradually gained more freedom through the reduction of *in loco parentis,* the rise of the elective system for choosing courses, and the establishment of extracurricular activities under their own control, mostly in the period since the Civil War.

Changes have taken place, but the basic structural characteristics of a strong board, a relatively strong president, a largely monolithic internal structure, and a large role for private organizations from outside academic life remain about as they were in 1900 and in some respects in 1636.

The Pressures for Change

Substantive issues may or may not be settled easily and peacefully; but redistribution of power is always fought out with difficulty. The campus is currently passing from a concentration on individual issues growing out of interests to a confrontation over power growing, in part, out of principle.

There are more claimants for power than ever before, and there is no more power to be divided. Someone must lose if others gain—a zero-sum game. One gainer is the government, state and federal. The major shift in influence since World War II has been to public agencies. The reasons are clear. More of the institutions of higher education are under public control, and more of the money in both public and private institutions is public money. Public interest in higher education has also risen. More young people attend from more strata of society, and the actions of higher education, in research and service and dissent, increasingly affect more of the population. Higher education has become everybody's business. The campus is no longer on the hill with the aristocracy, but in the valley with the people.

State governments are exercising more fiscal control and more influence over direction of growth, usually through coordinating councils, than was the general situation historically. And, currently at least, there is a renewed state interest in the appropriateness of the relationships of students and faculties to political issues and to political action.

But the great new force since World War II has been the federal government. It now supplies one-fourth of all funds spent by institutions of higher education. It has contributed more than one-fourth of the new initiatives: toward science, toward residence halls, toward more equality of opportunity to attend college, and in many other ways. And it, too, has an interest in the conduct of the campus within the political arena. Federal interest as yet is fractionized among many federal agencies and several congressional committees, contrary to the situation in most other nations and contrary also to that in the fifty states where control is more unified; but this interest is increasingly concentrated in the Department of Health, Education and Welfare.

Less power and less influence on the direction of change now reside on campus, the big losers, particularly in domination of the budget, have been the board and the president. Their best instrument of control is now shared with others, and the American pattern is approaching the world pattern.

The public campus in disarray internally is particularly open to further intrusions from the state and the federal government. Internal harmony is the price of autonomy, and this price is not now being paid.

Less power and less influence on the direction of change now reside on campus; on campus, the big losers, particularly in domination of the budget, have been the board and the president. Their best instrument of control is now shared with others, and the American pattern is approaching the world pattern. challenging the inner sanctum of the campus where the faculty and the administration have ruled supreme, challenging control over the curriculum and the use of the budget. Earlier they had asked for more freedom for themselves; now they wish to reduce the established authority of others. This is a harder challenge. The initial loser before this new force is the dean of students and then the president; before long, it may be the faculty. The sharpest challenges may come to be between the faculty which once supported the students against the administration and the students who, having disposed of the administration as an intervening power, directly confront the faculty. On campus, the students are the new men of power.

The faculty is in a less clear position. It is gaining power from the administration in those segments of higher education where it has had little—the state colleges, the community colleges, and the lesser of the liberal arts colleges. About half of all faculty members are at such institutions. Gains take the form of stronger academic senates and faculty councils, but also, and potentially more significantly, of union organization. For the first time, unionization is penetrating higher education on an important scale, sometimes aided by state laws that favor unions and look upon academic senates as company-dominated organizations. When this happens, not only is some power shifted to the faculty, but it also comes to be expressed in the new form of employee-employer relations rather than the older collegial sharing of certain authority. There is a change in locus of power and in the philosophy of its expression.

In some places the faculty will gain power from the administration, often in major ways; but it may also lose to the students, sometimes in major ways. The net effect could possibly be a negative one for the faculty in terms of total power. It should be noted that not only are nearly all faculty members happy to take power from the administration, but also that some of them are happy to turn power over to the students. This is particularly true of younger faculty members who see the power of the older faculty members being taken away, and not their own—for they have little. Thus, while the faculty may lose power on a net basis, this does not mean that it will necessarily be unanimously unhappy about this shift.

The least clear trend in governance is what will happen to faculty power vis-à-vis the students. Students are historically changeable in their interests, and it is not certain how long the drive for influence in traditional faculty areas of dominance will continue. Also, faculties are historically conservative, and their capacity for resistance to change is quite substantial. Additionally, the public backlash against student activism can potentially strengthen the hands of the faculties as it did in Bologna centuries ago (and strengthen the hands of the public authorities at the same time). A crucial question will be the degree of unity within faculty ranks. Student seizure of faculty authority is likely only when it draws substantial support from within the faculty itself. Faculties recently have been on the run in the face of the sudden student attacks. If and when they consolidate their new positions, they may be virtually unmovable.

The two net losers are clearly the board and the president. The board is in an increasingly difficult position. Federal and state agencies make decisions it once made. The campus, particularly in the case of the universities and larger state colleges, is now too complex and too dynamic to be subject to detailed decision-making; yet many boards historically have been managerial boards. It is difficult to become a performance review board since nobody knows exactly what kind of performance is being reviewed: There is no quarterly test of profit or loss. The campus concentrates on inputs, not outputs, and performance is concerned with outputs, with value added to inputs. As a consequence, many boards respond to the special interests of their members and the current headlines.

The president loses to everybody, partly because he has had the most to lose originally, but also because he has no firm base of support in the power struggle, no natural constituency of his own. He long ago ceased to have much of what Veblen called "erudition"; he now ceases to be much of a "captain."

New outside groups also seek influence, chiefly the cities and the minorities, and they are not so discreet in their approaches as agriculture and the alumni have learned to become.

Several special situations exist. The Catholic colleges are moving from religious to secular control and from dominaton by the president to a sharing of authority with the faculty. Negro colleges are seeing the once masterful presence of the president—indispensable ambassador to the white power structure—reduced in stature as both faculty and students are less impressed than they once were. State colleges and community colleges, where the president historically has personally done all the hiring and firing, are witnessing faculty insurgence, and at some places even the commuter students have now become activist. Administrative authority is being reduced particularly in these three segments.

The forces that have the operative influence are those that can get the changes they want. Since World War II, these have been particularly the federal government and now the students. It is their changes which have prevailed and are prevailing. Nor is this surprising. The public interest in higher education has grown, and the methods of influence have always existed. The influence of youth has arrived on the "tidal wave" of numbers and the new tactics of confrontation. So much of the recent history of higher education has been written by federally sponsored science and by rising numbers of students that governance could not well escape these forces.

The nature of the power struggle has changed. Formerly it was the faculty demanding freedom from the authority of the president and the board in the name of academic freedom with the American Association of University Professors determining the basic lines that divided freedom from unwarranted control. Now it is the campus asking for autonomy from the government and, as yet, the lines have not been clearly drawn nor the protective agency devised that will differentiate autonomy from undue domination. The battle has moved to another part of the terrain, and there are new contestants.

Another change has been that part of the conflict has been internalized. The administration has always been looked upon as being partially foreign and thus subject to attack. The internal academic community has been viewed as composed of teachers and students. And now there is conflict within that community. Some of the students are against some of the faculty, and the faculty itself is divided. The academic community historically has faced its enemies outside and to the right. Now it finds attacks coming also from inside and mainly from the left. The "community of scholars" is now fighting within itself. The battle is not over a hated fascism without, but rather over a partially cherished syndicalism within.

A Confusion of Forms

The campus is a Tower of Babel in many ways, including governance. And Hell hath few terrors like confusion sharply challenged—which is where higher education finds itself today.

A. J. Muste once wrote that a trade union had a divided soul. It was an "army," but also a "town meeting" and a "business enterprise." It could not be all of these things at once and yet it had to be. So also the university: It is many things to many people and many things to itself. It is a guild where masters train apprentices, where expertise is supreme, a guild run by the masters, by the faculty. It is also a market place where students choose one campus instead of another and move from one campus to another, where they choose one course of study and one professor rather than another. Campuses and professors offer their wares, and students individually express their preferences. The customers pick and choose. The rules of the market place apply, even though the curriculum does provide a good many "tie-in" sales.

The university is also, to some degree, a democracy. Decisions are made that require the consent of the governed; rules are issued; and discipline is exercised. In a democracy, one man has one vote and is entitled to a jury of his peers; and the students are in the majority.

It is a corporation with property, endowments, a reputation, a permanent life to preserve as against the difficulties of the moment. A board of directors should have the competence to manage the institution and look out for its long-run welfare. No group that comes and goes has the knowledge or the interest to do so. The directors represent the integrity of the institution.

It is a bureaucracy with rules to be applied impartially, accounts to be kept, and books to be stored as efficiently as possible. The executive runs the administration. It is a series of semiautonomous service bureaus. Each bureau provides information to interested persons in industry, government, and agriculture. It needs an executive secretary working under a committee of the people being served. It is an agent of the state that spends state money and provides society with the research, skills, and consultation that are so essential to the progress of an industrial economy.

It is a church with a religion. It believes in the unfettered search for truth, in free expression of opinion without fear, in preservation of the past, including all books however offensive they may be currently, and in access on merit and the granting of grace on merit. Its principles are more important than service, or rules, or votes, or consumer preference. It is the keeper of the good, the true, and the beautiful; of culture. It perpetuates a spirit of inquiry and integrity. Its religion is not subject to compromise.

It is also a community, and the essence of community is that it is voluntarily held together by the common standards and interests of its members. Community follows the "will of the meeting" which requires more than a majority vote, and it is based upon a consensus about purpose and process. Traditionally, the academic community has been marked by tolerance among its members in their daily relations and by mutual persuasion as the basis of change; the application of power has been muted in the conduct of its internal affairs.

The university is all of these things, but it is also none of them in total. Perhaps most of all it has been a community with an implicit consensus that the guild of the faculty ran the curriculum and the research; the market choices of the students helped determine which campuses and which areas of study grew and declined; the democracy of the undergraduates governed extracurricular activities; the board watched out for the capital investment and the brand name; the president ran the day-to-day administrative affairs; the deans kept the students and the parents and the farmers and the doctors reasonably happy; the society was served in fact, but attacked on principle and expected to keep its distance; and everybody respected the academic faith and showed tolerance toward his fellow believer. Each element had its own domain. All elements had a common concern for the purposes of the community and the welfare of their fellow participants.

Much of this is now being challenged. The consensus is fading, and in some places, at some times, it no longer exists. The new crisis of governance is located in the dissolution of the old consensus. Without consensus, the campus can perish.

If Governance Followed Function

The functions of higher education are diverse, more so than the unholy trinity of teaching and research and service implies. And these functions are not inherently best subject to the same form of governance.

The main groups of functions are these. First are those associated with production: the talent hunt before and during college, the provision of professional and technical training, the conduct of research, and the extension of service. Second are those associated with consumption: the creation of opportunities for a general education, the invention and maintenance of interesting communities for daily living on campus, the provision of custodial services like medical care and counseling and guidance, and the provision of a holding operation where students can drop in and out as they change career and life plans. Third are those associated with citizenship: the provision of remedial work for people deprived at earlier levels of education, the conduct of basic "acculturation" to democratic principles and cultural patterns, and the development of commentary upon, criticism about, and dissent toward the surrounding society.

The faculty would seem to be in a particularly good position to govern professional and technical training, research, and dissent–these are the areas where expertise is or should be supreme–and to consider general policy for "acculturation" (if anyone can). The students are in an advantageous position to share in the governance of general education (with the interested faculty) and of community life (with sympathetic administrators); the administration is most suited to govern the talent hunt (with faculty advice), the service activities (with advice from the groups specifically to be served), the custodial functions (with student advice), the holding operations (with faculty advice), and the remedial activities (with faculty advice).

Important qualifications are necessary. As two examples, the balance of research effort and its conduct without secrecy are of concern to the entire community, and community life must be conducted within the limits of the general law applicable to all citizens.

This particular functional distribution of governance would mean major changes from common practice: The faculty would assume authority over the rules governing dissent (such campus rules will only be effective anyway with faculty approval); and students would share substantial authority over the preprofessional curriculum and over community life on campus–authority that now resides with the faculty for the former and the administration for the latter.

Two of these shifts of authority would run counter to current public opinion: that to the faculty on dissent when the public has its suspicions, and that to the students on community life when the public has its fears. But the only viable rules on dissent will be faculty rules and public law, and the only viable community life will be responsive to the students and acceptable to them. One of the problems of governance today is that changes which the campus requires are changes which much of the public abhors; and that the changes affecting political action and styles of life which find broad public support are anathema to the campus.

A missing link in governance in the United States is an overall council of the total campus community–students, faculty, administrators, trustees, alumni–charged with discussing common concerns, such as academic freedom, institutional autonomy, continuity and integrity of operations, overall functions, and governance. Such a council would seek to evolve and preserve a consensus about the community as a whole and to protect the academic faith. The Australian universities have done and are doing particularly well in providing such councils.

The board, composed largely of lay members, should, I believe, be kept, with some changes in some situations. The board, when properly constituted, can serve as a buffer against improper external pressures. It can be, and often has been, a dynamic force in assuring progressive change as against the conservatism of the faculty. Additionally, it brings competence in handling many business and financial matters, and serves as the guardian of the long-run interests of the institution. Its role often needs clarification—particularly as to how it may best review performance; and its membership needs scrutiny—particularly as to how members may best be chosen to assure an understanding of and devotion to the institution in its myriad aspects.

Clarification is also necessary of both the legitimate interests and the limits of interference of state and federal governments.

All the points raised have certain implications for different types of institutions. The faculty would have even more authority over the university; the students would assume more influence over the liberal arts college or the "cluster" college on a university campus; and the administration would maintain much of its predominance in the community college. Nevertheless, the central suggestion is that governance should be related to a careful consideration of functions.

The crisis over governance is due, in part, to the rise in importance of certain functions—the rise of the consumption functions as pressed by the students and the rise of the dissent function as pressed by students and some faculty. The existing system of governance has not been well adapted to these new emphases.

A Pragmatic Pluralistic Strategy

The problems of governance in higher education are so complex that no single solution is possible—situations vary from campus to campus and within a campus from one major function to another. Nor are perfect solutions likely—perfection from one point of view is imperfection from another. Nor are permanent solutions likely—institutions change and the interests and roles of their several constituencies change, and, also, experience accumulates.

Attempted solutions on the basis of ideology—all power to the faculty or all power to the students or all power to the regents who represent the people—are fraught with danger. There can be no clear preference for one solution versus another solution on principle, given the nature of the academic institution; and ideological solutions tend to be absolutist, authoritarian, and across-the-board in a situation that calls for tolerance, a large measure of individual freedom, and the precise fitting of governance to special situations. Attempted solutions on the basis of power alone—on who has the money or the votes or mob pressure—can tear a campus apart, and once torn apart it is hard to put together again.

A practical, pragmatic approach seems more sensible. An effort should be made to sort out the general issue of governance into its component parts, and then to approach each part in the light of the total problem. Area by area, the central questions should be who has an interest in the problem and who has competence to deal with it. The test should be performance. If performance is good, the argument for change is reduced. If performance is bad, the argument for change is enhanced. As an example, the undergraduate curriculum for nonmajors is a disaster area on many campuses. The faculty as a whole has little or no interest in it, and many students are dissatisfied with it. Here is an area where the faculty cannot be proud of its record, and where the students have a great interest and some competence. Where the faculty has done well, as in some liberal arts colleges, the case for student participation is less persuasive.

This practical, pragmatic approach can lead to a whole series of agreements, area by area, at any moment of time. In fact, this approach is being followed, hesitantly and too slowly, in the United States, but particularly in Britain, Canada, and Australia. France and Germany, by contrast, are searching for across-the-board solutions of one-half power to the students or one-third power to the students in all areas. A more pragmatic series of solutions might lead to the conclusion that power should be total in some areas and zero in others.

Governance problems are best handled function by function. Also, academic governance is best conducted on a face-to-face basis within small communities. This suggests that separate institutions should be created to handle separate functions (particularly when the functions are not compatible—as, for example, specialized research versus general education for the nonmajors). Where several functions are combined in single institutions, there should be considerable decentralization of governance. It also suggests that institutions, both in total and in their component parts, should be of modest size. Structure and governance are interrelated.

Massive size is an enemy of effective governance in the academic world with its great variety of activities, interests, and personalities. A campus of large size might best be viewed as a series of communities within a common environment, rather than as a single monolithic community; this is how Harvard is organized.

Higher education in the United States is now reexamining the system of governance given to it by history. A new series of consensuses is needed—not one overall "best" solution, not one single preferred form. Variety in solutions should match the variety of situations, and this is almost infinite. Many small agreements will come closer to providing effective governance in totality than will any global approach. An examination of functions is essential to the success of the endeavor. The task is to match the form of governance with the function—to use the guild where the guild works best, democracy where democracy works best, and so forth. We are fortunate in having a variety of forms available to match against the variety of functions. The test of the matching will be found in the performance—let the governance fit the functions. Clarity about functions is becoming essential to sanity in governance now that the consensus which embraced the confusions of the past has disintegrated into conflict.

Charles Frankel

THE QUESTION OF ACADEMIC DEMOCRACY

Charles Frankel agrees with critics of the status quo *to the extent that he believes universities ought to be democratic institutions. He, however, does not believe that they ought to be regulated according to the principle of "one man, one vote." There is every reason, he contends, to take account of degrees of competence along with a due regard for the egalitarian ideal.*

The claim that students should participate in the major decision-making processes of colleges or universities is a political one. Its justification, if it has any, is the same as that which lies behind the demand of subordinate groups who constitute a majority in other domains of society to have a say about the conditions of their life and work. The justification, in short, is the general one that democratic principles call for the establishment of student power in higher education.

But is this what "democratic principles" do entail? Indeed, do they apply to institutions of learning? Are colleges and universities sufficiently like cities or national governments, or unions or factories, to justify the use of the same political arguments in relation to them? Or are they so different that a different set of principles applies to them, in part or in whole?

Weaving through most demands for "student power," or, for that matter, some demands for "faculty power," there are recurrent assumptions. They are worth listing.

1. A university consists of separate groups or blocs. Administrators and trustees form one bloc, the faculty a second, the students a third. The relationships between these blocs are essentially like the relationships between other groups in a political situation. Power is the name of the game, and each fights to get a larger share of it. If justice is to be served, therefore, the subordinate groups have to fight for more power. In a university, this means that faculty and students form a natural alliance. They are, in effect, the workers and peasants of the university, facing its entrenched ruling class, the trustees, together with their paid lackeys, the administrators.

2. Universities are not democratic organizations, but they should be. It is a sign of the hypocrisy of present-day society that it talks about individual rights and majority rule but denies the members of the largest group in the universities —the students—any voice in their government.

3. Accordingly, government by a board of trustees, supported by an administration, must be abolished or radically altered. Students and professors should make the major decisions, and the administration should be reduced to doing the housework. At the very least, trustees and administrators should be forced

to share their power. For it is not clear what trustees do, or why they have any rights over a university.

All of these assumptions have an initial plausibility about them. Yet the first, it seems to me, is a portrait of a university painted with an axe. The second is a tangle of laudable ideals and loose political philosophy. As for the third, it makes some interesting practical recommendations that are worth discussing. But if we are going to pursue them, it is important to do so for the right reasons, and most of the reasons that are given are wrong.

There are, of course, some characteristics of "class conflict" within universities. Professors bargain for their salaries with administrators. The general level of faculty salaries is influenced by pressures from the faculty. Conditions of work, such as the number of courses taught, are subjects of negotiation. The faculty as a group maintains a watchful eye over the administration to be sure that it does not trample on the faculty's rights. Professors think that administrators don't know what's going on. Administrators think that professors don't understand them. All of this resembles an employer-employee relationship.

Yet the resemblance is limited, and if it is taken as the clue to the essential nature of the relationship between faculty and administration, it is violently misleading. The professor has tenure: After he has passed certain signposts, he cannot be fired from his job short of misconduct, and not always then. His equity in his job is as firm as if he had bought it. And the president of his university can give him fewer orders about what to do with his job than his town council can give him about what to do with his house and land.

There is a fundamental respect in which the administrators of a university are in a different position from the managers of a company. The university administrators cannot create a total plan of work, define jobs within it, and then assign individual workers to them. Of course, now that labor unions have the power they have, managers cannot do this as easily as they once could. But the difference between their position and that of university administrators is nevertheless very great. The product of a factory is a corporate product to which individuals contribute. The product of a university is many separate, individual products, for which the corporate arrangements provide protection and support, but for which the individuals have basic responsibility.

The university administrator, by and large, has to deal with people who are intent on their own work, who have bargaining power in their own individual right, who have entrenched positions and feudal retainers around them, and who carry with them bundles of traditional freedoms and antique privileges on which they can call in time of trouble. Usually, it's no contest: The administrator is out of his league. By cajolery, by the allocation of funds, every once in a while by the power of his ideas, he can try to bring some system and purpose into the division of faculty labor. But he doesn't run the plant. This is a reason, perhaps it is the most important reason, why students so often fail to get a fair shake educationally. Universities are intensely individualistic in their structure and spirit. It is not impossible, but it is difficult to bring the individualists that compose them together to study and agree on their collective business.

In brief, a university, though a hierarchy, is a discontinuous hierarchy. The faculty is one hierarchy, the administration another, and the two hierarchies do different things, generally speaking. Where their activities overlap or conflict, there has to be a settlement. But on the whole, universities manage to keep going because each group recognizes its place. The relation between administration and faculty is not a relation between superiors and subordinates and certainly not a relation between employer and employees. It is a constitutional arrangement for the separation of powers.

The model of employer-employee relations, with its overtones of "class conflict," probably applies best, indeed, not to the relations between administration and faculty, but to the relations between senior professors and junior members of the teaching staff. Here some of the traditional—indeed, the nineteenth-century—powers of the boss over the worker apply. The junior teacher's assignment is given to him, and he depends on his boss for his bread and career. Because there has been a shortage of labor in the academic marketplace in recent years, junior teachers have a somewhat better bargaining position than they once did. Nevertheless, the young instructor or professor without tenure is the closest thing we have, in a contemporary American university, to the old-fashioned exploited worker.

Where, then, do students fit into this situation? The fact is that there is no analogy from any other human collectivity that quite applies to their position in a university. Consumer, worker, recipient of favors, protected son—the student is all of these, and none. He is a consumer, yes, but an unlucky one: He has to pass tests laid down by the seller before he is allowed to leave with the prize he came to purchase. Is he a worker? There are similarities. He has to submit to the rules and regulations of the management, and produce what it wants him to produce. But he does not turn over what he produces and get a wage in return. What he produces—certain skills and attitudes, a demonstrated mastery of a field of knowledge, a set of qualities of mind he did not have when he entered—these are his, not the management's, and they are presumably for his principal benefit, not the management's.

Is he, then, in the position of a beneficiary, a recipient of favors, an object of philanthropy? The student cannot entirely dodge this analogy. Even when he pays for his education, he doesn't pay its full cost, and he certainly receives a great many services intended to keep him healthy and happy. And yet, as a citizen in an affluent democracy, as a twentieth-century man with a full quota of human rights, the student is only receiving what the society, it is now generally held, is under a fair obligation to give him. Besides, it needs him for its own purposes, and it needs him trained.

So perhaps a better analogy is that the student is like the protected son in the family, loved and guarded while he is prepared for his future role. In English-speaking countries particularly, the university has in fact been expected to serve some of the functions of a surrogate family, and the student has been expected to submit to some of the restraints of living in the parental nest. But one need only state this analogy to see that it illuminates only a part of the story. All along people have known that, as Mr. Dooley said, at the age when a boy is fit to go to college, he isn't fit to be kept at home. The college has represented the parents, but it has also served the social function of easing the student out of the family and into the public world.

Probably the best analogy is simply that of the apprentice in the old medieval guild. It applies in certain ways to graduate students. The difficulty, however, is that it does not really apply to undergraduates. Essentially, undergraduate students are going through the first initiation rites of the scholarly guild. But they are going through them with a difference. Very few of them go on to full membership in the guild, and no one administers these rites to them with the expectation that most of them are in training to be full-time scholars. What has happened, apparently, is that the scholarly guild has managed to convince the other guilds that its initiation rites are generally useful to everybody else, and not least to the initiate himself. This may be right, or it may be wrong; but it means that the college student is not an apprentice in the traditional sense.[1] We are forced to the conclusion that students are—students! It is a status all to itself, and no other word describes it as well.

This may seem, undoubtedly it does seem, an exceedingly long way around to a tautology. But taking this long way around is illuminating. For most of the odd, novel, or shocking things that are being said about the condition of students in the United States today, and many of the discussions taking place about the reallocation of powers within universities, depend on the application of loose and unexamined analogies, drawn from other types of social organization, to the structure of institutions of learning.

Thus, to take a doctrine that has achieved growing currency, students are not an "exploited" group. It is possible to say other things about them: for example, that they are in the grip of a punishing and misconceived examination and admissions system that puts too many of the wrong kinds of pressure on them; that they are neglected; that, in many places, they are perversely miseducated; that they are harassed, constrained, and subject to indignities ranging from Victorian rules in dormitories to forced service in the army. Some or all of these are defensible statements. But they do not mean that students are "exploited," if the word means that anyone is profiting from them at their expense. As those who have experienced exploitation know, it usually involves a condition more painful to endure than boring or "irrelevant" classes. When this doctrine is propounded by students in revolt, or by middle-aged people who claim to speak for them, it can encourage, among those who remember the Depression, a feeling that there really is a "generation gap." And to students who are today trying to rise out of poverty, and to struggle against exploitation, it can give the impression that members of the more fortunate middle class are indeed insulated from reality.

Nor is the larger version of the doctrine of the exploited student any more persuasive. The word "exploitation" has been stretched so that it is used to describe the process by which young men and women, in the best years of their lives, are educated not for purposes of their own but for the external purposes of an alien social order. The university exists, it is said, simply to provide highly trained labor to the corporations, the government, or the knowledge factories. It is, therefore, an instrument of exploitation, a tool of the military-industrial complex or the one-dimensional consumer society. This sweeping proposition falls to the floor under its own weight. A sharp line cannot be drawn between the individual's "own purposes" and the purposes of the social order. A young man who wants to be a mathematician draws his own pleasure from that

[1] This may seem to apply only to students in liberal arts colleges and not to those in vocationally oriented schools like those of agriculture, nursing, or home economics. But even in these schools, the emphasis is on the mastery of general skills and broad fields of learning and not on picking up the tricks of a trade.

profession; the fact that it happens to be a useful profession does not mean that he has been dragooned into it against his will. To be socially useful is not to be exploited, and there is no society, existing or conceivable, which does not demand that its members make some contribution to the collective good.

The difference between one society and another lies in large part in the kinds of exception they make to this general rule and in the flexibility and scope of their conceptions of social utility. From that point of view, contemporary American society is one of the more, rather than less, generous social orders. Of course, it is also true that in any society there are some jobs to which people have to be force-fitted. They may be useful jobs, but they satisfy no esthetic or moral craving of the individual who holds them. It is hard to see, however, how all such jobs can be eliminated—nor is it even plain that all people want to be stimulated by their work. Einstein said, towards the end of his life, that if he had to do it all over again, he would be a plumber. It was simple, self-respecting work, free from the constant pressure to produce and be "creative." But in any case, college and university education are the best avenues that exist in our society to the kind of work that combines personal commitment and social utility. Of all the groups in society to whom the word "exploitation" is least applicable from this point of view, college and university students would seem to be the most conspicuous.

Of course, the deeper assumption in the charge that higher education is "exploitative" is that it trains students for work which is frivolous or harmful, not useful. The basic purposes of the society are wicked, and its fundamental arrangements misconceived. But we need not examine that very large proposition here. True or not, it cannot be used to indict universities. For the universities are themselves the major centers in which that proposition, in its extreme or more moderate forms, flourishes. They shelter the teachers and students who express and propagate this view of American society. That in itself makes it impossible to denounce universities as unequivocal instruments of the status quo. At any rate, it makes it impossible if one respects facts.

And besides, what system of higher education in the world grants more freedom to students in their choice of studies than the one that now exists in the United States? What system has provided more room for individual variation, more flexibility in programs of study, more diversity in standards and style, more friendliness to eccentricities, rigid and unimaginative though many of its aspects may be? Assume the worst: Say that the larger economic system is "exploitative"; say that it chains people to routines and purposes to which they have not consented and which they do not approve. Still, of all the parts of the existing social order, this indictment applies least of all to institutions of higher education. Very few of them fail to offer a viable alternative to the student who refuses to be co-opted into the system: He need merely study music, philosophy, and poetry, and join some protest group. And the chances are good that he will be offered a job by this "exploitative" system which will allow him to go on doing the same things after he has graduated.

Whatever may be wrong with American colleges and universities—and there is plenty—calling them "exploitative" is demagoguery. The war and the draft have changed the objective relation of students to their colleges, and have altered their inner feelings about the experience of education. These are real but circumscribable evils. Broadside attacks on the university system as such merely lead people away from effective action against these specific difficulties.

In sum, the case for student power cannot be presented as a case against tyranny and oppression. Nor can it be justified on the basis of fundamental student rights. It is highly desirable for a dozen reasons, I think, to give students a larger share of responsibility in the government of the institutions which they attend. But the issue is a matter of practical educational and political practice, not of the rights of man. And this distinction is important. To do something because it is desirable is not the same as to do it because it violates people's rights not to do it. The logic is different, and the consequences are different. Students are indeed members in good standing of a university community. But this community is a hierarchical human organization, based on the premise that some people know more than other people and that the community cannot perform its tasks effectively unless these gradations in knowledge are recognized in its form of government. Allowing for certain qualifications, the rights which people acquire within this community are earned rights which they have to show that they merit.

This is not an abuse of "democracy." The right of a citizen of the larger society to vote just as the next man can, without regard to hierarchy, is based on the premise that, where the major policies of the State are concerned, where the nature of what is good for society is at issue, only extreme inadequacies, like illiteracy or a criminal record, are disqualifying. The basic reason for this view, according to the believer in democracy, is that there are no reasonably defensible general procedures by which the citizenry can be divided into the class of those who know enough to have an opinion worth counting or an interest worth expressing, and the class of those who don't. And, in addition, majority rule is accepted in democracies only because its range is restricted. Individuals have rights against majority rule, and all sorts of associations exist which are insulated against majority rule.

In contrast, while universities are democratic organizations in the sense that individuals have a broad array of personal rights within them and that there is a play of opinion inside them which has a massive effect on their evolution, they are not democratic organizations in the sense that majority rule applies to them. For within a university there are acceptable procedures by which people can be graded in accordance with their competence, and grading people in this way is essential to the conduct of the university's special business. The egalitarian ideal does not apply across the board in universities any more than it does in any other field where *skill* is the essence of the issue. To suggest that it should apply is to make hash of the idea of learning. This involves, as the very language of the learned community suggests, the attainment of successive, and increasingly higher, *degrees* of competence. If there is a case to be made for student participation in the higher reaches of university government, it is a case that is not based upon *rights,* but upon considerations of good educational and administrative practice.

To examine this case, it is best to begin by looking at the status quo—the government of colleges and universities by trustees. Does the discussion we have just concluded imply that the present system is a good one? No; but it helps to put the examination of this system in perspective.

The case which is generally presented against trustee control of universities mixes truths with exaggerations. It is true that most trustees tend to be preoccupied with other matters than education, that they are inaccessible to teachers and students, and that a dispiriting number of them have reached an age and station in life calculated to protect them against fresh ideas. It is not surprising, therefore, that professors and students are sparing in the confidence they lavish on trustees. The government of American universities by boards of trustees is not an example of government by the consent of the governed.

However, neither is it an example of tyranny. The powers of trustees are severely limited by custom and law, and by the realities of a university. In any well-established university, trustees normally leave educational decisions to the faculty. One of their primary educational functions, indeed, is simply to provide the educational community of the university—its students and faculty—with protective insulation. The trustees throw their mantle of influence and respectability around it, deflecting and absorbing criticisms and denunciations, and thus guarding the community's freedom. Indeed, it is doubtful that faculties and student bodies, in many parts of the country, could by themselves, and without the help of trustees, successfully defend their autonomy, even assuming that their economic problems could be solved. It is odd that trustees should be attacked as though their presence was in contravention of academic freedom. Their presence is usually a condition for it.

On the whole, indeed, trustees of private colleges and universities probably have a better record with regard to respecting the autonomy and freedom of faculty and students than do boards of regents, chosen by popular vote or appointed by a governor or other public official. Those who call for "democratic control" or "democratic participation" in the government of universities should reflect on the fact that there is a second version of the idea of "democratic control," not less acceptable than theirs, and perhaps somewhat easier to bring into being. If government of a university by private trustees is a form of despotism, why not turn over the government of the university to public control? This is certainly what is likely to happen if private funds are removed, and only tax revenues are available for supporting the institution. Yet most of the evidence suggests that when the general public, through its political processes, exercises control, the autonomy of the faculty and students tends to be put under greater pressure than when private trustees are in control. When a legislature votes the budget, it is usually much more insistent on knowing why Professor X, the mathematician, is sounding off on the glories of Cuba, or how that ragged crowd of students who took over the Administration Hall could ever have slipped through a decent admissions procedure.

The comparison between the record of boards of trustees and that of boards of regents should not, of course, be pushed too hard. In most parts of the United States, public higher education is not now significantly different from private education with respect to the academic freedoms it provides. What is different, however, is the story behind that equal academic freedom. The presidents of public universities generally have to conduct a much severer campaign of public education, and spend a good deal more of their time defending the rights of individuals, than do the heads of large private institutions. If there were no private institutions, this task might well be even more difficult. The private institutions help set the standards. The government of some universities by private trustees is a general condition for maintaining the variety and independence of American education at large.

Still, whether we are discussing boards of trustees or boards of regents, it can be asked whether this form of government is the best form for a college or university. Trustees (or regents) do make educational decisions, even if most of these are only indirect. They allocate resources, do more for one field of learning than for another, and make arrangements affecting the relation of the university to the larger society which bear on the daily lives of teachers and students. Would it not be better if trustees continued to do their work of finding the money, but surrendered the other powers they exercise to the people who really constitute the university—namely, its students and teachers? Obviously, it is doubtful that many trustees would accept this proposal that they should supply the money but keep quiet about the way it is used. Just to see where the argument goes, however, let us imagine that trustees have a capacity for self-immolation not conspicuous in most human beings. Would it be a good thing for them to retire from the scene?

Not entirely. They are the buffers of the university against external pressures. As we have seen, an educational institution requires such protection. Most organizations, furthermore, benefit from having a lay group of critics with deep commitments to them, who are nevertheless not part of their daily operations. In addition, since universities must maintain relations with the surrounding society, they require people on their board of governors who have interests and experience in that society. And it is always well to remember that, though education, like the law, is in part a professional business, it is also everybody's business. If students have a stake in what happens to them, by the same token, so do their parents and so do lay members of the community. In courts of law, juries are not composed of professional lawyers. On the university scene, the outsider, though he should not have as decisive a place as a juror has, also deserves to be represented.

In part, this function is served by the activities of alumni, and by the presence of alumni on most boards of trustees, and, in principle, it could be served by restricting the "outside" membership on such boards only to alumni. But only in part. Alumni bodies are immensely varied. The main source of private funds for some universities is the alumni, but this is not true for others. And alumni represent only one relevant point of view. There are other "outside" constituencies which a university should serve, and which should be represented on its governing board. In general, the needs of most universities justify the proposition that they should be ruled, at least in part, by people who are not active members of them, including people who have not studied at them.

Yet these same considerations call for change in the composition of most boards of trustees. They call, equally clearly, for changes in the manner in which they communicate with the communities they govern. Boards of trustees ought to have more younger people on them, and poorer people. They ought to have recent graduates, and not only older ones. They ought to have people who have not yet arrived, and not only those swollen with success. The surrounding neighborhood should, if possible, be represented. That is not always easy to arrange because there are so often disagreements about who is "representative" of whom. But if it can be done without creating quarrels that did not exist before, then it should be done. And students and faculty members should either be represented on the board or should be assured of regular consultation with it.

The case for such changes is not open and shut. Faculties lose some of their cherished independence if they share with trustees the burdens of budget-making, real estate deals, and community politics. The extension of university self-government almost certainly involves the proliferation of still more of the committees which are the bane of many professors' lives; there can come a day when professors—and students on their committees—will curse the people who demanded "democracy" in the university, and yearn for the "despotism" under which they once suffered. Almost certainly, self-government in a university is not likely to be an enterprise in which all will participate. It should not be. A large number of professors are likely to think, and with reason, that they have other and better things to do. A large number of students may have the same idea.

But for those who want to participate, there should be an opportunity to do so. There are clear advantages to giving members of a faculty the assurance that they are represented in the decision-making procedures of their institution. The sense of distance from the institution's center has had at least something to do with the increasing mobility of professors, their lack of interest in the collective business of their institution, and their orientation towards professional organizations or community problems off the campus. The inaccessibility or uncommunicativeness of administrators is the single largest cause of declining morale in a college or university. The only thing worse, perhaps, is an excessively accessible and communicative administrator who is a simpleton. How to guarantee faculty communication with administrators and trustees—whether this should be done by guaranteeing faculty representation on the board of trustees or by other means—is a question to which answers will vary because situations are variable. But it is difficult to argue against the proposition that trustees and faculty should be in continuing communication, and that this has not been the normal pattern.

The participation of students in the supreme governing bodies of a university raises issues that are equally subtle. Students are inexperienced. They are present on a campus for only a short period, and could serve on committees and boards for only a shorter period. It takes time, on most boards and committees, before new members learn enough to become genuinely useful. Student generations change in their styles and opinions, furthermore, and sometimes very quickly. Students, therefore, bring an element of discontinuity, a shortened perspective and sometimes a short fuse, into the consideration of matters of policy. In educational institutions particularly, continuity of perspective and some sense of the time-dimension are essential.

Finally, student representation on the permanent governing bodies of a university poses a complex problem both practically and theoretically. How do we arrange this "representation" so that it is representative? In a liberal-arts college the problem is manageable. But in a university, with its scores of schools and faculties and its variegated student body, this is considerably easier to talk about in the abstract than to produce in the concrete. Nothing could do greater and quicker harm to the cause of "student power" than the complaint that the students officially representing their fellows are not really representative of them.

In sum, the idea of student membership on boards of trustees raises as many problems as it seems to solve. Nevertheless, the idea is worth experimentation, even though the number of students who belong to a board, or who sit with it when certain issues are discussed, should probably be small. And there is little question, apart from the formalities of representation on a board of trustees, that machinery for regular face-to-face meetings between students and trustees is desirable. Discontinuity in policy is dangerous, but so is automatic, thoughtless continuity. The long view is estimable, but impatience is useful too. And if inexperience is a handicap, so is experience: It dulls one to novelty. Trustees could learn from students things they will never learn from administrators or other trustees.

In the end, we are discussing not matters of right and justice, but matters of political wisdom. Trustees will not know what they should know unless they mix with the people who can tell them. The community they govern will not understand why the trustees have made the decisions they have, and will not have confidence in these decisions, unless it has its own trusted emissaries to keep it in touch with the board. Faulty communication is the heart of the political problem in the American universities that are today having trouble. Demands for "student power" and "faculty power," so interpreted, are more than justifiable.

One more word, however, is in order. The discussion we have just concluded turns on the distinction between students' *right* to be represented in the government of a college or university, and the desirability, for other reasons, of giving students closer access to the university's important decision-making procedures. The argument has been an argument from desirability and not from rights. But this should not be interpreted as meaning that, within a university, students have no rights. They have rights as citizens of the larger society, which they do not lose when they become members of a higher educational institution, and they also have rights that derive from their special status as students.

The term "power," when used in political contexts, has three levels of meaning. At the highest level, it can mean participation in the actual business of government. At a somewhat more restricted level, it can mean access to the people in authority so that one can advance one's own ideas or interests. At the most elementary level, it means that one possesses certain rights as against those who govern, and that one has what it takes to protect these rights. The most elementary meaning of "student power" is that students have such rights. As citizens, they have rights of free speech and association, and are free to exercise them, subject only to the impact on the rights of others. Similarly, students have the right to petition for redress of grievances; the right to organize legal political actions; the right to live their own lives when off the campus, subject only to the laws and the risks of the larger society. They also have a right, it seems to me, which is increasingly important today, and is too often violated: This is the right to control the use of their academic records.

As for the special rights which inhere in their status as students, they have, for example, the right to invite speakers of their own choice to address their organizations and to ask the university to provide the facilities required. So far as university authorities are concerned, this is not a matter of educational discretion, but of recognizing a valid claim. Students are captive audiences, forced to hear the opinions of their professors. Their right to free inquiry should imply that they have a right to seek alternative points of view. Other rights of the same kind—for example, the right to due process in disciplinary proceedings when they so request—also belong to them. These rights, as a day-to-day matter, are as important to students as the enhancement of their power over the decision-making functions of a university.

All or most of these rights are recognized, however, in all or most colleges and universities in the country. The live question now is not whether students should have them. It is how far they go. And that brings up the question of the tactics that have been employed at Columbia and many other institutions, ostensibly in the pursuit of student rights.

Daniel Bell

QUO WARRANTO?—NOTES ON THE GOVERNANCE OF UNIVERSITIES IN THE 1970s

The current controversy over university government, writes Daniel Bell, points to a fundamental "crisis in legitimacy" in which the aims and character of the university can no longer be taken for granted.

Quo warranto?—"By whose right?"—is an ancient legal challenge to authority. The controlling problem of the governance of universities in the 1970s will be the resolution of a crisis in legitimacy, in the definition of authority which justifies any use of power or command. Clearly, in the last two years, there has been an enormous erosion of authority. The cry of the angry student has been, "By what right—who gave you the right—to say so?"

To govern is to exercise authority. In *The Social Contract* Rousseau wrote, "The strongest man is never strong enough to be always master unless he transforms his power into right and obedience into duty . . . ." No institution can live free of the daily shadow of coercion without the freely given consent of its members. A university cannot rule by power. In fact, it has no power other than the reluctant threat of expulsion; and if besieged it has to resort to civil authority, an action that serves merely to confirm a rupture rather than resolve a conflict. The lack of power makes the problem of winning assent much more a question of agreement than of vote, for if a minority finds a situation immoral, or intolerable, a majority vote does not of itself provide legitimacy for action. The problem then is twofold: accepting the challenge to deal with the morality of specific actions; and recreating a generalized trust in the institution. Morality involves the redefinition of accepted, and often unquestioned, judgments. Trust derives from a belief in the worthwhileness—in short, the character—of an institution.

The older authority of the university (and therefore a definition of its character) was, in Max Weber's sense, of a "traditional" kind. It was rooted in the past and sanctified by its attachment to the central value system of the society. Its role was to exemplify and express those values. Those values were not, however, the ideology of any particular social body, but the maintenance

Reprinted in part with permission from *The Public Interest,* no. 19. Copyright ©1970 National Affairs, Inc., pp. 53-68. Notes deleted.

of a tradition of free inquiry and of a consensus about what constituted civility. Recently, particularly the past twenty-five years, the university has sought, again in Weber's sense, a "rational-legal" authority—namely the assertion of a particular expertise (as the source of rational authority) and a willingness to serve society in its pursuit of socially defined goals (the basis of its claim to legal support). These rational-legal claims as well as the traditional authority are being challenged today—first by the students and now in a growing voice by the faculty.

To say that the university must regain its authority is simply to say that the university must live. But live as what? True, there has been an erosion of authority in the society and, to the extent that the university is part of the society, it is subject to forces beyond its control; but there has been a loss of trust in the institution itself because something has happened to its character. I would suggest that the crisis of legitimacy in the university (to the extent that it is specific and not just societal) derives from its assumption of many new and contradictory functions and from its evident inability to fashion a structure appropriate to its purposes. For twenty-five years the American university has been a vast "dumping ground" for tasks that society could not fill elsewhere. The university did not resist—in fact, it often welcomed—the intrusions; but it failed to adapt its structure to the new tasks. Now, the major question is whether the university can fulfill these functions; and if it can not, what tasks should it legitimately assume.

Thus, we have a double problem: to redefine the character of "the university," and to create a system of governance appropriate to that character . . . .

The problem of governance is tied up with the question—increasingly an ambiguous one—of what a university is and, more broadly, what *a university system* is in the society. One can, for the purposes of analysis, identify four functions which have been and are being performed today by the university:

1. Custodian of the traditions of Western culture and the evaluation of claims to membership in this "great chain of learning." This is the oldest function, and it centered in the humanities. But this function is in process of dissolution. Ten years ago, a serious debate could take place about whether Nietzsche belonged in the canon of great works to be studied in a Humanities course—it actually took place at Columbia. Today, almost anything goes. During one of the sit-ins at Duke University, a student complained (on camera, during a TV news program) that his modern literature course only went up to the 1950s and did not include the 1960s.

2. The search for truth through inquiry and scholarship: the effort to assert the philosophical foundations of certified knowledge, the discovery of the laws of nature, the explication of the norms and rules that govern human behavior. These inquiries still go on, though they have become, necessarily, more technical and specialized.

3. The training of a large number of people as professionals in specific fields. A hundred years ago, one learned on the job. Now, with knowledge increasingly dependent on theory, one learns in a school and then takes a job. This function has been combined in recent years, with mass higher education and technical training on the junior college level.

4. The application of knowledge to social use. This includes, in earlier years, aid to agriculture; more recently it has been the service to military technology and to economic planning.

Since World War II, the third and fourth functions have expanded enormously, for many reasons: the fact that theoretical knowledge has become more intimately entwined with applied research and development; the needs of government and industry, etc. Whatever the reason, one sees the fruits of this in the multiplication of research institutes, centers, and programs in universities, the expansion of research and the service functions.

But all this brings us back to the root question: What is a university? It is startling to realize that we have not really had any adequate definition of a university. The university is ordinarily likened to an extended family, a secular church, to a corporation, to a community, or it is simply described as a microcosm of the society. And the multiplication of functions in recent years leads to increasing ambiguity and amorphousness about the nature of the beast—and this is one of the central reasons for the failure to define adequate governance. If it is like a family, then one kind of standard applies; if like a political community, another set of standards; if like a corporation, a third, and so on. But the very fact that all these metaphors and analogies are possible only multiplies the confusion and makes more difficult the question of asserting some justification—and therefore legitimacy—for authority in the university.

There are, it seems to me, two distinct justifications possible, each (as ideal types) representing markedly different roles for the university.

The first might be called the classical model. This is to say that the university is that institution in the society endowed with the special function (and the extraordinary immunity) of searching for truth and evaluating the culture of its times. In this sense, it is free to question everything—*in theory.* If it is to be true to its purpose, nothing is exempt from its scrutiny. But if it [is] to have the immunity from reprisal that goes with this power, it must obey the self-denying ordinance of remaining at the level of theory, of speculative discourse. The question whether anything is to be put into practice is a question, not for the university, but for the society. In this model, the university stands outside the society, and contains within itself all varieties of creeds and beliefs, and all kinds of persons, subject to the one qualification of competence in the world of learning and scholarship. These qualified individuals, scholars, are free to explore any question, and test all areas of human experience—in theory.

The second might be called the pragmatic model. Here the function of the university is primarily one of service to the society: service in training large numbers of persons, service in the application of knowledge, service of the members of the university in government and elsewhere, etc.

The legitimacy of each type is clear: the first, knowledge for the sake of knowledge; the second, social benefits. But the limitations of each view are also apparent. If one chooses the first, then one is barred, in the role as scholar and researcher (though not as citizen) from political advocacy and active partisanship. If the second, the question becomes: "Who shall decide?" Should the universities serve the military? Or the urban poor? Or the radicals? Should the criterion be national interest, social need, the command of money, the influence of power groups, or what?

While my formulation of the types is extreme, and somewhat abstract, the division is nonetheless real, and some choices will have to be made . . . .

One of the immediate reforms that must take place in many of our institutions of higher learning is the creation of juridical and representational bodies to deal with policy issues of the university. The university, today, faces a special problem. The idea of a small community of scholars (with senior common rooms and junior common rooms to mark the differences in rank) on the Oxbridge model is clearly inapplicable in the United States. Given its size and varied functions, the university today mingles a political model (as regards faculty self-governance and self-selection) with a bureaucratic model (in the relation of an administration to the students, often in the organization of research, relation to the community, etc.). The clarification of these differences—how far the university must go in being a political community, and how much bureaucratization is necessary—is one of the most pressing problems in the explication of university governance.

Clearly the university must become, more formally, a political community. The making of policy decisions must be open, subject to debate, and to some form of confirmation by the relevant constituencies in the university. There are, it seems to me, three major areas which require exploration:

1. *The structure of representation.* The problem will vary from school to school. In some unitary colleges there might be some kind of proportional representation between faculty as a whole, administration, and students; in other, federated institutions, there would be representation by federated unit, etc. So far as I know, there are no studies of the range of representational structures and the rationales for each.

2. *The relevant constituencies.* Who is to have a vote, and of what kind (with vote or without), in university deliberations? The librarians are pressing for faculty status. The teaching assistant wants to be considered as having a faculty role, though usually he is also a graduate student. Do nontenured and tenured personnel have equal voice on all issues? Again, there is here a major area in need of research and clarification of principle.

3. *The division of powers.* What decisions, if any, are reserved for the trustees, who are often the legal custodians of the corporation? What kinds of administrative action are subject to review, and by whom? To state these questions is to indicate again how little discussion there has been of these most crucial issues of university life.

Beyond all these problems, one crucial consideration—which most people accept as metaphor, yet rarely explore in practice—has to be observed: that all these problems take place within a change of scale unprecedented in the history of the university. A change of scale is not simply a linear extension of size. As Galileo once defined it in his square cube law, a change of *size* is a change in *form,* and consequently in institution. Most of our older discussions of rights and responsibilities, the allocation of powers and the devolution of responsibilities, are modeled on an organizational form whose size is of a vastly smaller magnitude than our own. It is this change of scale, in all its dimensions, and for all its consequences, that still has to be explored.

* * *

6

An Overview

Sanford A. Lakoff

PRIVATE GOVERNMENT IN THE MANAGED SOCIETY

If private government is a useful concept, how is it that political scientists have all but ignored the subject until recently? Sanford A. Lakoff suggests two reasons: (1) Early analysts, preoccupied with the transition from feudalism to liberalism, neglected associations standing midway between the individual and the state; (2) Later analysts, fastening on the study of "organizations," have subjected private associations to an essentially apolitical mode of analysis. The organization theorists, he suggests, have succumbed to the lure of a managerial ideology instead of examining the prospects for democracy in private as well as public government.

I

In a liberal democracy students of politics are bound to be preoccupied with the definition of freedom and with its actual expression in social and political life. No such inquiry can avoid the principle of the separation of public and private.[1] However ambiguous a principle it may be, however diverse and shifting its applications, to dispense with it is virtually to dispense with the very idea of liberty. But there is a corollary to this principle which, although it is no less important, has not yet received adequate recognition: The separation of public and private implies and generates a dual system of government—public and private. Both sectors of government regulate the affairs of members, both exercise an influence over nonmembers, and both serve as contexts for the expression and resolution of conflict. To estimate the ordinary prospects for autonomy in any society it is therefore essential to analyze the structure and operation of both types of government and the pattern of their interaction.

The validity of this corollary is in no way impaired by a recognition of the differences in character and scope of action that distinguish public from private government. We need only show that these differences are not so radical or qualitative as to justify the inference that only public associations have the true characteristics of polity or government. There are usually said to be two essential differences: First, the private association cannot exercise the ultimate sanction

[1]This principle is the critical concern of at least two major recent studies, Henry S. Kariel, *The Decline of American Pluralism* (Stanford: Stanford University Press, 1961); and Grant McConnell, *Private Power and American Democracy* (New York: Alfred A. Knopf, 1966). It also figures prominently in Peter Bachrach, *The Theory of Democratic Elitism: A Critique* (Boston: Little, Brown, 1967), esp. pp. 102-05, William Kornhauser, *The Politics of Mass Society* (New York: The Free Press, 1959), and John Kenneth Galbraith, *The New Industrial State* (Boston: Houghton Mifflin, 1967).

Reprinted from J. Roland Pennock and John W. Chapman, editors, *Voluntary Associations: Nomos XI* (New York: Atherton Press, 1969);

of physical force[2] which, as the legitimate monopoly of the state, is said to make the public association unique; second, membership in the private association is voluntary, while citizenship is commonly thought compulsory.

Both contentions have a certain undeniable analytical validity, but as a practical matter they fall far short of establishing an absolute distinction. As to the first, the fact is that private associations may have recourse to potent sanctions short of physical force while the public government is often unwilling or unable to invoke its ultimate sanction. The threat of excommunication, to take an extreme example, may seem more consequential to a communicant than any secular penalty.[3] The threat of exclusion from a vocation or a livelihood, to take the more common case, may well be regarded as a far more serious threat by the recalcitrant member of a trade union or a professional association than any of the ultimate sanctions of public authority. Business corporations, especially when they enjoy monopolistic or oligopolistic conditions in which they can administer prices and all but control both supply and demand, regularly exercise an economic power which is no less coercive than the threat of physical force. Because of their economic power, or because they represent significant segments of the electorate, well-organized interest groups frequently determine public policy in areas of direct concern to them, even though the right to legislate is formally reserved to public authority.[4]

The private sphere may also enjoy a certain power at the expense of public authority in cases of conflict. A well-disciplined trade union located in a strategic sector of the economy will sometimes defy an antistrike injunction because its leaders know that public government will hesitate to bring ultimate sanctions to bear, for fear of antagonizing other trade unionists and for fear of exposing the fragility of the consensus upon which it must, in the last resort, rely for its own survival. Although the public authority may have the sole right to utter the sovereign's "last word," it is usually mute so long as private associations do not pose an immediate threat to the safety of society and so long as they exercise their power without flagrant resort to illegal or corrupt methods.[5] There are vast areas of social life, in other words, into which public government never

[2] Except, of course, for illegal societies like the Mafia. But to speak of "the private government of organized crime" (see "Robert Kennedy Defines the Menace," *New York Times Magazine* [Oct. 13, 1963], 15), which seems to imply that only outlaw associations have political characteristics, is to put too much weight on the sanction of physical force and too little on more subtle forms of coercion.

[3] Cf. McConnell, op. cit., p. 125, and generally his admirable chapter on "Private Government," pp. 119-56, where many of the points raised in this section are discussed.

[4] "The market power which large absolute and relative size gives to the giant corporation is the basis not only of economic power but also of considerable political and social power of a broader sort . . . . That we pay, in the form of percentage depletion, an outrageous subsidy to the oil and gas business (which goes to the many small producers as well as to the giant integrated oil firms) is a phenomenon of no different order than that we pay nearly outrageous ones to farmers." Carl Kaysen, "The Corporation: How Much Power? What Scope?" in Edward S. Mason, ed., *The Corporation in Modern Society* (Cambridge, Mass.: Harvard University Press, 1959), p. 99. Kaysen also notes the considerable influence over foreign policy exercised by large firms with foreign branches and subsidiaries.

[5] "When the threat is aimed at the very life of the state, government commands as of right —as it did in the general strike of 1926, . . . or as it did during the war. But in most instances it is properly chary of even the display of force—unless that is made necessary by violence." William Y. Elliott, *The Pragmatic Revolt in Politics* (New York: Macmillan, 1928), p. 103.

dispatches the army, the marines, or the national guard, and in these areas private associations certainly enjoy a considerable share of effective sovereignty.

The distinction of public from private associations according to whether membership is compulsory or voluntary is, if anything, even more dubious as a practical matter.[6] (Indeed, it is even weak on theoretical grounds: in a government by consent, authority rests on "will not force," in T. H. Green's phrase.) Ideally a citizen can choose to leave one political jurisdiction for another. If he is no longer likely to find an hospitable haven in Locke's fabled vacuis locis, he may at least emigrate to another country. Practically speaking, he may find it hard to leave, even if circumstances in his native land are oppressive, and he may anticipate such serious hardships that he will decide not to go.

The situation is in principle no different with respect to membership in many private associations. Ideally a frustrated executive may leave one business corporation for another and an embittered professor may transfer from one university to another. Practically such moves may be difficult, especially if the executive's pension rights are vested only after lengthy service or if the professor's options are uncongenial and his children are enrolled in a nearby *lycée française.* A dissident trade unionist will almost never be able to join another union (for dual unionism is indeed "a cardinal sin within the American labor movement")[7] although he may find life easier in another local or another district. A physician who leaves or is expelled from one of the societies of the American Medical Association will find himself deprived of access to facilities and of other vital benefits such as professional comity and inexpensive malpractice insurance.[8] In such instances, where what is at stake is nothing less than the deprivation of the means of livelihood, membership in a private association is virtually as compulsory in character as citizenship. Among churches and sects, especially within the Protestant denominations, there is perhaps a greater possibility of mobility than in other types of association, but this mobility is often tied to economic and status considerations.[9] In order to exercise his freedom to leave one church and join another, the communicant must risk a very considerable social alienation under settled conditions. The voluntary character of private associations, then, is at most a severely limited one and certainly no basis for a radical distinction between public and private associations.

Furthermore, the question of whether the private association differs from the public because the sanction of physical force cannot be invoked and because membership is voluntary should not be allowed to obscure the plain and simple fact that while they belong to private associations people are being governed by them. In some instances, such as those involving fraternal or community service organizations, the adherent may consider his membership a trivial matter.[10]

[6] Cf. McConnell, op. cit., Chap. 5, and Christian Bay, *The Structure of Freedom* (Stanford: Stanford University Press, 1958), pp. 288-89.

[7] McConnell, op. cit., p. 150.

[8] See David R. Hyde and Payson Wolff, "The American Medical Association: Power, Purpose and Politics in Organized Medicine," *Yale Law Journal,* 63 (May 1954), 938-1022.

[9] For the classic study of this relationship, see Liston Pope, *Millhands and Preachers: A Study of Gastonia* (New Haven: Yale University Press, 1942).

[10] Indeed, even in hobby clubs and fraternal associations, personality involvement may be so intense that as Bay notes, op. cit., p. 289, people may be reluctant to quit when they feel they are being "pushed around."

But in many instances the functions performed by private associations are far from trivial, since they may vitally affect the livelihood of members and the welfare of nonmembers as well as the realization of personal values.

Although the issue of democracy in private associations is not one that has been much considered in political theory, it arises in many contexts in contemporary society. For a long time the great demand of working men was that the right of the trade union to engage in collective bargaining be recognized and protected. Now that this right has been secured, the demand that is increasingly heard from the rank-and-file members as well as from academic critics is that unions be required to guarantee the right of participation, the right of dissent, and the right to meaningful elections to all their members.[11] In corporations the movement for "shareholder democracy" led by such activists as Lewis D. Gilbert and Wilma Soss may well be unjustified and impractical,[12] but there is a growing recognition that the power of the managers of the modern corporation to control the business association must be made responsible and accountable to the constituents of the corporation—the consuming public, employees, shareholders, suppliers, distributors, and the communities in which its plants are located.[13] In the churches a considerable ferment is brewing over the role of the lower clergy and the laity in the government of the church and over the role of the church in society.[14] In the universities, trustees and administrators must now contend with the demands of faculty and students for a greater voice in the decisions by which the academy is regulated. Questions have also been raised over the right of professionals and professional groups—such as the "scientific

[11] See Clark Kerr, *Unions and Union Leaders of Their Own Choosing* (New York: Fund for the Republic, 1957). Especially pungent comments of activist dissenters are reported in Paul E. Sultan, *The Disenchanted Unionist* (New York: Harper & Row, 1963).

[12] On the limitations of shareholder democracy, see especially Eugene V. Rostow, "To Whom and for What Ends Is Corporate Management Responsible?" in Mason, op. cit.; Earl Latham, "The Body Politic of the Corporation," ibid., p. 223; and Richard Eells, *The Government of Corporations* (New York: The Free Press, 1962), pp. 258-61. The case for more effective shareholder democracy is propounded in Frank D. Emerson and Franklin C. Latcham, *Shareholder Democracy, A Broader Outlook for Corporations* (Cleveland: The Press of Western Reserve University, 1954); and Lewis D. Gilbert, *Dividends and Democracy* (Larchmont, N.Y.: American Research Council, 1956).

[13] Richard Eells, op. cit., argues cogently that the modern corporation is in the throes of a "constitutional crisis" over the question of the accountability of management to its various constituencies. See also his earlier *Corporation Giving in a Free Society* (New York: Harper & Row, 1956) for a good statement of the case for the exercise of the "corporate conscience" through financial contributions. For critical views of this argument, see Theodore Levitt, "The Dangers of Social Responsibility," *Harvard Business Review* 36 (September-October 1958); Andrew Hacker, ed., *The Corporation Take-over* (New York: Harper & Row, 1964); Andrew Hacker, "When Big Business Makes Gifts (Tax-Deductible)," *New York Times Magazine* (November 12, 1967); and Michael D. Reagan, *The Managed Economy* (New York: Oxford University Press, 1963).

[14] To cite only a few of many instances reported recently in *The New York Times:* the successful campaign for equal representation for women in the House of Deputies of the Episcopal Church (September 19, 1967), Bishop Fulton J. Sheen's experiments with the use of lay boards to screen applicants for the priesthood (September 14, 1967), and the dispute between Cardinal McIntyre of Los Angeles and the Sisters of the Immaculate Heart of Mary over "the nuns' right to decide on matters of their personal life" (November 14, 1967).

estate"—to influence and even determine major issues of public concern.[15] In all these practical controversies there is clearly at issue a vital and inadequately understood series of problems stemming from the underlying fact that private associations are no less systems of government than the state itself, and that as such they and their spokesmen exercise power in society.

II

If the principle of the separation of public and private necessarily implies a dual system of government, and if private associations exercise such a demonstrably significant variety of power over members and nonmembers, why has it taken so long for these conditions to be recognized and to be treated as fit subjects of investigation by political theorists and political scientists?

Probably the best single explanation is that both the theory and the empirical study of politics have until recently been strongly influenced by perspectives originally developed by earlier generations of analysts whose vision was fixed upon the transition from feudal corporatism to modern individualism. Private associations of all sorts were so thoroughly distrusted, as enclaves of privilege and hierarchy and enemies of representative government, that they were all but denied a place in the theory of the modern nation-state. Hobbes warned against "the great number of corporations; which are as it were many lesser Commonwealths in the bowels of a greater, like wormes in the entrayles of a naturall man."[16] Locke simply ignored them; one may search the *Second Treatise* with the help of all the learned authorities and still find not a single reference to private association. Like Hobbes, Locke apparently believed that men must choose either to live in an insecure state of nature, without a common judge, or

[15]For the role of scientists in politics, see Don K. Price, *The Scientific Estate* (Cambridge, Mass.: Harvard University Press, 1965); C. P. Snow, *Science and Government* (Cambridge, Mass.: Harvard University Press, 1961); Ronald W. Clark, *Tizard* (Cambridge, Mass.: M.I.T. Press, 1965); S. A. Lakoff, "The Tizard Record," *Bulletin of the Atomic Scientists* 20 (January 1966); Robert F. Gilpin, Jr., *American Scientists and Nuclear Weapons Policy* (Princeton, N.J.: Princeton University Press, 1962); Albert Wohlstetter, "Strategy and the Natural Scientists," in R. F. Gilpin, Jr. and Christopher Wright, eds., *Scientists and National Policy Making* (New York: Columbia University Press, 1963); J. Stefan Dupré and S. A. Lakoff, *Science and the Nation: Policy and Politics* (Englewood Cliffs, N.J.: Prentice-Hall, 1962), Part Two; S. A. Lakoff, ed., *Knowledge and Power: Essays on Science and Government* (New York: The Free Press, 1966); Eugene B. Skolnikoff, *Science, Technology and American Foreign Policy* (Cambridge, Mass.: M.I.T. Press, 1967); Daniel S. Greenberg, *The Politics of Pure Science* (New York: New American Library, 1968); and Harold K. Jacobson and Eric Stein, *Diplomats, Scientists, and Politicians* (Ann Arbor: University of Michigan Press, 1966).

[16]*Leviathan*, W. Pogson-Smith, ed. (Oxford: Oxford University Press, 1909), 2, 29, pp. 256-57. In keeping with his belief in unitary and absolute sovereignty, Hobbes contended that whatever is applicable to "bodies politique" such as "the government of a Province, or a Colony," also applies to "an Assembly for the Government of a Town, an University, or a College, or a Church, or for any other Government over the persons of men." Ibid., 2, 22, p. 177. Curiously, however, he seems to have made an exception for the merchant company, describing it as an "Assembly of all members" which only becomes a "body politique" if it is granted a monopoly. Ibid., pp. 177-78.

they must join together to form "one Body Politick under one Government."[17] Adam Smith, for all the acuteness with which he saw the development of the market system, had only anathemas to pronounce upon economic associations, which he thought of as retrograde mercantilist monopolies.[18] Even Rousseau, whose extreme idealization of the face-to-face community has been attacked as hopelessly romantic (when it has not been attacked as a convenient myth for dictators), left no room within these communities for the formation of still more primary subgroups, perhaps because it seemed to him they would have posed an even greater danger to the expression of the general will than the self-interest of unorganized individuals.

As the persistent reality of group life forced itself upon the attention of more practical observers, the initial response was to think of private associations as a necessary evil. The classic example is, of course, Madison's treatment of the dangers of faction in the tenth *Federalist.* When he defined faction as a group of citizens united to pursue a particular interest *adverse* to the interest of others, Madison was simply echoing the conventional wisdom on the subject of private associations. But when he went on to argue that the radical cure of totally eliminating faction would be worse than the disease (since "liberty is to faction, what air is to fire, an aliment, without which it instantly expires") and that the division of powers, coupled with the size of the new republic, would be a sufficient check,[19] Madison gave the private associations a legitimacy, however

[17] *Two Treatises of Government,* Peter Laslett, ed. (Cambridge: Cambridge University Press, 1964), *Second Treatise,* Chap. 8, 97, p. 350. Locke's failure to treat lesser associations may simply reflect his preoccupation with other matters. He was anxious to show that only civil government could protect private property and he wished, as Laslett has shown, to refute Sir Robert Filmer by drawing a sharp distinction between natural government, which was paternal, and civil government, which was based upon compact and majority rule. See particularly *Second Treatise,* Chap. 15, 169, pp. 398-99. But his silence on this issue is nevertheless remarkable inasmuch as English law early recognized a distinction between public government and the government of private associations. Thus the anonymous author of *The Law of Corporations* (London: Cleve, 1702) could write: "The General Intent and End of all Civil Incorporations is for Better Government; either general or special. *** Special Government is so called because it is remitted to the Managers of Particular things, as Trade, Charity and the like; for Government whereof several Companies and Corporations for Trade were erected." Quoted in Adolph A. Berle and William C. Warren, *Cases and Materials on the Law of Business Organization (Corporations)* (Brooklyn: The Foundation Press, 1948), p. 3. The "concessionist" theory implicit in this statement was made explicit by Blackstone: "With us in England, the consent of the crown is absolutely necessary to the erection of any corporation, either impliedly or expressly given." Sir William Blackstone, *The Commentaries on the Laws of England* (London: John Murray, 1867), Vol. 1, p. 450.

[18] "The pretence that corporations are necessary to the better government of the trade, is without foundation." A. Smith, *The Wealth of Nations* (New York: Modern Library, 1937), p. 129. Cited by Dom Votaw, *Modern Corporations* (Englewood Cliffs, N.J.: Prentice-Hall, 1965), p. 1. Edmund Burke exceeded Smith, but with better insight, when he attacked the East India Company as "a state in the guise of a merchant." Quoted by W. J. Bate, introduction to *Edmund Burke Selected Works* (New York: Modern Library, 1960), p. 19.

[19] Alexander Hamilton, James Madison, and John Jay, *The Federalist or, the New Constitution,* Max Beloff, ed. (Oxford: Basil Blackwell, 1950), Number X, pp. 41-48. Compare the definition of party by Halifax as "a conspiracy against the nation" quoted by John Plamenatz, *Man and Society* (London: Longmans, Green, 1963), Vol. I, p. 334. *"Party* and *faction,"* Plamenatz comments, "were still mostly used in a pejorative sense, to suggest something narrow, selfish and unpatriotic." Ibid., p. 335.

grudging, that represented a considerable advance in political thinking. Even so, it was only a limited advance, for Madison still thought of group activity solely in terms of its influence upon public government and not as a device for enhancing the opportunity of self-government or as a source of power that might affect others directly rather than indirectly through its influence on public policy.

As the new American nation began to develop a characteristic political style, it was possible to see the role of private associations in a democracy in a more realistic light. As usual, it is to Tocqueville that we must credit the next major advance. Perhaps it took the eye of a French aristocrat, accustomed to the shadows of authoritarianism, to see the significance of private associations to democracy, as it had previously taken a Montesquieu to realize the importance of the "intermediary powers" to an earlier form of government. Struck by the tendency of Americans to form associations of every kind,[20] Tocqueville sought an explanation that would accord both with the social conditions of the new society and the beliefs of the inhabitants. The Americans, he concluded, could not depend upon the benevolence of aristocratic patrons, and they did not want to depend upon the benevolence of a paternalistic government. Wherever possible, therefore, they would undertake to perform public functions in voluntary associations. Tocqueville thought there were two potential benefits to be looked for from this tendency. Private associations, like local governments, could provide a training in the responsibilities of democratic citizenship. As relatively autonomous centers of power and initiative, they could also serve as surrogates for the absent intermediary powers (such as the estates, the free cities, and the church) which had combined to check absolutism in predemocratic times. Thus, the existence of these associations would help to prevent a slide toward Caesaristic mass society which seemed the inevitable fate of democracy in Europe.

Tocqueville's acute insight into the positive functions of private associations in a democracy represented a step forward toward a more sophisticated and comprehensive understanding. But the same perspective which endowed Tocqueville with such insight also constricted his vision. Because he was so concerned to save democracy from itself, he was able to recognize that private associations could help prevent overcentralization and could enable individuals to withstand the tendency for government to engulf the whole of social life. But because he

[20] In Tocqueville's own luminous description: "Americans of all ages, all conditions, and all dispositions, constantly form associations. They have not only commercial and manufacturing companies, in which all take part, but associations of a thousand other kinds, religious, moral, serious, futile, general or restricted, enormous or diminutive. The Americans make associations to give entertainments, to found seminaries, to build inns, to construct churches, to diffuse books, to send missionaries to the antipodes; and in this manner they found hospitals, prisons, and schools. If it be proposed to inculcate some truth, or to foster some feeling by the encouragement of a great example, they form a society. Wherever, at the head of some new undertaking, you see the government in France, or a man of rank in England, in the United States you will be sure to find an association." *Democracy in America,* P. Bradley, ed. (New York: Alfred A. Knopf, 1963), Vol. 2, p. 108. See also Vol. 1, Chap. 12. Tocqueville comments: "Governments, therefore, should not be the only active powers; associations ought, in democratic nations, to stand in lieu of those powerful private individuals whom the equality of conditions has swept away." Ibid., Vol. 2, p. 109.

was not himself committed to the democratic ideal—at least not to the extent that an avowed exponent of democracy would have been[21]—he never thought to ask whether private associations offered a valuable opportunity for self-government or whether their actual operation would be such as to raise a threat of oligarchy and to frustrate the will to autonomy, both within the associations themselves and within the context of the larger society.

The ambivalent character of private associations, from the point of view of their effect upon freedom, only began to be clearly exposed early in this century in the controversy generated by the work of the European pluralists.[22] The pluralists went to the opposite extreme of the early liberal theorists by insisting that the "omnicompetent state" was a thoroughly illegitimate invention and by attempting to reduce the claims of the state to sovereignty to a point at which the state would be thought of simply as one association among many competing for the allegiance of the individual. In this frontal assault on conventional thought, the pluralists succeeded in compelling an awareness of the important functions served by private associations like churches and trade unions in providing a course of identity, fulfillment, and power to individuals who would otherwise pursue their beliefs and interests without protection against an arbitrary government or a tyrannical majority. But as many of their critics noted,[23] the logic of the pluralist position led either to an anarchy of competing groups or to a reconstitution of the state in a weak and impractical form as a mediator among groups. Worse, the pluralists naively imagined that private associations inevitably provided the individual with a far better opportunity for grass roots democracy, for self-government and self-fulfillment, than he could find in the state. They completely ignored the likelihood that in many cases these associations could be even more oppressive than the state, because they were not subject to the restraints of formal procedure, judicial review, and public scrutiny, and because they could claim (often more plausibly than the state) that threats to the very existence of the association justified repression of dissent and concentration of power.

The debate over the contentions of the pluralists opened opportunities for research and analysis, but many of the most important of these opportunities were ignored. The "analytical pluralists" chose to pass over the internal workings of groups and to concentrate instead upon examining their impact on public policy. Like the normative pluralists, they too went overboard, arguing that interest or pressure groups were the only real constituents of the political process and that all ideals, constitutional formalities, and legal procedures were metaphysical clouds, best ignored by the serious analyst. "When the groups are adequately stated," A. F. Bentley laid down in a memorable excess of enthusiasm,

[21] A view elaborated in S. A. Lakoff, *Equality in Political Philosophy* (Cambridge, Mass.: Harvard University Press, 1964), pp. 158-76.

[22] Notably Gierke, Maitland, Figgis, Laski, Cole, and Duguit. Pluralistic thought may of course be traced farther back in time. For the German development, beginning with Fichte and Hegel, see especially R. H. Bowen, *German Theories of the Corporative State, with Special Reference to the Period 1870-1919* (New York: Whittlesey House, 1947).

[23] None more acutely than W. Y. Elliott, op. cit. See also Earl Latham, *The Group Basis of Politics: A Study in Basing-Point Legislation* (Ithaca: Cornell University Press, 1952), Chap. 1.

"everything is stated."[24] The result was a growing concern, especially intense among American students of politics, with the role of pressure groups. Some sought to expose their unsavory efforts at corruption, others merely to replace an inadequate theory of politics as a competition among atomistic individuals with a similarly laissez faire theory in which the individual was displaced by the group. But rarely did it occur to these investigators to examine or comment upon the internal workings of private associations or their role in the democratic system.

The first major effort to answer the need for such analysis arose from the study of a species of association midway between public and private: the political party. Robert Michels and Moisey Ostrogorski examined the inner workings of the political party because they were skeptical of the notion entertained by radicals and progressives that the political party, as a popular movement, could escape the tendency toward bureaucratization and irresponsibility that appeared to be endemic in public government. In fact, they sought to show, the political party was itself a prime example of this very tendency. The "iron law of oligarchy" to which Michels gave currency, but which both he and Ostrogorski found in operation in the political party,[25] was offered as a principle applicable to any organized effort to pursue a specific goal—which is to say to all social associations, public and private.

Much subsequent research has been directed at the examination of this thesis as it affects other political parties,[26] but no comparable effort was made for some time to extend the study to include unmixed private associations. It was not until 1942 that a noted political scientist, Charles E. Merriam, issued a call for such studies in a series of lectures at Indiana University.[27] Merriam pointed out that although in common parlance it was customary to speak of "church politics" or "office politics," political scientists had confined their attention to public government and had neglected to study private government. Such neglect, he contended, was scarcely justified: If churches operate under ecclesiastical law, if a corporate board of directors functions like a cabinet (and the shareholders as a constituency), if in universities the faculty senate checks the administration,

[24] Arthur F. Bentley, *The Process of Government: A Study of Social Pressures* (Chicago: University of Chicago Press, 1908), p. 208. He adds: "When I say everything, I mean everything." Bentley was quite aware that corporations and trade unions were (as he said of corporations) "government through and through" and he thought further study might be warranted: "Possibly there are as many forms of corporate government as there are of political government, and possibly these corporate government forms can ultimately be classified on the very lines used for the classification of political governments. I do not know they can be, I only suggest it. Certain methods which political government uses, as, for instance, hanging, are not used by corporations, generally speaking, but that is a detail. Corporation activities often put people to death by carelessness or by parsimony: this is not a judgment upon the corporation, but merely a statement of fact." Ibid., p. 268.

[25] See Robert Michels, *Political Parties; A Sociological Study of the Oligarchical Tendencies of Modern Democracy* (New York: The Free Press, 1966); and M. Ostrogorski, *Democracy and the Organization of Political Parties* (New York: Macmillan, 1902), especially "Conclusion," Vol. 2, pp. 607-741.

[26] See *inter alia* Seymour M. Lipset, *Agrarian Socialism* (Berkeley: University of California Press, 1950); and Robert T. McKenzie, *British Political Parties: The Distribution of Power within the Conservative and Labour Parties* (London: Heinemann, 1955).

[27] Charles E. Merriam, *Public and Private Government* (New Haven: Yale University Press, 1944).

then these associations were political and in need of examination. In the wake of Merriam's call, a number of studies began to appear. One, indeed, had already appeared. Oliver Garceau's examination of the AMA concentrated on its role as a pressure group but did not neglect its internal structure and paved the way for at least one fuller study.[28] Earl Latham prefaced his study of the basing-point controversy in the steel industry by a discussion of the nature of private government and later addressed himself to the theory of corporate government.[29] The most extensive empirical study of the government of a private association was and remains the inquiry into the International Typographical Union by Seymour Lipset, Martin Trow, and James S. Coleman.[30]

The study of the ITU was valuable not only because it was extensive (and because the methods of inquiry were refined and the conclusions carefully framed) but also because it was undertaken with the insights of Tocqueville, Michels, and other social theorists very much in mind. It was assumed that trade unions were more likely than many other private associations to be concerned with achieving democracy because they represent a movement opposed to privilege and committed to the solidarity of the most numerous class in society. They therefore would be uniquely concerned to offer a serious opportunity to ordinary people to participate in resolving common concerns, to develop and exchange opinions without actually meeting each other and to learn the techniques of democratic government. As powerful associations they could serve to mediate between the otherwise omnipotent forces of industry and the state and the otherwise impotent individual. Indeed, the authors contended, the vitality of the trade union and of other private associations was bound to be a critical factor in determining whether the future held in store a mass society—in which individuals would be without the protection of relatively autonomous groups which might shelter them from the power of the state and from the effects of the social pressure to conform—or a pluralism in which the power of the state would be tempered, broken, or modified by private associations and in which differences of identity and interest would remain acceptable.

Lipset and his associates concluded that the ITU, with its two-party system and its well-developed tradition of worker involvement in union affairs, was not typical of unions generally, but nevertheless provided an example of how such opportunities might be made available to members of private associations. Following Tocqueville, they noted that, whether or not they are internally democratic, private associations serve a useful function in pluralizing power and preserving a sense of group autonomy. Other studies have emphasized the damage strong private associations do to the possibility of self-government by the larger society. Grant McConnell has shown convincingly that the American Farm Bureau Federation overrepresents wealthier farmers and exerts an influence upon both legislation and the policies of the Department of Agriculture that

[28] Oliver Garceau, *The Political Life of the American Medical Association* (Cambridge, Mass.: Harvard University Press, 1941); and Hyde and Wolff, op. cit.

[29] Earl Latham, *The Group Basis of Politics;* "Anthropomorphic Corporations, Elites, and Monopoly Power," *American Economic Review,* 47, 2 (May 1957); "The Body Politic of the Corporation," in Mason, op. cit.; and "The Commonwealth of the Corporation," *Northwestern University Law Review,* 55, 1 (March-April 1960).

[30] Seymour Lipset, Martin Trow, and James S. Coleman, *Union Democracy* (Glencoe, Ill.: The Free Press, 1956).

upon both legislation and the policies of the Department of Agriculture that is often detrimental to the public interest.[31] Henry S. Kariel, echoing Thurman Arnold's attack on the "folklore of capitalism," points out the absurdity of thinking of giant private organizations like the AMA, the Teamsters Union, General Motors, and the Farm Bureau Federation as extensions of private individuals, endowed with a fictitious personality making them immune from public control and interference. The current problem of pluralism, he argues, is "not how to strengthen the hierarchies of organized power, but rather how to control them by some means short of establishing an illiberal political order."[32]

Much more needs to be known about the actual forms and practices of private governments, however, before it will be possible to draw definitive judgments on their internal and external effects. It is surprising how little work has been done by political scientists on the government of churches, for example, especially considering that they range in form from the monarchical through the episcopal to the congregational, offering an inviting spectrum for comparative analysis. It is surely time that we had a more up-to-date account of church government than we may find in Hooker's *Laws of Ecclesiastical Polity.*[33] The professions have only recently come in for serious study and the same is true for philanthropic foundations.[34] Corporations have been subjected to study from a wide variety of scholarly viewpoints, but the information on the comparative government of corporations and trade associations is still sparse. Studies of federalism in the "multiversity" are also badly needed. Given the time it has taken for political scientists to recognize the reality of private government, it may be reasonable to expect that it will only be a matter of more time before this research will be undertaken. But what is reasonable is not necessarily inevitable. In fact, for other reasons that have to do with the development of the social sciences and with the development of society itself, there has lately emerged a rival to the study of private government which aspires to examine the same phenomena under a new and more comprehensive rubric—the study of "organization."

III

When Merriam issued his call for the study of private government, he noted in passing that the study of organization was attracting considerable attention in all the branches of the social sciences. In political science it was the concern

[31] Grant McConnell, *The Decline of Agrarian Democracy* (Berkeley: University of California Press, 1953).

[32] Kariel, op. cit., p. 2.

[33] See, however, the pathbreaking work of Léo Moulin, "Policy-making in the Religious Orders," *Government and Opposition,* 1 (October 1965); and *Le monde vivants des religieux* (Paris: Calmann-Levy, 1964).

[34] For professions, see especially Corinne L. Gilb, *Hidden Hierarchies, The Professions and Government* (New York: Harper & Row, 1966). For foundations, see Warren Weaver, *U.S. Philanthropic Foundations: Their History, Structure, Management, and Record* (New York: Harper & Row 1967); Marion R. Fremont-Smith, *Foundations and Government* (New York: Russell Sage, 1965); and F. Emerson Andrews, *Philanthropic Foundations* (New York: Russell Sage, 1956).

of students of public administration, in economics it attracted specialists in the behavior of the firm as well as academic and practical people interested in business administration. For some psychologists it seemed an ideal framework for examining human needs and "interpersonal relations" and for some sociologists it seemed to provide both a general category and a small-scale model for the study of the social system.

Merriam did not foresee that there would be any conflict between the study of private government and the study of organization. But now that organization studies have multiplied to a point at which it is possible to begin to assess their significance, it is becoming clear that there are critical differences between the two approaches. These differences arise both at the theoretical level and in the actual execution of the inquiries. As a theory, the concept of organization derives from the concept of bureaucracy. It is therefore at once more comprehensive in scope and more limited in its political character than the concept of private government. The organization theorist is not ordinarily concerned to distinguish between public and private governments. Nor indeed is he likely to be interested in knowing whether the organization operates in a democratic or a totalitarian context. His focus is entirely upon the decision-making system, wherever it arises and whatever ends it serves.

In a certain sense, to be sure, the focus on decision-making seems to make the study of organization eminently political, inasmuch as the question of how power or influence is exercised is often said to be the essential question of all politics. But this turns out upon examination to be a misleading inference, for the study of organizational decision-making studiously avoids asking the kind of questions that would render the study of decision-making genuinely political. It does not ask what constituencies are involved, or how the legislative is related to the executive, or how the authority of the decision-maker is made accountable to those he represents. It does not ask whether the system is constitutional or just, legitimate or illegitimate. Instead the study of decision-making in organizations is confined to the question of whether and to what extent the functions of management are exercised rationally. The stress, in other words, is clearly on *administration* rather than government, on the integrative function of social organization, on improving the efficiency of the decision-maker. There is practically no attention paid to the question of whether people who are members of the organization or who are served by it have or ought to have control over it, whether they have any right (a term which would probably be considered altogether unscientific by students of organization) to be consulted in the decision-making process or indeed to decide what form the process will take.

In this conventional sense organization study, despite its focus on decision-making, is quite apolitical. This is apparent even in the attempts to define the concept of organization—although it must be said that these attempts are often vague and divergent from each other. Herbert Simon and James March, in what is generally taken as a leading text on organization theory, prefer to avoid definition. "It is easier, and probably more useful," they assert at the outset of the work, "to give examples of formal organizations than to define the term."[35] (Thus U.S. Steel, the Red Cross, and the New York Highway Department are

[35] James G. March and Herbert A. Simon, *Organizations* (New York: Wiley, 1958), p. 1.

offered as examples, but there is no indication what it is that makes these good specimens or whether others that one could think of would be excluded.) A few pages later they do venture a definition (but only after warning that it must not be taken "too literally or too seriously") with a quaintly Spencerian ring: organizations are "assemblages of interacting human beings and they are the largest assemblages in our society that have anything resembling a central coordinating system."[36] Apart from this half-hearted and scarcely probing venture, Simon and March content themselves with citing an earlier definition by Simon, Smithburg, and Thompson according to which an organization is said to be "a system of interrelated social behaviors of a number of persons whom we shall call *participants* in the organization." The rather startling tautology of this definition does not escape Simon and March, but they seem to find in this some mysterious confirmation of its validity: "the theory," they note, "like many theoretical generalizations, verges on the tautological."[37] Not only is it tautological, but just as significantly it skirts any consideration of the organization as a political system.

The same is true for the definitions offered in the *Handbook of Organizations,* the most ambitious effort so far made to provide a survey of the field. Once again tautology is very much in vogue and once again political questions are studiously ignored. "A defining characteristic of the social entity known as an organization is, as the name suggests, its state of being organized." So writes Dorwin Cartwright in the opening essay.[38] The organization, he adds, is "an arrangement of interdependent parts, each having a special function with respect to the whole." In this arrangement members adhere to schedules, the range of each is limited and stable as well as predictable; and the activities of all the participants tend to produce "accomplishments."[39] It is, of course, impossible to know from such a definition whether what is under study is a trade union, a crematorium, or an automatic factory. But the omission of such distinctions appears to be quite deliberate. When even rudimentary distinctions are introduced, they only divide the practitioners. W. Richard Scott contends that organizations may be distinguished from aggregates (such as age groups, market competitors, communities, and families) because "subjects in organizations are bound together in a common network of relations."[40] But an economist, Thomas A. Marschak, is nevertheless convinced that markets are organizations,

[36] Ibid., p. 4.

[37] Ibid., p. 84. The same fascination with tautology also marks the hypotheses offered to explain behavior in organizations. Among them (complete with cross-referential numerology): "The greater the group's *permissiveness* toward individual achievement (3.83), the more individual needs will be satisfied in the group." [3.66:3.83].

"The greater the *independence of individual rewards* (3.74), the less competition among group members [3.67:3.84]. Contrariwise, where individuals are, in effect, engaged in a zero-sum game in which some must lose in order for others to gain, competition is increased and identification decreased." Ibid., p. 70.

[38] "Influence, Leadership, Control," in J. G. March, ed. *Handbook of Organizations* (Chicago: Rand McNally, 1956), p. 1. In this volume, however, the prize for tautology can go only to the unabashed entry of Donald W. Taylor, "Decision Making and Problem Solving," ibid., p. 81: "Ill structured problems are those that are not well structured."

[39] Cartwright, ibid., p. 1.

[40] "Field Methods in the Study of Organizations," ibid., p. 424.

"perhaps the longest studied of all human organizations."[41] One definition stresses the importance of technology: "Organizations are systems which utilize energy (given up by human and nonhuman devices) in a patterned, directed effort to alter the conditions of basic materials in a predetermined manner."[42] Others stress goal-direction as the defining characteristic: "the organization provides its members, both men and machines, with programs or constraints to direct the behavior of those components toward the goals of organization."[43]

From an enterprise which prides itself on its social-scientific ecumenicism and on respect for the "niceties of operationalism,"[44] such vague and incoherent efforts at definition are disconcerting. But the aim of the movement is nevertheless clear. The organization theorists are convinced that only by studying the process of decision-making in a wide variety of contexts using the methods of all the social sciences will it be possible to determine the variety of rational structural alternatives open to purposive associations of all sorts.[45] There is a strong implication in this belief that all earlier thinking about this subject was cloudy and unscientific. Thus March, in his preface to the *Handbook,* notes that the study of organization is recent in origin, having arisen, as he puts it, in an "immaculate conception" occurring sometime between 1937 and 1942 in the work of Barnard, Roethlisberger, Dickson, and Simon.[46] He admits that the problems of managing organizations have been noted by many eminent figures in earlier times but chides them for not having been reluctant "to solve such problems in the course of determining the ultimate destiny and primordial nature of man." The modern student can only regard these early and overambitious efforts with curiosity, but it would apparently be a waste of time to take them seriously. "We offer them the same reverent condescension that typifies a modern musicologist's consideration of the Platonic theories of music."[47] Even

[41] "Economic Theories of Organization," ibid., p. 424.

[42] Charles M. Perrow, "Hospitals: Technology, Structure, and Goals," ibid., p. 913.

[43] Julian Feldman and Herschel E. Kanter, "Organization Decision Making," ibid., p. 619. For a similar emphasis, see also Arthur Stinchcombe, "Social Structure and Organizations," ibid., and Amitai Etzioni, "Organizational Control Structure," ibid.

[44] March, "Introduction," ibid., p. xiii.

[45] Bay, op. cit., p. 287, rightly stresses Philip Selznick's definition: "Formal organization is the structural expression of rational action." "Foundations of a Theory of Organization," *American Sociological Review,* 13 (1948), 25. But although this is indeed a good summary of the original intention of the school, much recent work has gone, paradoxically, into an effort to show that organizational behavior should not be thought of as wholly or even primarily rational, as Weber's "classical" theory of organization seemed to imply. See Cartwright, in March, *Handbook,* p. 2. In this paradox lies the major explanation of the difficulty contributors to the *Handbook* have in arriving at a common definition. Having originally sought to define organizations as expressions of rationality, they now tend to be preoccupied with showing that the prospects for rational decision-making in organizations are usually severely limited and constrained. The point is amplified below.

[46] March, ibid., pp. xii-xiii.

[47] Ibid., pp. ix-x. How reverent a condescending piety can be may be judged from Cartwright's travesty of the development of the concept of power in the history of political thought: "For a great many years it was fashionable to postulate a unitary and universal motive, or desire, for power. The writings of Hobbes (1651) and Nietzsche (1912) provide outstanding examples. While Russell (1938, p. 274) agrees that 'this desire is an essential part of human nature, and in energetic men it is a very large and important part,' he introduces [sic] a distinction between 'power desired as a means and power desired as an end in itself.'" Ibid., p. 7.

Weber's theory of bureaucracy is generally regarded as the "classical" theory of organizations, because it put too much stress on centralization and rational rules.[48]

It is ironic, in view of their disdainful attitude toward earlier theorists, how often the students of organizations seem to be involved in nothing so much as the rediscovery of the most hoary of political truisms, well known to the ancient and modern philosophers. Aristotle, as everyone knows who has read his *Politics* or *Rhetoric,* was well aware of the contrast between the determinate nature of neatly constructed logical problems and the indeterminate nature of political questions. That is why he counseled prudence and was suspicious of utopian schemes involving all-wise philosopher-kings. It would scarcely have been news to him to learn that the prospects for rational decision-making in society were limited or, as Simon has put it, "bounded."[49] Similarly, it is not in the least surprising that Julian Feldman and Herschel E. Kanter should have come to the same conclusion by examining the possibility of rational decision-making in organizations. After pointing out the difficulty faced even by advanced computer systems in searching out all conceivable alternatives that may be open, they note that prospects for rationality are further limited by the inability to predict the responses of others to decisions:

In most decision situations . . . the problems involved in determining consequences of alternatives are greater than the problems involved in computation. The additional problems arise because of the indeterminacy of the consequences. The decision-maker does not know exactly what will happen if prices are raised or advertising expenditures are increased or an island is blockaded.[50]

This is, of course, precisely why Aristotle thought politics required the deliberation of contingents rather than the demonstration of necessity. The same Plato who preferred the rule of an ideal statesman even to a government of laws knew —without the help of RAND Air Defense simulation experiments—that

operational flexibility is the most important characteristic of the ideal organization. To obtain this . . . humans must play an important role in the system and . . . the organization must encourage these people to adapt their actions and procedures to the immediate situation. In particular . . . fixed-procedure systems, the ultimate of which are completely automated systems, are [not considered]

[48] Ibid., pp. 1-4, passim.

[49] "Bounded" rationality means that "the capacity of the human mind for formulating and solving complex problems is very small compared with the size of the problems whose solution is required for objectively rational behavior in the real world—or even for a reasonable approximation of such objective rationality." Herbert A. Simon, *Models of Man* (New York: Wiley, 1957), p. 198. Another of Simon's widely adopted neologisms—and one that is generally thought equally novel and profound—is what he calls "satisficing." Thus "the key to the simplification of the choice process . . . is the replacement of the goal of *maximizing* with the goal of *satisficing,* of finding a course of action that is 'good enough.'" Ibid., p. 204. Both definitions are quoted by Taylor in March, *Handbook,* pp. 60-61.

[50] Feldman and Kanter, ibid., p. 624.

ideal organizations, because they lack operational flexibility and because they do not adapt effectively to unstable task environments.[51]

The problem of ideological perspective, well known to theorists of the sociology of knowledge, from Marx to Mannheim and beyond, is discovered anew by Charles M. Perrow, who finds that some studies of hospitals reflect a utopian radical view of hospital organization as a conflict between rational-legal bureaucracy and patient self-government. Thus, as he notes perceptively, a "curious emphasis upon the rationality and sanity of mental patients and the irrationality and sometimes repressive behavior of doctors, attendants and nurses is a key theme in much of the current literature."[52] But Perrow, for all his insight into the biases of others, falls into the opposite and equally ideological error of imagining that "bestial practices" toward mental patients simply reflect "a faulty organizational structure."[53] It is one thing to criticize the intrusion of bias but another to imagine that systems of authority, even in therapeutic contexts, are not affected by political values and by the distribution of effective power and interest.

Precisely this tendency to deny the relevance of political considerations and to concentrate instead on rational problem-solving as the index to all social experience is the predominant characteristic—and the fatal weakness—of most organization study, even when the inquiry is conducted by such an exceptionally astute analyst as Perrow. Although students of organization claim to recognize the importance of the distribution of power in the social system (generally they conclude that it is the most important of all questions), they persist in examining its manifestations as though these were problems of logic instead of problems of social relationships, with all the indeterminacy this implies.[54] They rarely trouble to distinguish between types of organizations or between the political-

[51] Kalman J. Cohen and Richard M. Cyert. "Simulation of Organizational Behavior," ibid., p. 329.

[52] Perrow, ibid., p. 936. Perrow offers an interesting description of this literature: "The term 'communication' threads its way through virtually every account (it is always blocked): the attendants and their illegitimate, abused power are the villains of nearly every piece; the psychiatrists are castigated for failing to be good administrators, for clinging desperately to a two-person model of therapy, and for being aloof from nurses and attendants; the business side is usually accused of hoarding supplies, frustrating attempts to change physical conditions or even to transfer patients around, and making the good workers indispensable. The whole hospital structure is neatly characterized as 'paranoid' . . . , 'granulated,' 'authoritarian,' and so forth. The therapeutic goals have always been displaced by custodial ones." Ibid., p. 924.

[53] Ibid., p. 934.

[54] William H. Starbuck enters a proper note of warning: "Of course, logical analysis is only one part of the theorist's problem. And often a secondary part at that. Before phenomena can be described by a set of theoretical statements, causal relations must be disentangled and significant variables distinguished from insignificant ones. Valid data, meaningful insights, and intimate familiarity with the referent situation are at least as important as logical rigor, and there is very little difference between empirically relevant but logically inconsistent theories and logically taut but empirically irrelevant theories." But it is significant that this caution appears in the conclusion of a paper devoted to "Mathematics and Organization Theory," ibid., p. 381, and that Starbuck does not consider the possibility that rigorous mathematical statement may be inherently inappropriate.

cultural contexts in which they operate.[55] They rarely examine cases of conflict and conflict-resolution in organizations (however defined).[56] Whenever possible they prefer to structure their experiments so as to eliminate the clutter of the real world, to simulate real conditions rather than examine them in the raw, and to extrapolate from their controlled laboratory experiments conclusions that are said to be applicable to "behavior in organizations." They have shown no interest whatever in examining the relationships among organizations or the ways in which organizations, public and private, affect nonmembers. For all their allegedly scientific scrutiny of the "needs" of factory workers and other members of the organization ("human and nonhuman"), they have never given serious thought to the one fundamental need of all men everywhere—the need for autonomy.

Unlike the study of private government, therefore, the study of organizations never succeeds even in posing what are perhaps the central political dilemmas of the modern liberal democracy: can ordinary people realize the desire for autonomy in the midst of the large and complex units of organization which are increasingly predominant in modern society? Is a genuine and viable pluralism of associations possible, even when the lines between public and private are breached and when certain associations become extraordinarily powerful vis-à-vis others? Must we conclude that under modern conditions most people must become the dependents of vast impersonal bureaucracy, doomed to exchange liberty for services and utterly incapable of seriously affecting or controlling the decisions by which they will live?[57] Because it fails even to pose such questions—

[55] Most organization theorists do not seem particularly aware of any need either to consider political context or to justify their neglect of it. Anthony Downs, in formulating a theory of bureaucracy as a special class of organization, is at least explicit in denying any significance to the general social milieu. "The basic institutional setting of this theoretical world can either be democratic, totalitarian, monarchical, or traditionalist, or can have any other form in which bureaus are likely to be found. As pointed out by Max Weber, bureaus probably require a money economy rather than a barter economy . . . . But there are no other particular constraints on the type of society to which the theory applies." *Inside Bureaucracy* (Boston: Little, Brown, 1967), p. 3.

A French student of bureaucracy, Michel Crozier, has criticized just this readiness of (American) students of organization to ignore variations in social and political culture. "It seems possible to elaborate a general and universal theory of organizations dealing with the differences between social and cultural systems only parenthetically. However, as soon as one embarks on the study of the pathology of organizations, cultural analysis becomes an indispensable tool which permits the delineation of the global theory and its application in different cultural contexts." *The Bureaucratic Phenomenon* (Chicago: University of Chicago Press, 1964), p. 7. Crozier also criticizes the tendency of those organization theorists committed to notions of "interpersonal interaction" to "shy away" from any treatment of the allocation of power inside organizations. Ibid., p. 165.

[56] This becomes especially apparent if the March *Handbook of Organizations,* with its emphasis on the abstruse issues of rational decision-making, is compared to the earlier public administration casebook edited by Harold Stein, *Public Administration and Policy Development; A Case Book* (New York: Harcourt, Brace, 1952), which stresses the importance of political conflict even in the administrative process.

[57] To conclude, as Downs does, that bureaucratization increases individual freedom because it provides more "behavioral options" (op. cit., p. 259) is to evade the problem bureaucracy poses with respect to *political* freedom. To increase the number of outlets available to a rat in his maze may give him more "behavioral options," but it does not give him any greater control over the design of the experiment he is compelled to participate in. Similarly, when bureaucracies succeed in imposing such additions to human behavioral

let alone answer them—the study of organization can be regarded only as a painful intellectual symptom of the passing of traditional liberal democracy. In this, however, lies its utility. If its findings cannot help to preserve or reconstitute a normative political order, at least its appearance and its increasing popularity provide presumptive evidence that fundamental changes are occurring which are not adequately examined or explained by conventional political theory and political science.

IV

For the inference which begs to be drawn not only from the study of organizations but from much that is obvious in daily life is that the normative order of liberal democracy to which our political theory and political science are largely attuned is being eroded and undermined both in the private and the public sectors. As the United States in particular becomes a mature industrial society, with all that this implies in scale, complexity, and interdependence, inherited conceptions of the most hallowed variety—such as individualism, democracy, and pluralism—come to seem archaic and inadequate. Yet, however paradoxical it may be in the face of such novelty, recent analyses suggest that we can best understand the modern condition by referring to conceptions even more remote than these. Thus it is sometimes proposed that we are entering into a "new feudalism." Hans Morgenthau uses this term explicitly, although he seems to mean by it only that private interests have grown so powerful that they can and do threaten the ability of the state to protect the public interest.[58] Don K. Price, after having first tried to assimilate the new involvement of government with science to conventional theory—in his concept of "federalism by contract"—has lately fastened on the analogy between the feudal estates and the modern professions.[59] He is careful to warn, however, that this analogy should not be understood as a theory of cultural reversion but only as a device to highlight the new role of professionals in ostensibly democratic politics. Similarly Corinne Gilb finds certain striking parallels between modern and feudal experience. The path from status to contract tends to be reversed as individuals must find places in collectivities and hierarchies. The separation of public and private, having arisen out of a sharp distinction between the state and the individual, is now increasingly blurred. Instead, public and private governments meet in a continuum marked by partnerships, amalgamations, and substitution of roles—a continuum reminiscent more of feudalism than of liberalism.[60]

options as "better highways" and "supersonic aircraft"—two of the more unfortunate examples Downs cites—it is no wonder that people adversely affected by these decisions should feel frustrated and resentful over their inability to affect the decisions by which their options are determined.

[58] Hans Morgenthau, *The Purpose of American Politics* (New York: Alfred A. Knopf, 1960), pp. 274-92.

[59] Compare Price's *Government and Science: Their Dynamic Relation in American Democracy* (New York: New York University Press, 1954) with his later work, *The Scientific Estate,* op. cit.

[60] *Hidden Hierarchies,* "Introduction," pp. 1-24. Cf. also Kariel, op. cit., for a similar discussion of parallels with feudalism.

But the parallel with feudalism is only useful up to a point, as those who propose it are aware. Precisely because modern society is industrial, it can never wholly be made congruent with the feudal model. By comparison with the society we know today, the feudal system must have been a serene and slow-moving affair, a network of loosely connected enclaves whose demands upon members and whose links to each other were generally casual and fixed by custom. Because modern society depends so much upon an incredibly ramified and rapidly changing technology, it is profoundly different from earlier systems. Neither the patriarchal authoritarianism of feudal and prefeudal times nor the democratic individualism of a more recent period could possibly provide an adequate form of authority for a modern society—a society in which the central challenge is the problem of coping with the effects of extraordinarily rapid and unsettling changes in technology. The degree of organization, integration, and active decision-making required in such a society means that the single most important goal of the political system must certainly become the achievement of successful management.

As yet we do not know enough about the nature of the emerging managed society to be able to set forth a fully developed theory of managerialism.[61] But we can at least point to the ample evidence that such a phenomenon exists. Nowhere is there more such evidence than in the private sector. Because of the separation of ownership and control, effective power in large business corporations devolves upon the executives.[62] In trade unions the declining interest in democracy among the rank and file, coupled with their growing dependence on full-time staff and expert negotiators, has similarly led to a concentration of effective power in a virtually permanent leadership cadre.[63] Control over universities has passed for the most part from the hands of wealthy contributors —those whom Veblen colorfully described as the "captains of education"—and from the hands of state legislators as well, to those of the professional academic

[61] There is, however, a considerable literature bearing directly or indirectly on this subject, beginning with James Burnham, *The Managerial Revolution* (New York: The John Day Company, 1941). But although Burnham recognized the pervasiveness of the phenomenon he directed his analysis primarily at "the managerial world system of superstates" and gave only passing attention to the management of business corporations and other private associations, as Eells notes in *The Government of Corporations,* op. cit., p. 298n. For more contemporary and more comprehensive treatments, see Clark Kerr, John Dunlop, Frederick Harbison, and Charles A. Myers, *Industrialism and Industrial Man; The Problems of Labor and Management in Economic Growth* (Cambridge, Mass.: Harvard University Press, 1960); Michael D. Reagan, op. cit.; and Andrew Hacker, "Liberal Democracy and Social Control," *American Political Science Review,* 51, 4 (December 1957).

[62] The classic statement of this development is that of A. A. Berle, Jr. and Gardiner C. Means, *The Modern Corporation and Private Property* (New York: Macmillan, 1932).

[63] See Will Herberg, "Bureaucracy and Democracy in Labor Unions," *Antioch Review,* 3 (Fall 1943); Richard A. Lester, *As Unions Mature: An Analysis of the Evolution of American Unionism* (Princeton, N.J.: Princeton University Press, 1958); William M. Leiserson, *American Trade Union Democracy* (New York: Columbia University Press, 1961); and the studies of the government of particular unions by Michael Harrington, Morris A. Horowitz, Leo Kramet, Mark Perlman, Sam Romer, Melvin Rothbaum, Joel Seidman, Jack Stieber, and Lloyd Ulman, all published by Wiley in 1962.

administrators.[64] In the churches, even in those with a commitment to congregational democracy, authority comes to rest for all practical purposes in the clergy, especially the upper ranks.[65] Even in the large-scale charitable foundation, it is not the benefactor or the volunteer aides but an intermediate corps of professional managers—aptly dubbed "philanthropoids"[66]—who decide how the surplus capital and energy of the donors will be distributed among deserving recipients.

It must be stressed that this new managerialism is not some new form of dictatorship. On the contrary, the managerial ethic is inherently benevolent. Since the manager is in no sense an owner, either economically or politically, his sole interest is to achieve a result satisfactory to those he serves. Above all, he must be concerned to gain accommodation, compromise, and consensus, for if he fails in this he fails in his task as a manager. The manager, in short, is a mediator, as his predecessor was an autocratic entrepreneur. Again the evidence is readily available throughout the private sector. In the trade unions the quiet negotiator comes to replace the militant demagogue.[67] In industry the generation of the robber baron is succeeded by that of his philanthropic progeny and their allies and instruments, the almost anonymous managers.[68] In the universities the innovating administrator tends to be succeeded by the would-be (they are not always successful) conciliator.[69] Though the evidence is sparse, there is reason to think that the same shift in leadership style affects the clergy, where

[64] To the radical eye, however, *plus ça change plus c'est la même chose.* Bettina Aptheker, in *Big Business and the American University* (New York: New Outlook Publishers, 1966) appends a series of charts headed "The Web" showing the ownership and directorship interests of members of the Regents of the University of California and the members of the Harvard Corporation and Board of Overseers. These boards are said to be the managers of "knowledge factories," with "the employees as the faculty; and the raw material as the students." p. 13.

[65] See William S. Salisbury, *Religion in American Culture: A Sociological Interpretation* (Homewood, Ill.: Dorsey, 1964), pp. 104-08, 131-34; and Gibson Winter, *The Suburban Captivity of the Churches* (New York: Doubleday, 1961).

[66] By Dwight MacDonald in *The Ford Foundation: The Men and the Millions* (New York: Reynal, 1956).

[67] See Kerr et al., op. cit., and studies of particular cases such as Michael Harrington's discussion of the "benevolent paternal stewardship" of the leaders in *The Retail Clerks* (New York: Wiley, 1962); and Irving Howe and B. J. Widick, *The UAW and Walter Reuther* (New York: Random House, 1949).

[68] Berle and Means predicted that the large corporate management might well "develop into a purely neutral technocracy balancing a variety of claims by various groups in the community and assigning to each a portion of the income stream on the basis of public policy rather than private cupidity." op. cit., p. 356. Quoted by Eells, *The Government of Corporations,* op. cit., p. 297n. By 1961 Kariel could write: "It now appears that the foremost managerial aim of corporate leaders is not so much to maximize immediate personal profits as to negotiate equitably with whatever interests compose the large firm—including those which, from a purely legalistic point of view, are not incorporated at all. Today, its function is to conceive of the corporation's constituencies in the broadest terms and to deal with them in statesmanlike fashion." Kariel, op. cit., p. 33. On the relative public anonymity of the managerial leadership, see Andrew Hacker, "The Making of a Corporation President," *New York Times Magazine* (April 2, 1967).

[69] See Clark Kerr, *The Uses of the University* (Cambridge, Mass.: Harvard University Press, 1963).

the job of satisfying the diverse needs of different member-groups and engaging in "ecumenical dialogue" with nonmembers requires a pacific rather than an unyielding or dogmatic temperament.

On the whole, though there are occasional exceptions, the rule of the managers is generally accepted by the membership. One reason has already been indicated: the manager's sole interest is in placating the membership as best he can, and to the extent that he succeeds his authority is not questioned. Another reason seems to be that in most cases members of private groups do not look upon their membership as an opportunity for self-government. They seem to prefer to receive the services that membership provides—much as "members" of an automobile club—without having to decide policy questions or even to judge the qualifications of those entrusted with this task. We might expect that union members would resent the superior status and grossly higher pay of many of their officials. In fact they tend to be content, sometimes even with corrupt leadership, so long as that leadership "delivers the goods." Nor is the situation any different in the business corporation. No significant group of stockholders is likely to question the pay or the perquisites of management so long as the dividend rate and the price of the stock are maintained at satisfactory levels.

When the clients are not satisfied with the services provided by the managers, they may well become balky. But dissatisfaction in private associations does not necessarily lead to the same results as in public government, where electoral procedures allow the citizenry to vote out leaders with comparative ease. Because democratic procedures and safeguards are often merely nominal in private associations, it is far harder to "throw the rascals out." The result is that political activity in private associations more often than not falls into the category of "protest politics."

Proxy contests led by dissident shareholders are rare and successful proxy contests rarer still. A few especially persistent malcontents (or die-hard believers in "shareholder democracy") may try to harass the management by causing embarrassing incidents at annual meetings or instituting stockholder suits, although these have become costly and difficult to win. Union dissidents find that it is almost impossible to unseat an entrenched leadership, given all the advantages available to the incumbents and the handicaps that limit the effectiveness of campaigns against them. The lack of confidence in democratic processes is evident in the widespread cynicism felt by ordinary union members —a feeling that sometimes expresses itself in acts of defiance directed against their own leadership, such as the calling of wildcat strikes by union locals, the insistence of premature strike votes, or the rejection of bargaining settlements strongly recommended by the leaders. In the universities a similar sense of frustration sometimes develops among faculty and students, but although academics can be especially articulate in voicing their grievances, they do not often find it any easier than it is for the unionists to do more than stage a protest. They cannot easily replace an administrative leadership with one they prefer or compel a reform of the university constitution giving them a voice in the election of administrative leaders who would be responsible to them as well as to public and private sources of support.[70] In the churches the recent call for

[70] At least one social critic, Paul Goodman, has seen signs of an impending academic revolution. "I do not think that there are any other institutions of established society

the unionization of the Roman Catholic priesthood is eloquent evidence of the frustration felt by members of organizations who find themselves without effective means to influence the policies laid down by their leaders.

Managerialism, moreover, is not a phenomenon confined to the internal operation of private associations. It is also evident in their external relations. The most striking evidence is the tendency toward mergers in almost all areas of the private sector. Business corporations were the first to exhibit the trend and, although the concentration of ownership in large corporations has grown steadily, the end of the process is not yet in sight. But the same tendency is now apparent in other subsectors as well. Thus denominations and churches which have long prided themselves on their doctrinal purity and independence now rush to extend the "hand of fellowship" to each other. Long-embattled unions have agreed to settle their jurisdictional disputes and to join in creating larger and more effective federations, notably of course in the long-deferred reunion of the AFL and the CIO. To a degree the same process is evident in colleges and universities, especially where the disadvantages of size and independence have become economically and educationally untenable. Even professional athletics has not been immune to the merger fever, especially when rival leagues have had to recognize the futility and costliness of unregulated competition.[71]

Although the merger movements offer perhaps the most dramatic evidence of a managerial drive for accommodation and the dampening of rivalry and conflict, in the long run the development that may prove to be a kind of paradigm of an emerging managerial democracy is the new pattern of relations that has arisen out of public support for research and development. Because science and technology are in a figurative sense the leading sectors of the advanced industrial society, what happens with respect to them may well indicate the shape of more general developments. The overall phenomenon has been variously described, but the essential facts are not in dispute.[72] Universities, whether public or private, have come to depend upon federal and state funding not only for the support of their research activities, but also increasingly for the support of their educational functions. Industry and government, traditionally suspicious of each other, have entered into contractual agreements—arranged by negotiation rather than through advertisement and bidding—by which public funds pay for a large proportion of the "R & D" work performed by private industry. In certain cases large corporations have become completely or almost completely dependent upon this public support, since virtually all their contracting is done with government defense agencies. Whole subsectors,

in which a subversive anarchy is quite so near the surface as in the faculties of colleges. And the students ready to follow hard after." *The Community of Scholars* (New York: Random House, 1962), p. 24. Experience since Goodman wrote these lines would seem to suggest that like Marx he was wrong about the proletariat but right about the peasantry.

[71] Witness the recent merger of the National and American Football Leagues. Some rivalries are more intractable, such as that between the Amateur Athletic Union and the National Collegiate Athletic Association, which has so far resisted all efforts at resolution—and that between the National Education Association and the American Federation of Teachers, which seems to have risen in intensity.

[72] See, among other accounts, Dupré and Lakoff, op. cit.; Greenberg, op. cit.; and Harold Orlans, *The Effects of Federal Programs on Higher Education: A Study of 36 Universities and Colleges* (Washington, D.C.: Brookings Institution, 1962).

such as the complex known as the aerospace industry, rely heavily on public government both for their regular business and for the support of innovation in such products as space vehicles and systems and supersonic aircraft.

Where a contractual relationship between government and private industry has been deemed inadvisable, as in the management of military systems research or in matters in which the public and private interest would collide head-on, new public-private "hybrids" have been created. Among these are the RAND Corporation, a nonprofit, privately managed but publicly funded "think factory" providing technical information and advice to government agencies.[73] Another such hybrid is the Communications Satellite Corporation (Comsat), which represents a venture in cooperation joining the public and private sectors in the development of space communications.[74] In time the precedent created by the establishment of these hybrids may well lead to further applications of the same principle. Independent technical advice would be useful at all levels of government and the same need for cooperation between public and private which led to Comsat surely exists in other areas, such as housing and urban renewal.

The implications of these developments in connection with science and technology have aroused more than a small degree of uncertainty. There have been warnings that universities dependent upon government funding may lose their autonomy and therefore their ability to protect academic freedom and to pursue the kind of free inquiry to which they ought to be devoted. The dependence of industrial contractors upon public funding is said to give them an incentive to lobby for military spending and to put the public in a position in which it is simply subsidizing private profiteering. Evidence could be cited in support of these allegations, but it should also be noted that efforts have been made, often successfully, to check the abuses in the "research partnership" and to preserve the independence of all parties. It is easy to criticize the actual operation of this system of support for research through grants and contracts, which is bound to be untidy at the very least, but it is more difficult to suggest an acceptable alternative. A strict separation of public and private and with it a total reliance for progress in science and technology on one sector or the other would be far less appealing, on realistic as well as ideological grounds.

Thus both the evidence of internal developments in private associations and the pattern of external relations evident in the research partnership point in the direction of what has been described as managerialism—the tendency toward accommodation, cooperation, and consensus and away from conflict and the struggle for power. If this tendency proves to be as permanent and as powerful a force as it now seems to be, the analytical value of the concept of private government is bound to be affected for the worse. In a managed society it is not at all clear that a serious degree of political autonomy is possible either for private individuals or for groups. This is surely the reason that the concept of organization, with its stress on rational decision-making and on the accommodation of member needs, seems to some to be the most appropriate mode of analysis.

[73] See Bruce L. R. Smith, *The RAND Corporation: Case Study of a Nonprofit Advisory Corporation* (Cambridge, Mass.: Harvard University Press, 1966).

[74] See Roger A. Kvam, "Comsat: The Inevitable Anomaly," in Lakoff, ed., *Knowledge and Power.*

But to concede the implicit assumption of students of organization is not only to neglect the temptations of power inherent in the political process but also to underestimate the social capacity for creative self-renovation. In recent years a number of practical proposals have been offered with a view to improving the environment for democracy in private associations. Some have already been implemented. The Landrum-Griffin Act of 1959 contains provisions designed to protect the right of union members to participate in free elections by secret ballot as well as their right to dissent without fear of reprisal. It also limits the power of union leaders to abuse the trusteeship device as a means of silencing opposition.[75] Certain unions have themselves moved to protect the appeals process in disciplinary proceedings by creating public review boards.[76] Universities are beginning to consider structural revisions that will engage both faculty and students in certain aspects of administration and that will give both groups more control over their own affairs.[77] Many proposals have been advanced for "constitutionalization" of corporate power, including the appointment of public members and stockholder representatives to boards of directors and further experiments along the lines of the "Scanlon Plan" and German "codetermination" by which employees are given a voice in management.[78] In the churches efforts are being made to assign greater responsibility to laymen and to the lower orders of the clergy. The external relations of private associations with each other and with the public government pose an even more difficult problem. It will not be easy to preserve and promote a healthy tension among them at the same time as efforts are made to bring about the integration and cooperation that technological necessity requires. But the effort need not be thought impossible, inasmuch as the functions and personnel of the separate elements even in an integrated scheme remain distinct and to some extent committed to cross-purposes.

In the first instance the democratization of private government can be looked upon as an end in itself, valuable because it would provide greater opportunity for self-expression and self-government in a significant area of social life. As the ordinary citizen finds that he can participate in public government only

[75] The provisions of the act and related issues are treated in Marten S. Estey, Philip Taft, and Martin Wagner, eds., *Regulating Union Government* (New York: Harper & Row, 1964). See especially the essays by Joel Seidman and Sar A. Levitan and J. Joseph Loewenberg.

[76] Among them the United Automobile Workers and the Carpenters' Union. See Jack Stieber, Walter E. Oberer, and Michael Harrington, *Democracy and Public Review: An Analysis of the UAW Public Review Board* (Santa Barbara: Center for the Study of Democratic Institutions, 1960).

[77] For the results of a survey of Canadian experience and proposals for reform, see James Duff and Robert O. Berdahl, *University Government in Canada, Report of a Commission Sponsored by the Canadian Association of Universities and Colleges of Canada* (Toronto: University of Toronto Press, 1966).

[78] For such proposals, see particularly the writings of Earl Latham, previously cited, and the conclusions of Richard Eells in *The Government of Corporations.* See also Frederick Lesieur, ed., *The Scanlon Plan: A Frontier in Labor-Management Cooperation* (Cambridge, Mass.: The Technology Press of M.I.T., 1958); Herbert J. Spiro, *The Politics of German Codetermination* (Cambridge, Mass.: Harvard University Press, 1958); Werner M. Blumenthal, *Codetermination in the German Steel Industry; A Report of Experience* (Princeton, N.J.: Princeton University Press, 1956); and Abraham Shuchman, *Codetermination: Labor's Middle Way in Germany* (Washington, D.C.: Public Affairs Press, 1957).

by periodically registering his frustrations on a voting machine, such opportunities may become more meaningful than ever. The problems posed by the advent of the managed society are, to be sure, as serious in the public sector as they are in the private. But at least public politics benefits from the detailed scrutiny of political scientists and from the constant efforts of reform groups. The same cannot be said of the private sector. Too little is known about private governments, and too little is being done to reform them. Political theory and political science have neglected the subject far too long. As a result it has fallen prey to an apolitical mode of analysis which, although it may reflect powerful tendencies in society itself, cannot provide the insight or the practical help that a free society needs if it is to implement and sustain its most cherished commitment.

1 2 3 4 5 6 7 8 9 10 11 12 13 14 15 16 17 18 19 20 21 22 23 24 25 80 79 78 77 76 75 74 73 72